Books by Marshall Sprague

THE BUSINESS OF GETTING WELL

MONEY MOUNTAIN

MASSACRE: THE TRAGEDY AT WHITE RIVER

NEWPORT IN THE ROCKIES

THE GREAT GATES: THE STORY OF THE ROCKY MOUNTAIN PASSES

A GALLERY OF DUDES

A GALLERY OF DUDES

A GALLERY

By Marshall Sprague

OF DUDES

LITTLE, BROWN AND COMPANY · BOSTON · TORONTO

Published simultaneously in Canada
by Little, Brown & Company (Canada) Limited

PRINTED IN THE UNITED STATES OF AMERICA

For my beloved dude
EDNA JANE
who went West and won it

FOREWORD

THOSE TWIN MONUMENTS to linguistic scholarship, the *Oxford English Dictionary* and the *Century Dictionary,* appeared in the late 1880's with a brand-new word, "dude" — origin unknown. "A factitious slang term," the *Oxford* stated, "which came into vogue in New York about the beginning of 1883, in connection with the 'aesthetic' craze of the day — a name given in ridicule to a man affecting an exaggerated fastidiousness in dress, speech and deportment." The *Century* called the word "a slang term said to have originated in London, England. It first became known in general colloquial and newspaper use at the time of the so-called 'esthetic' movement in dress and manners in 1882-83. . . . A fop or exquisite, characterized by affected refinements of dress, speech, manners, and gait, and a serious mien; hence by an easy extension, and with less of contempt, a man given to excessive refinement of fashion in dress." I would extend the meaning further. By 1883, the word was being used to describe a "fop or exquisite" seeking new experiences in the North American West.

That is what the dudes in my gallery sought. Prince Maximilian was lured to the Dakotas and Montana by the chance of scientific discovery. The gay blade Lord Milton crossed Canada in search of health, with the sturdy Dr. Cheadle trying — not always successfully — to keep him out of trouble. Captain William Drummond Stewart and Lord Dunraven were mighty hunters who had exhausted the hunting grounds of Europe. Stewart in addition sought escape from domesticity, to which he had committed himself quite by accident in Perthshire. Grand Duke Alexis yearned for thrills after a tiresome goodwill tour of the eastern United States for his father, Czar Alexander II. Miss Isabella Lucy Bird wanted material for travel books, and also to get away from her sister Henrietta, who was on the dull side. The Marquis de Mores and Count Pourtales wanted to make money to restore their ancient heritages in Europe. Young Theodore Roosevelt went West for all sorts of reasons — to hunt, to write, to build up his biceps, to get over a cold, to forget about New York politics. He went a second time to recover from the awful shock of his first wife's death.

My dudes were as comic in their foppishness as only dudes can be. Isabella Bird wore Turkish trousers and Hawaiian bloomers to Estes Park. Sir William Drummond Stewart took his tea in a scarlet tent every afternoon on Green River. Count Pourtales wore Bavarian knickerbockers on the mine dumps of Cripple Creek. Grand Duke Alexis broke out a magnum of champagne every time he shot a buffalo in Nebraska. Lord Milton baked an English plum pudding spiced with gunpowder at Jolie Prairie. Theodore Roosevelt wore regulation blue jeans and silk neckerchiefs on the Little Missouri but they were so flashy that the cowboys figured his tailor made them in New York.

My dudes were comic, but they had more than comedy to offer. They were highly educated, and they had traveled widely. Most of them saw the West in a broad and fresh perspective. They saw the incredible space, the potential wealth, the limitless opportunity. They saw people uplifted by a new kind of freedom and they realized that this unique freedom would spread by its own vitality to the ends of the earth to inspire discouraged people everywhere.

They wrote well about what they saw and their writings helped Americans to evaluate themselves at a time when they were too busy building a new world to have time to think. Theodore Roosevelt's zestful books on Western hunting and ranching taught a whole generation to appreciate the splendor of the land. Lord Dunraven's hilarious tales of camping and pack mules and Yellowstone geysers brought international attention on the joys of Western life, including "the joyous freedom to be filthy." Nobody has described the beauty of the Rocky Mountains half as well as Isabella Bird did in the 1870's.

My dudes' objective views of the Indians were a valuable balance to the American idea that the race was subhuman. "The perceptions of an Indian," Dr. Cheadle remarked, "are so nice." Sir William Drummond Stewart recommended bringing a few Indian girls to Scotland for breeding purposes to improve the Scottish strain. Dunraven found no difference between "savage" Indian warfare and the Oxford-Cambridge boat race. Maximilian's two volumes on the Upper Missouri contain sympathetic Indian studies which remain standard.

I have quoted copiously from the writings of my dudes, and not because I was too lazy to write about them myself. They said it far better than I could.

They went West between 1833 and the 1890's, and they all seemed to know about each other, as international skiers do now, and mountain climbers, and chess players. Captain Stewart and Prince Maximilian became friends at William Clark's home in St. Louis. Isabella Bird went to Colorado on the advice of George Kingsley, Dunraven's hunting companion. Roosevelt borrowed Tolstoy novels from his neighbor on the Little Missouri, the Marquis de Mores. Dunraven and Grand Duke Alexis had mutual friends in General Phil Sheridan and General George A. Custer. There were hangouts in New York where such dudes congregated in the '70's and '80's — Delmonico's, the Knickerbocker Club, the Brevoort House and the Hotel Brunswick.

I wrote this book at the prodding of an old friend of mine, Mitchell A. Wilder, who is director of the beautiful Amon Carter Museum of Western Art in Fort Worth, Texas. At the Amon Carter, Mr. Wilder has been mounting annually a big exhibition on some Western topic, and sending it to other museums around the country after its Fort Worth showing. He wanted a book about dudes to accompany his 1967 show, also titled "A Gallery of Dudes." It was my good fortune to be permitted to decorate my book with reproductions of paintings and photographs appearing in this Amon Carter exhibition. I am very grateful. They were gathered for me by Miss Barbara Tyler, the museum's research-historian. I extend my heartfelt thanks to Miss Tyler for all her help.

MARSHALL SPRAGUE

Colorado Springs
March 1, 1966

CONTENTS

FOREWORD ix

SCOTSMAN ON THE GREEN 3

THE TRAVELS OF PRINCE MAX 33

ORDEAL OVER YELLOWHEAD 67

A GRAND DUKE FOR DENVER 95

LOVE IN THE PARK 119

THE DUDE FROM LIMERICK 147

O TEMPORA! O MORES! 181

THE MAKING OF A PRESIDENT 215

THE MILKMAN OF BROADMOOR 247

NOTES AND SOURCES 273

AN ACKNOWLEDGMENT 285

INDEX 287

LIST OF ILLUSTRATIONS

Sir William Drummond Stewart at forty-nine — 2

Alfred Jacob Miller, a self-sketch — 5

Flirting with danger — 10

Stewart sights "buffler" — 13

Ugly Crow Indians — 14

Loch Drummond (New Fork Lake), Wyoming — 16

Sunrise of the hunter's day — 19

Tom Fitzpatrick's caravan — 20

Gift from Tona to the captain — 24

Death on the plain — 27

Moonlight — Camp Scene — 31

New Harmony, Indiana — 36

The steamer *Yellowstone,* grounded — 39

Fort Pierre in June 1833 — 41

Prince Maximilian has callers — 45

Dancing Mandans near Fort Clark — 49

Fort Union — 51

"King David" Dreidoppel stalks *Ursus horribilis* — 55

An Indian battle outside Fort McKenzie — 57

Down the Missouri in a Mackinaw boat, mid-May 1834 — 59

The Stone Walls — 61

Maximilian after his return to Germany — 63

Fort Milton, winter 1862-1863 — 66

Lord Milton and company — 77

Fort Edmonton — 79

O'Byrne sits out the forest fire — 81

Lord Milton and Cheadle urge Bucephalus up a trail   82

The view up the Athabasca from near Jasper House   84

The Assiniboine saves Bucephalus from drowning   85

O'Byrne hangs on to Bucephalus's tail crossing Canoe River   86

Trouble on a raft   87

The headless Indian   89

Lord Milton safe in San Francisco   91

Grand Duke Alexis, aged twenty-one   94

How Alexis might have killed his first buffalo   103

The grand duke hunting buffalo, a page of cartoons   105

Denver's gala ball for the grand duke   108

Alexis with his escort, General George A. Custer   113

Alexis and entourage in Topeka   114

The grand duke in his later years   116

Isabella Lucy Bird holding her mare Birdie   120

Chalmers's northern route into Estes Park   123

Isabella's cabin in Estes Park   127

Isabella's view approaching Longs Peak   131

The Lava Beds (Boulderfield) on Longs Peak   134

The Continental Divide near Breckenridge Pass   139

Lord Dunraven and Dr. George Kingsley, 1871   146

The guide Texas Jack Omohundro   151

Dunraven and Sandie hunting bighorn sheep in Estes Park   154

Dunraven and Kingsley hear a Crow brave's tale   161

Indians approach the Dunraven party   164

Mammoth Hot Springs, Yellowstone Park   166

Upper Geyser Basin, Yellowstone Park   167

Packing the mules   169

Camping in the rain   171

The artist Albert Bierstadt   172

Bierstadt's painting *Longs Peak*   173

The English Hotel   175

Lord Dunraven in the late 1880s   177

Dunraven in later years   178

The Marquis de Mores   182

Medora von Hoffmann   185

The Chateau de Mores   191

The marquis "armed like a battleship"   195

William Van Driesche, English valet   197

The meat-packing plant in Medora   199

A bit of a "We Never Sleep" report   203

Medora, Dakota Territory, in 1886   206

The bedroom of the marquise as she left it in December 1886   209

The marquis's statue in De Mores Memorial Park   213

Theodore Roosevelt at Harvard   214

Alice Hathaway Lee, Rose Saltonstall, Roosevelt   219

The dude from New York   222

Nobody called him a dude any more   223

The log house at the Maltese Cross   227

Roosevelt as cow hand   229

The Elkhorn Ranch house   233

The fearless posse   242

And they got their men!   243

Count James Pourtales   249

Berthe de Pourtales   251

Views at Broadmoor Dairy Farm   253

The Brown Swiss champion William Tell, Jr., manager Duncan
    Chisholm looking on   257

For his bride, Pourtales built a fine home   259

Cheyenne Mountain Country Club   260

An artist's sketch of Broadmoor Casino   263

A photograph of Broadmoor Casino   263

Buena Vista Mine   267

The Broadmoor area today   270

LIST OF MAPS

Maps by SAMUEL H. BRYANT

The Stewart Country	8-9
The Prince Maximilian Country	42-43
The Route Taken by Lord Milton and Dr. Cheadle	70-71
Western Tour of the Grand Duke Alexis	96-97
Isabella Lucy Bird's Routes	118
Dunraven's Route	149
Town of Medora	180
Bad Lands Ranches in the 1880's	217
Colorado Springs and Broadmoor	255

A GALLERY OF DUDES

Sir William Drummond Stewart was forty-nine when he left the Green River country forever to live out his days dully and respectably on the Tay of his forefathers. This portrait was done in 1844 at Murthly by the American, Henry Inman, who spent that year abroad painting only important people including William Wordsworth and Lord Macaulay. Stewart liked the painting because it showed him to be noble, wise, intelligent, handsome — and yet not to be trifled with. The Joslyn Art Museum, Omaha, owns the painting.

1

SCOTSMAN ON THE GREEN

CAPTAIN WILLIAM DRUMMOND STEWART, a tall, complex and rather stern aristocrat from Perthshire, was doing nothing unusual in 1832 when he left the family castles on the Tay to dude it in the American West. Ever since Napoleon's defeat at Waterloo in 1815, well-to-do Europeans had been crossing the Atlantic in quantity to see what transpired in this peculiar new land of popular government.

They went for all sorts of scientific and romantic and commercial reasons, and some of them returned home disillusioned. Frances Trollope, mother of the English novelist, spent two years — 1828 to 1830 — running a dry-goods store in Cincinnati and wrote an outrageous and enormously popular book about Cincinnati's boors, *The Domestic Manners of the Americans*. Count Alexis de Tocqueville, the elegant French dude, got to Lake Michigan in 1831 and had some tart comments in his *Democracy in America*. Harriet Martineau, the English freethinker, published *Society in America* after a year in the East and echoed Mrs. Trollope's complaint about the American want of refinement.

Captain Stewart had heard such reports but they didn't discourage him at all. He was sick to death of refinement, and had been almost from the day of his birth on December 26, 1795, in a gloomy Scotch castle called Murthly. The place stood near the Tay at the center of three family estates totaling 32,000 acres and it fitted the lugubrious aura which Shakespeare's *Macbeth* had brought to these Sidlaw Hills. Birnam Wood was twelve miles northwest. Close on the east was Dunsinane Peak, where Macbeth, murderer of King Duncan in the eleventh century, vowed to have no "taint" of fear "till Birnam Wood removed to Dunsinane." The Stewart line traced back at least as far as Duncan's, but the spreading family tree did not seem to bring much pleasure to the present generation. Young William's father, Sir George, the seventeenth Lord of Grandtully and fifth Baronet of Murthly, could not stand his wife Catherine, daughter of Sir John Drummond of nearby Logiealmond. Catherine was bored by her five sons and daughters, who had no particular affection for each other. As Sir George's second son, William, grew older he came to despise the eldest boy, John, who would inherit the lands and castles by primogeniture, the inflexible law of entail.

William was educated by tutors on the Murthly estate but he was released from confinement at seventeen when his father bought him a cornetcy in the fashionable Sixth Dragoon Guards (cornets had charge of the Dragoon flags). He saw three months of action in Spain and Portugal, and was with Wellington as a lieutenant at Waterloo. Five years later he was promoted to captain in the Fifteenth King's Hussars, retiring soon afterward on half pay. His next decade was spent roaming around the fast-disappearing hunting grounds of Europe and fuming at the injustice of being a second son trying to live like a lord on five shillings a day. When Sir George died in 1827, he left three thousand pounds in trust to William. But his brother — now Sir John, sixth Baronet of Murthly — was trustee and he gave William just enough money to encourage him to stay away from the castle.

Occasionally the captain visited his friend Lord George Glenlyon of Blair Atholl some twenty-five miles north of Murthly. In *Scotsman in Buckskin,* Mae Reed Porter and Odessa Davenport have told how Stewart was strolling by one of Blair Atholl's tenant houses and "here in the courtyard he saw an extraordinarily beautiful girl, her skirts tucked up until they barely covered her knees. . . . A contemporary said, 'He fell in love with her nether limbs when he saw her tromping blankets in a tub.' " The lovely laundress's name was Christina. The sight of her nether limbs inspired the captain into what for him was a novel kind of action. Up to this thirty-fourth year of his, he had paid

He was only twenty-six, this amiable, Paris-trained Alfred Jacob Miller, when Captain Stewart found him in New Orleans and took him West to paint the Green River country for remembrance. Miller did not know, and would not have cared if he had known, that he was the first artist to fully paint the Rockies. He made this pencil sketch of himself on the back of a trapper painting. (Northern Natural Gas Collection at Joslyn Art Museum, Omaha, Nebraska.)

just enough attention to women to establish his manhood without entangling himself. He associated mainly with males to avoid the emotional complications which women required. But Christina in the tub caught him off guard. He wasted no time investigating those nether limbs, and within a year Christina produced a considerable complication — a son named George. Three months later, Stewart married the girl in Edinburgh "for purposes of legitimization," with George Glenlyon on hand as an interested witness. Having done the right thing, William installed Christina and their son George in an Edinburgh apartment and took steps to remove himself as far away as possible — to St. Louis, Missouri.

In 1832 the primary interest of this distinguished veteran of Waterloo was hunting — any kind, anywhere. He had heard of a happy hunting ground west of St. Louis which was infinitely larger and richer than those on the Continent. Its name was the Louisiana Purchase. Its beautiful prairies and rivers extended west a thousand miles to the Continental Divide in the Rocky Mountains, where Atlantic and Pacific waters divide. The states of Louisiana, Arkansas and Missouri were being carved out of the Purchase by the 1830's, but most of it remained pure wilderness, ruled by a few superb hunters such as William Sublette, Robert Campbell, Tom Fitzpatrick and Jim Bridger. Actually the hunting kingdom of these merry mountain men spread far beyond the Purchase itself, into Mexico's Utah and the British-American no-man's-land of Idaho and Oregon.

Captain Stewart landed in New York from Liverpool in May of 1832, and spent the summer canalboating across New York State to Lake Erie, on the Ohio River by the brand-new Ohio and Erie Canal, and so to the Mississippi. He found St. Louis to be a bustling, cosmopolitan town of six thousand people, with broad streets, large homes, rambling warehouses and enough taverns to keep everyone in a good humor most of the time. Its riverfront was a pageant of ferries, skiffs, pirogues, barges, keelboats and schooners, all scurrying about on romantic business. Stewart called at once on General William Clark, who had crossed to the Pacific in 1805 with Meriwether Lewis and who supervised the Western wilderness as superintendent of Indian affairs. Next he met Pierre Chouteau, Jr., the St. Louis Frenchman who ran John Jacob Astor's American Fur Company (AFC), and met also

General William Ashley, founder of the Rocky Mountain Fur Company (RMF). Since the mid-1820's, these two firms had been battling each other for the wilderness fur trade, and had competed with England's Hudson's Bay Company based in Oregon. Stewart learned that the AFC had a string of fixed trading posts along the 2500-mile length of the Missouri River, to which the Indians were expected to bring their furs. By contrast, General Ashley had invented for the RMF the more accommodating rendezvous system. His traders and their successors trailed their wares from St. Louis to the Indians and free white trappers, instead of urging these customers to come to a fixed post.

The retired Ashley was pretty much King Arthur as far as the round table of buckskin knights of the RFC was concerned. He put Stewart on to his former field agent, William Sublette, an able Kentuckian who sent goods to the Green River area of present Wyoming for each summer's shifting point of rendezvous. Sublette's partner was the Scotchman Robert Campbell, who had come to the American West from Northern Ireland to cure his tuberculosis. Campbell would be in charge of the RMC pack train of baubles, hardware and booze to meet Indians and whites wanting to mix business and pleasure at the July rendezvous for 1833. For the privilege of going along with Campbell, Stewart paid the partners five hundred dollars out of his small allowance from the sixth baronet of Murthly. In addition, Stewart performed a curious errand for Sublette. In March, 1833, he went back East to the home near Cincinnati of the old Indian fighter General William Henry Harrison, collected a thousand dollars from him, and gathered up his wayward son, Dr. Benjamin Harrison, who was drinking too much. The money was the partners' fee for taking Benjamin to Green River on the chance that it would get him off liquor as it had gotten Campbell off tuberculosis.

So Stewart, Campbell and Harrison said farewell to St. Louis on April 13, 1833. Their goods train consisted of forty men, one hundred and twenty pack mules, a large remuda (saddle horse herd), a flock of sheep for food, and two bulls and four cows. Their route would be known in another decade as the Oregon Trail — up the Missouri, Kansas and Little Blue Rivers to the Platte, North Platte, Sweetwater and over South Pass, which they crossed at the south end of the Wind River Mountains on July 2. In three more days, the train reached rendezvous at present Daniel, Wyoming, around the junction of Green River and

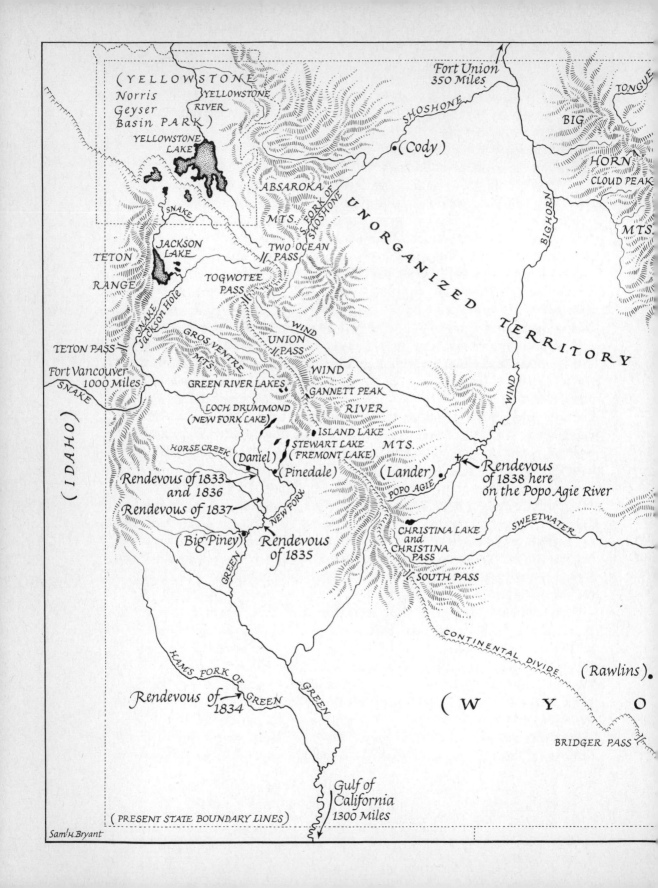

(YELLOWSTONE

Norris
Geyser
Basin P A R K)

YELLOWSTONE
RIVER

YELLOWSTONE
LAKE

SHOSHONE

Fort Union
350 Miles

TONGUE

(Cody)

BIG

HORN

CLOUD PEAK

ABSAROKA

MTS.

TETON
RANGE

JACKSON
LAKE

SNAKE

TWO OCEAN
PASS

TOGWOTEE
PASS

U N O R G A N I Z E D   T E R R I T O R Y

BIGHORN

MTS.

TETON PASS

Fort Vancouver
1000 Miles

SNAKE

(I D A H O)

GROS VENTRE
MTS.

UNION
PASS

WIND

WIND

GREEN RIVER LAKES

GANNETT PEAK

RIVER

LOCH DRUMMOND
(NEW FORK LAKE)

ISLAND LAKE

HORSE CREEK

(Daniel)

STEWART LAKE
(FREMONT LAKE)

MTS.

(Lander)

Rendevous
of 1838 here
on the Popo Agie River

Rendevous of 1833
and 1836

(Pinedale)

POPO AGIE

Rendevous of 1837

NEW FORK

Rendevous
of 1835

CHRISTINA LAKE
and
CHRISTINA
PASS

SWEETWATER

(Big Piney)

GREEN

SOUTH PASS

CONTINENTAL DIVIDE

(Rawlins).

HAMS FORK OF GREEN

Rendevous of
1834

GREEN

(W   Y   O

BRIDGER PASS

Gulf of
California
1300 Miles

(PRESENT STATE BOUNDARY LINES)

Sam¹ H. Bryant

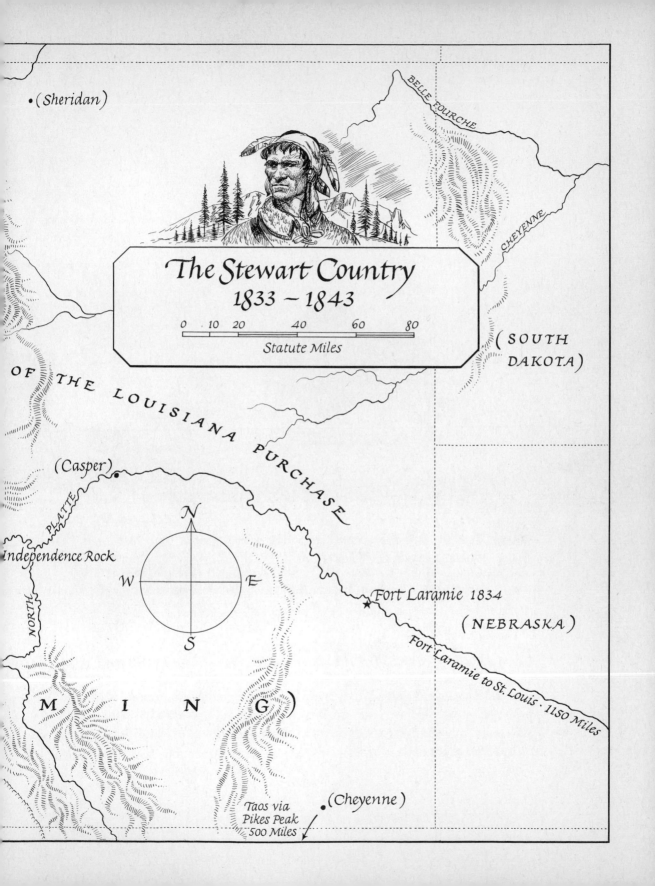

• (Sheridan)

BELLE FOURCHE

CHEYENNE

The Stewart Country
1833 – 1843

0   10   20   40   60   80
Statute Miles

(SOUTH
DAKOTA)

OF THE LOUISIANA PURCHASE

(Casper) •

PLATTE

Independence Rock

N

W   E

S

NORTH

Fort Laramie 1834

(NEBRASKA)

Fort Laramie to St. Louis · 1150 Miles

M   I   N   G)

Taos via
Pikes Peak
500 Miles

• (Cheyenne)

Young Indians, Miller observed, were like young people the world over. They loved best of all to flirt gaily with danger. This Miller pen-and-ink sketch, published for the first time, shows several of them teasing an enraged buffalo. The sketch belongs to the Amon Carter Museum of Western Art.

Horse Creek — beautiful cold clear waterways rushing through rich pastures. Stewart had enjoyed the long trip across the prairies. He was well equipped physically for his flight from primogeniture and Christina — a slender, lithe athlete just under six feet with sharp blue eyes, a long nose and ruddy cheeks. He had endurance, and a digestion as tough as a goat's.

Green River was all that he had dreamed it would be. There was the warm, fragrant sage plain, rolling in purple ridges for a breadth of fifty miles. Eastward, he gazed on the snow-streaked blocks and towers of the Wind River Range, where Green River began its two thousand miles of flowing to the Gulf of California. Just beyond the glaciers at the crest, Wind River set out on a much longer trip to the Gulf of Mexico. The Wind River peaks which we call Gannett (13,785) and Fremont and Sacajawea and Washakie were bathed in blue, and they rose behind an enticing shelf of spruce and pine forests half a mile higher than the Green River plain — the lake-bejeweled terminal moraine of today's Bridger Wilderness Area near Pinedale. In the west was the soft line of the lower Wyoming Mountains. Northward was the Gros Ventre Range, beyond which Stewart would find Jackson Hole, the Tetons and present Yellowstone Park.

Years later, in *Altowan,* the first of the two autobiographical novels which he would write about Green River, Stewart noted: "In these high plains, unknown to cloud or damp, the pure air elevates and frees the spirit." Such enthusiasm was unusual for the captain. He seemed to forget about the burden of Christina and the bitterness of his remittance-man role beneath these placid skies, deep blue by day and sparkling with stars by night. The sights and sounds of the rendezvous entertained him — the tents of the traders and white trappers, and the big hide tipis of the Indians in miles of villages along the willowed streams. The fine physique of the Indian men inspired him to write that "the best models of Greek sculpture had sprung into life in these wilds." He watched short, stocky Utes from Colorado's uplands; tall Crows from the valleys of the Bighorn, Yellowstone and Tongue; Snakes from Idaho's Salmon River; Blackfeet from eastern Montana and from Canada; Nez Percé and Flatheads from the Bitterroot Range. He admired their dress, their art, their nature worship, their foods and medicines and hygiene, their pride and courage, and concluded that many features of their Stone Age society contributed more to the joy of living than the ways of Europe.

Being primarily a hunting man and not an acute observer, Stewart would put much romantic nonsense about these Indians into his novels. But they make lively reading even so. In *Altowan* he described the male homosexuals and explained their function in the households of the chiefs, keeping the squaws in line "like the eunuchs of the seraglio."

This scene was Miller's rather Polynesian idea of how Crow Indians looked in 1833 when they threatened Stewart and Antoine Clement near present Sheridan, Wyoming, below the Big Horns. The recumbent lass at right has features similar to those of "the ductile Idalie" described by Stewart in his novel Altowan. A Walters Art Gallery painting.

financiers, began a long Army leave in 1832, ostensibly to trade. However he made clear to Stewart that his real mission was to examine potentials for national expansion westward into Oregon and California. Another man at the Horse Creek rendezvous who seemed to be promoting something important was the young Boston ice merchant, Nathaniel Wyeth. Stewart found him to be boiling with schemes to create an American industry in Oregon based on Columbia River salmon, Indian trade, agriculture and shipping to the Orient.

WHEN RENDEZVOUS ENDED in late July of 1833, the captain joined Tom Fitzpatrick and Jim Bridger on a seven-hundred-mile RMF trapping trip to the short-grass Crow country on the north and east sides of the Big Horn Mountains. Today's motorists see much of the beauty of this trail as they drive along the east flanks of Wind River Range and Absaroka Range from South Pass City, Lander and Thermopolis to Cody, Wyoming. From Cody, the old route goes over Pryor's Gap to Pryor and then to the Bighorn River at Hardin, Montana. In September, Stewart and the twenty Fitzpatrick trappers crossed from the Bighorn eastward in the golden glow of fall cottonwoods and willows. It was the spacious land of the Little Bighorn, Rosebud Creek and Tongue River, where General Custer would meet disaster in 1876. Near today's Sheridan, Wyoming, below the massive Big Horns, their trip ended unpleasantly. A band of Crows got into camp while Stewart was trying to guard it, and walked off with everything loose, including Stewart's watch and his best horse.

From the Big Horns, Stewart and Jim Bridger seem to have ridden south to spend the winter in Taos, that gay village of New Spain where trade and festival had reached a glamorous stage, after two centuries of practice. Their route paralleled today's roads from Sheridan to Casper, around the Laramie Hills to Cheyenne, past Pikes Peak to the majestic Spanish Peaks and over Sangre de Cristo Pass to San Luis Valley and Taos. That made eight hundred miles of travel, especially charming in autumn. When spring came, the two men broke out of hibernation and moved north through Colorado's high parks. They crossed Bridger's Pass in southern Wyoming and reached rendezvous, which was taking place this time at Ham's Fork of Green River, a hundred miles south of Horse Creek.

Today's New Fork Lake north of Pinedale, Wyoming, was Stewart's be-
loved Loch Drummond, named for his mother's family. Of the two snowy
peaks, the one at the right resembles Gannett, Wyoming's highest at 13,785
feet above sea level. Miller did not strive for realism in his landscapes. To
him, romance was the important thing. A Walters Art Gallery painting.

The Sublette-Campbell pack train arrived there for business on
June 18, 1834. It was followed by Nat Wyeth's big caravan, featuring
dudes in dismaying quantity. How long, Stewart wondered, could his
hunting paradise last with new people coming in at this rate? In
Wyeth's train were the missionaries Jason Lee and Daniel Lee, plan-

ning to carry the Methodist kind of Christianity to the Pacific; Thomas Nuttall, the great curator of Harvard College's Botanical Garden; his fellow academician, the ornithologist from Philadelphia, John Kirk Townsend, who had just discovered at South Pass "a beautiful new species of mocking bird" (Townsend's solitaire); and Captain Joseph Thing, Wyeth's Boston navigator, who was measuring the length of the future Oregon Trail by the stars. The Ham's Fork rendezvous was shorter and more brawlsome than the year before, reflecting everybody's worry over lower beaver prices. Stewart was glad to get it over and continue west with Wyeth and his dudes by way of Bear River, Portneuf River, Snake River and on over the Blue Mountains to the Columbia — the embryo Oregon Trail, of course. They reached the Hudson's Bay Company post, Fort Vancouver, in mid-September, making those thousand miles from Green River in sixty-four days. They had been delayed a trifle on Bear River, where Stewart and Wyeth had a celebration with Captain Bonneville and finished his last keg of alcohol and honey water.

At Fort Vancouver (today's Portland) the travelers were taken in by Dr. John McLoughlin, head of the Hudson's Bay Company for the Columbia drainage. McLoughlin, a huge, quiet, Quebec-born Scot, loved pomp, culture and personal honor. His baronial castle reminded Stewart of Sir John's Murthly on the Tay — blazing logs in the great hall, fine paintings, a big library, exquisite silver and china, vintage wines, and a bagpipe band. It had a house crew of olive-skinned Sandwich Islanders, also. Stewart was McLoughlin's guest from September until he left for Green River at the end of January, 1835 — a period of peace marred briefly when Nat Wyeth's tailor, Mr. Thornburg, got into a drunken fight and wound up dead. The captain was sad about it, but John Townsend was sadder still when he found the source of Thornburg's liquor. He had been nipping at the whiskey Townsend used as a preservative in the jars holding his Townsend solitaire and specimens of lizards and snakes.

Stewart worked his way slowly eastward with some HBC trappers. He reached Snake River in mid-June and Green River a month later by way of Teton Pass, with the Teton Mountains soaring above Jackson Lake in divine panoply. The rendezvous of 1835 took place in mid-August around the mouth of New Fork River, twenty-five miles down the Green from Horse Creek and near today's site of Big Piney,

Wyoming. Antoine Clement joined the captain there. More Oregon-bound missionaries arrived — the Presbyterian physician, Marcus Whitman, and the Congregationalist preacher, Samuel Parker. But when Stewart told him all the things he would need to build an Oregon mission, Dr. Whitman turned back for more supplies, sending Parker on to the Columbia. The captain watched the big, handsome Whitman start his career as a Western hero by removing an arrowhead from Jim Bridger's back which had got there during an argument with some Blackfeet in 1832. Whitman asked Old Gabe why the arrowhead hadn't caused a fester. Jim replied to the effect that "meat don't spoil in the Rockies."

By November, Stewart was back in St. Louis, physically blooming but in poor financial shape. Sir John's remittance from Murthly was approaching zero. Soon after Christmas, the captain was forced to borrow from William Sublette to keep alive, so he hurried down to New Orleans and began cotton speculations with a young Texan named E. B. Nichols. He made money. Soon he could afford the gay spots of Chartres and Bourbon Streets again. He even financed a winter vacation in Cuba, and a return West through Charleston, Washington and Cincinnati. Somewhere along the line he picked up a German dude, Mr. Sillem, who signed with him to go up the Platte in Tom Fitzpatrick's caravan. It formed in early May at Bellevue, near present Omaha, Nebraska.

As Fitzpatrick's train crept west along the familiar route, the captain had periods of worry. Because of his cotton profits, he had assembled an outfit in St. Louis for this trip which was mollycoddling to say the least. It consisted of a four-horse wagon loaded with fine foods and liquors and a two-horse wagon full of English hunting clothes, Persian rugs, sable blankets, two expensive Manton rifles and a big chest of soaps, salves, pills and purges. He had three servants, two hunting dogs, two race horses, and Mr. Sillem for elevated conversation. Heretofore, he had prided himself for holding his own with the best of the mountain men in the wilderness. He had learned to eat raw buffalo meat, drink mule blood, sleep out in any weather, face charging grizzlies, cheat at cards, fix horse races and bed down with Indian girls. Jim Bridger, Bill Sublette and the rest trusted his judgment in a crisis and told him that he had a "ha'r of the Grissly in him."

The captain was a somber man but even he felt a happiness during the sunrise of the hunter's day, its freshness enhanced by a breakfast of buffalo steaks and tea. Artist Miller has painted Antoine Clement at Stewart's right. A Walters Art Gallery painting.

By the summer of 1837, Captain Stewart (on white horse, center) was used to scenes like this which Miller made of Tom Fitzpatrick's caravan bound for Green River from St. Louis. The red-haired Narcissa Whitman had graced the caravan in the previous year so Stewart knew that the great days of absolute freedom were ending. Women, even beautiful women, spoiled everything. The Joslyn Art Museum, Omaha, owns this watercolor drawing. (Northern Natural Gas Collection at Joslyn Art Museum, Omaha, Nebraska.)

Was the Waterloo veteran softening up now, as he slipped into his forties? If so, he could argue that the times were softer too. The old dangerous route to the Pacific was becoming known as the safe and sound Oregon Trail. How else could he explain the presence in this train of someone like Narcissa Prentiss Whitman? Narcissa was Marcus Whitman's bride — a lovely face and a fine fluid form which she displayed without modesty. Whitman's party of missionaries included the Reverend Henry Spalding and *his* bride, Eliza, a plain girl who had the bad luck to be matched against a goddess. Spalding had wooed Narcissa first, in upstate New York, and had lost her. He still trembled before her tumbling red-gold hair and warm smile. Stewart could imagine what her impact would be on American expansion when people back East read about her light Dearborn carriage on the Oregon Trail, her farm wagon of furniture, and laundered petticoats billowing on a line above the wagon like banners to the pioneer spirit. Senator Benton himself would not excite the country more about its manifest destiny out West.

When Fitzpatrick's train paused in eastern Wyoming at Fort Laramie, which Sublette and Campbell had built in 1834, Stewart celebrated the new trend of wilderness life by asking Narcissa and Eliza to tea. Later, he helped to carve their names on Independence Rock. And he was their bodyguard at the Horse Creek rendezvous in mid-July when a crowd of Snakes in full undress honored the first white women in the Rockies with dancing and a wild ride-around.

It was an interesting rendezvous. But the captain was relieved when it ended and Green River became wild and peaceful again.

STEWART SPENT THE WINTER of 1836-1837 in New Orleans, gambling in cotton with E. B. Nichols and showing Antoine Clement the sights of the city. Spring came, and with it startling news from Scotland. The captain's despised brother, Sir John, was dying of cancer in Paris. Sir John's wife was unable, or unwilling, to produce an heir. When Sir John got around to expiring within a year or so, the captain would become Sir William Drummond Stewart, seventh Baronet of Murthly, nineteenth Lord of Grandtully, and master of those gloomy castles and quaint villages on the Tay between Birnam Wood and Dunsinane.

On a sunny April morning, Stewart, sternly handsome in stovepipe hat and frock coat, strode down Chartres Street trying to adjust to the prospect of lordship. He would be a wealthy man, and that was good. But he would have to give up Green River and all its joys and return to Murthly to represent that millennium of Scotch nobility. He would miss his mountain men, and the Indians too — noble souls, all of them, within the frame of their environment. It occurred to him that Scotland would be improved if he imported a few Indian girls like Tona and Idalie to invigorate the ancient Scotch blood lines. It could not happen, of course. And still the thought absorbed him as he walked along Chartres Street trying on the phrase "Sir William." And perhaps it was then that he began plotting his novel *Altowan,* which he would bring to a climax with the arrival in Perthshire of Idalie to marry Lord Roallan.

In *Across the Wide Missouri,* Bernard De Voto described how Stewart just then approached a Chartres Street linen store and paused to examine a painting in the window by an artist upstairs. It depicted a Baltimore scene, and he liked its gay quality — warm twilight tones stressing the ideal and blurring the city's ugliness. He climbed the stairs to the studio and expressed his approval — "I like the management of that picture" — to the artist, Alfred Jacob Miller. Some days later, Stewart returned and hired Miller to go with him to Green River that summer to record in the same romantic style the life he was going to have to give up.

Miller, a native of Baltimore, was a slight, amiable man of twenty-six years, full of boyish zest and a kind of sweet, naive interest. He had spent two years in Paris studying wines and copying old masters, and he had been pleased when, on his way home in 1834, French police seized his copies, believing them to be originals. Thereafter he had developed an American style of his own, owing little to European techniques. He had hiked from Baltimore to New Orleans, painting portraits for his keep, some months before Stewart hired him for his Green River trip.

The opportunity was comparable to being invited today to go tripping to the moon with an astronaut. In late spring of '37, Miller and his watercolors ascended the Platte past Fort Laramie with Stewart and Antoine Clement, accompanying Fitzpatrick's caravan again. Stewart rode a big white horse this time. Also along were his valet, his cook, three packers, a guide and three wagons carrying fancy goods ranging from tinned sardines to a medieval iron breastplate and helmet for Jim Bridger to protect him from arrowheads. Miller made hundreds of sketches as he went, without premonitions of destiny. He had no interest in the West as a historical phenomenon. He loved to paint as he loved to breathe, because it came naturally. He did not know that he was the first man in all time to fully paint the actual Rockies.

The artist's joy in his work was Stewart's good luck that summer. Miller was producing exactly the romantic impressions the captain wanted for mementoes on the walls of Murthly. He sketched splendid Sioux warriors and the busy society of Fort Laramie. He used the great Turner's palette to suggest the heady yellow glare of the Sweetwater-South Pass region. The July rendezvous was held on the Green between New Fork River and Horse Creek. Attendance was in the thousands, but the mood was in a nostalgic key. Indians and mountain men alike suspected that this was the last big fur festival of the series which General Ashley's trappers had started so modestly in 1824. To catch the old spirit for Stewart, Miller painted the Snakes on parade, behaving as they had the year before to impress Narcissa Whitman.

Later, in August, the captain took Miller and a small party on a hunting trip of some weeks in that entrancing moraine which hung at an altitude of ten thousand feet, below the Wind River peaks and above the rendezvous area of the Green. Here was the setting of a sportsman's idyll. It still is, where pack trippers from Pinedale leave their cars behind to explore on horseback the Bridger Wilderness Area — fifteen hundred square miles of glacier lakes, singing streams among the lodgepoles and spruce, and gardens of granite beneath the crests of the Winds. Jim Bridger had guided the captain through, the summer before. This time, Stewart began with a bullboat tour of present Fremont Lake, naming it Stewart Lake. Then the group visited New Fork Lake (Stewart called it Loch Drummond after his mother) under Gannett Peak and rode to the north end of the moraine to look at Union Pass, on the old trail to Wind River, Bighorn and Yellowstone. They ascended Green River past its south-turning loop to Green River Lakes, and on below Squaretop Mountain to Green River Pass and Stonehammer Lake where the air was thin and vibrant and the ptarmigans walked about as tame as chickens. They camped at an unearthly alpine spot, Island Lake. Lieutenant Frémont would camp there in 1842, seeking glory for himself and his father-in-law, Senator Benton. Game was more plentiful than cattle on Green River ranches nowadays. Birds were everywhere — Townsend's solitaires, gorgeous western

Miller caught in his sketchbook a most attentive Captain Stewart. He is accepting a powder horn of water from a Crow Indian girl who must have been the fifteen-year-old Tona, described in Altowan as "a wild creature, scantily clothed, with well-formed limbs and a roguish eye." The sketch, published here for the first time, is owned by the Amon Carter Museum of Western Art.

tanagers, nutcrackers and jays, Lewis woodpeckers and pipits. The high meadows blazed with fireweed, beardstongue and rosy paintbrush.

Young Miller thought he was in heaven as he recorded all this beauty in watercolors. He created scenes also from Stewart's Green River past — Stewart hunting and butchering buffalo, Stewart watching nude Indian girls bathing, Stewart at campfire telling his trapper friends about life in Europe, Stewart arguing with the Crows who looted his camp in 1833. But the idyl had to end, as ice began filming on the little blue lakes and the wind moaned through the gold aspen leaves. Stewart led his men out of paradise early in September, over South Pass and on down the Platte past Fort Laramie. His thoughts turned to Perthshire as he brought his artist back to St. Louis and followed him to New Orleans for another winter.

By spring, Miller had worked up several paintings for Murthly from his sketches. Word came from Scotland that Sir John's condition in Paris was worsening. Nevertheless, Stewart decided to attend the rendezvous of 1838. In the caravan going out, he found as many missionary ladies as traders, and also a Swiss captain, John A. Sutter, who had a wild notion of farming in Mexico's California. The rendezvous was brief, and took place on the Popo Agie near Wind River, not even across the Continental Divide. As he was returning to St. Louis, Captain Stewart learned from a traveler that Sir John had expired on May 20.

So he was Sir William Drummond at last. But he was in no hurry to leave the land where he had found so much happiness. It took him nine months to wind up his Western career. In late April of 1839, he said good-bye to Bill Sublette and, with Antoine Clement, journeyed to New York by boat through the Caribbean. His baggage was remarkable. It included a thin cow buffalo, a fat young bull, and "a most noble" grizzly bear. There were packets of tree and plant seeds, a cage of red cardinals, and two live male Indians.

Sir William billeted the Indians briefly in the Long Island carriage house of an old New York friend of his, J. Watson Webb, editor of the *Morning Courier* and the *Enquirer*. He told Webb about the two novels, *Altowan* and *Edward Warren,* which he was in the process of writing. Webb was enthusiastic and promised to see to it that Harper and Brothers published them. He declared that Stewart's adventures on Green River would make charming reading for his young children. Sir William did not explain that the books would describe his sleeping with Indian maidens and the duties of homosexuals in upper-class Indian homes. Alfred Jacob Miller showed up soon at the Webb place with eighteen paintings for Murthly. Before Stewart sailed for Glasgow, he gave the artist permission to show the paintings at the Apollo Gallery. The exhibition drew huge crowds all summer.

Sir William and his exotic human and animal freight descended on Murthly in July. Antoine Clement and the Indians found life there dreary from the start. The old stone castle was a depressing depository of antiques. Though Bill Sublette sent still more buffalo and some deer from his farm near St. Louis, they soon fell into the museum mood and might just as well have been stuffed. Queen Victoria passed by them while on her honeymoon and was only mildly taken with "those strange humpbacked creatures from America." The red birds got out of their cages and flew away. The pines and spruce which Stewart planted on Birnam Hill seemed to die of listlessness. Antoine tried to wear kilts but felt foolish in them. His attempts to become a butler failed. When he and the Indians staged a rendezvous-style brawl in Dunkeld village, the citizens were not amused.

Artist Miller arrived from New Orleans in September of 1840 to finish more paintings but was sick much of the time and could not reproduce the vigor of the sketches he had made on Green River. Sir William himself was disillusioned with his efforts to bring the Rockies to Dunsinane, and went off to France a good deal. Actually, he was pining for Green River. At last, in August, 1842, he gathered up Antoine and the Indians and set out for New York and the Rockies. If he couldn't make Scotchmen out of them, at least he could return them to their homes, and have one last fling himself. Stewart wintered in New Orleans and then moved up the Mississippi to talk to Bill Sublette about a special spot he wanted to visit before he got too old.

OF COURSE HE WAS Sir William Drummond Stewart of Murthly now, and his caravan should have a commensurate style. Bill Sublette led it from St. Louis during that spring of 1843. Since Stewart could not persuade John James Audubon to join the train, he engaged a Scotch

At his best, Miller caught the feeling of the Wind River Range from the Green River side — the wavelike quality of peaks like Gannett, Sacajawea and Fremont, the mystery of the lower hills and the richness of the grasslands where the buffalo flourished. Here he shows Stewart, thoughtful and intent, as he watched a dying buffalo. A Walters Art Gallery painting.

naturalist, and two from Germany. He hired Matt Field, the popular New Orleans *Picayune* columnist, to keep a journal of the trip. Several youngsters from old St. Louis families came along, including the late General Clark's son, Jeff, and his nephew, Clark Kennerly. Baptiste Charbonneau drove a cart. He was the son of Sacajawea, who had hiked across the continent (with the infant Baptiste on her back) as a member of the Lewis and Clark expedition.

Bill Sublette wrote in his diary: "I took charge of the party of some 60 men. Sir William had 10 carts & one small 2 mule yankee wagon. There was some 30 other Carts and small 2 horse wagons in the Company belonging to Individual gentlemen, Some of the armey, Some professional Gentlemen Come on the trip for pleasure, Some for Health, etc. etc." Sir William's Scotch valet, Corbie, and two other servants from Murthly managed Sir William's remarkable tent. It was a bright crimson affair, fourteen feet square and furnished inside like a Soho apartment. Corbie had to put up the tent each day, in good time for Sir William's tea at five o'clock. If he didn't, his lordship would berate him and Corbie would try to counter with, "Why, I thought, Sir William — " bringing the explosion, "You thought! Well, whenever you get to thinking, there's the devil to pay."

Independence Day was celebrated near South Pass with sage juleps, two cases of Rhine wine and a huge plum pudding. In late July at Sir William's beloved Loch Drummond, the young St. Louis dudes astonished a band of Snake Indians with demonstrations of Stewart's electric-shock box, and they took turns paddling his India-rubber boat around the lake. Then it was time to head north for the special spot Stewart had longed to see ever since Jim Bridger had described its wonders in 1833.

Using Old Gabe's map, they rode from Loch Drummond up Green River to Union Pass, westerly down Fish Creek into Jackson Hole and up Pacific Creek to Two Ocean Pass. Yellowstone River began there. Stretching away before them as far as they could see was a high plateau which was, they thought, more magical, more stunning, more incredible than any other spot on earth. The plateau was a carpet of lodgepole forest and grassy clearings. Noble mountains surrounded it — the Absarokas east and north, the Centennials west, the breathtaking Tetons south above Jackson Hole. In its center was a beautiful lake, presiding over all like a great sapphire on the bosom of an empress.

They were seeing Yellowstone Park, of course — the first whites outside the trapping fraternity ever to see it. For two weeks, under Yellowstone's fairest of skies, they roamed about dreamily, shot elk and bear, fished in Yellowstone Lake, watched the thundering falls and bubbling cream paint pots and rainbow hot springs. In his *Persimmon Hill* reminiscences, written years later, Clark Kennerly told of chasing a white buffalo with Sir William and gave some impressions of the Norris Geyser Basin area:

On approaching, we had noticed at regular intervals of about five or ten minutes what seemed to be a tall column of smoke or steam, such as would arise from a steamboat. On nearer approach, however, we discovered it to be a geyser, which we christened Steam Boat Geyser. Several other geysers were found near by, some of them so hot that we boiled our bacon in them, as well as the fine speckled trout [they were cutthroats] which we caught in the surrounding streams. One geyser, a soda spring, was so effervescent that I believe the syrup to be the only thing lacking to make it equal a giant ice cream soda of the kind now popular at the drugstore. We tried some experiments with our first discovery by packing it down with armfuls of grass; then we placed a flat stone on top of that, on which four of us, joining hands, stood in a vain attempt to hold it down. In spite of our efforts to curb Nature's most potent force, when the moment of necessity came, Old Steam Boat would literally rise to the occasion and throw us all high into the air, like so many feathers. It inspired one with great awe for the wonderful works of the Creator to think that this had been going on with the regularity of clockwork for thousands of years, and the thought of our being the first white men to see it did not lessen its effect.

The explorers returned to Loch Drummond on August 17. As Matt Field wrote in the New Orleans *Picayune*: "We are the fattest, greasiest set of truant rogues your liveliest imagination can call up to view. We are the meanest, raggedest — perhaps you would add, the ugliest — set of buffalo butchers that ever cracked a rifle among the big hills of Wind River." And then the long trail home began. The ugly buffalo butchers looked meaner and more ragged still when they arrived in St. Louis toward the end of October. Sir William, described by Clark Kennerly as "a mighty hunter and a prince among sportsmen," gave a farewell banquet at Persimmon Hill for his whole caravan, topped off with Scotch whiskey and a tearful "Auld Lang Syne."

So MUCH FOR OUR Scotsman on the Green, one of the first of countless dudes to find adventure and happiness in the Rockies. In the spring of 1844 he returned by way of New Orleans and Long Island to Murthly, where he became one of the permanent museum exhibits, like the suits of armor and Alfred Jacob Miller's paintings. Nothing more happened to him during his long life except a few sardonic mishaps and the erosion of years. He remained brightly blue-eyed to the end, and slim, but a trifle bent. His dark brown hair thinned and grayed. By the time of his death in 1871 at seventy-five, his stiff military manner had degenerated into a gouty peevishness. His wife Christina died in the 1850's but Stewart had had nothing to do with her after investigating her nether limbs so successfully in the late 1820's, before their marriage. Their son George served with honor as an army captain and survived the heroic charge of the Light brigade in the Crimea. He did not succeed to the baronetcy because he died in 1869. Some said he died in a duel or drunken brawl. His uncle, Stewart's younger brother Archibald, spread a rumor that a certain Franc Nichols was involved somehow.

This Franc Nichols was the son of Stewart's old New Orleans business partner, E. B. Nichols, who had become a rail and shipping magnate in Galveston, Texas. Bernard De Voto has gone so far as to suggest that Franc may have been Stewart's son. Mae Reed Porter has described in *Scotsman in Buckskin* how Franc, aged fifteen, went to Murthly when Christina died, and acted as a sort of companion for Sir William. After George Stewart's mysterious death, Sir William adopted Franc and tried to make him his heir. But the law of primogeniture could not be circumvented and the baronetcy passed to Archibald Stewart. However, Franc went off to Galveston with pictures, jewels, silver and furniture from the castle valued at two hundred thousand dollars. In Galveston he called himself Lord Stewart and married a Houston debutante, Miss Ella Hutchings. But Miss Ella didn't want to be Lady Stewart for long and the marriage broke up. Franc died in San Antonio, Texas, in 1913, having disposed of most of the Murthly heirlooms by then.

On the long trail of fifteen hundred miles there was always yarning before bedtime. The mountain men told Captain Stewart stories of their survival in the Indian country. Stewart told of his survival on the streets of London and Paris and New Orleans. Life, it seemed, was exciting wherever there were people. Miller called this painting Moonlight — Camp Scene. It is owned by the Walters Art Gallery, Baltimore, Maryland.

You will have observed that Sir William spent his life avoiding women and consorting with men. During his Rockies years he always had males in tow, and yet, paradoxically, this preference for men derived from the fact that he liked women very much indeed — Anglo, Indian, Creole or whatever. He avoided them, socially at least, because the alluring Christina had taught him early in life what would happen to him if he didn't — the awful slavery of love, children and dear, dull domesticity. Until his retirement in 1844, he was far too egocentric and adventurous to endure such an existence. The deepening experience of connubial bliss was not for him and, for that reason, he lived and died a limited man. He settled deliberately for half a loaf.

But that half brought him seven summers of savoring paradise on Green River. Perhaps that was enough.

2

THE TRAVELS OF PRINCE MAX

THE THRILL of hunting buffalo and other strange beasts lured Captain Stewart to the mountain West in that first summer of 1833. At exactly the same time, an entirely different kind of dude was drawn to the wilderness by the lure of a different kind of adventure — the search for scientific discovery.

Alexander Philip Maximilian, Prince of Wied-Neuwied, was born in 1782 in one of those picturesque perching castles which make the Rhine between Bonn and Koblenz such a charming waterway. He came from a long line of royal scholars, including his father, Prince Friedrich Karl, who ruled his small harmonious principality from his castle in Neuwied, eight miles downstream from Koblenz. Karl taught his eighth child, Maximilian, to be dutiful, patriotic, proud and Protestant. The boy learned to study hard, to discipline himself and to require discipline from his associates. He could have developed into quite a prig but was saved by his passionate thirst for knowledge about the wonders of nature, birds and geography, plants, animals and people.

He began hoping to visit St. Louis and the West as early as 1803, when Meriwether Lewis and William Clark were preparing their transcontinental epic. The ambition of Napoleon wrecked his plans. The prince fought in the Prussian Army at Jena in 1806, was captured by the victorious French, imprisoned, exchanged and returned to Neuwied. Later, while Lieutenant Stewart was with Wellington in Spain, Maxi-

milian rose to major general in the allied Army, which struggled
through France during the winter of 1814 to capture Paris and destroy
Napoleon's First Empire. Soon afterwards, he was able to escape
soldiering at last, making it to Brazil as a substitute for North America, which was still unsettled by the War of 1812. He passed two happy
years seeing what transpired in Brazil's tropical forests, and a decade
more back on the Rhine writing two monumental books and compiling
an atlas. The publication of these works on Brazil in four languages
during the 1820's brought him great distinction as an exploring naturalist.

By 1832, Prince Max, as he was called, was turning fifty — much
too old for further adventuring. But the obstacle of age never occurred
to him. He was ready now to tackle the scientific objective of his youth,
even if it killed him. He had been gathering material about it, even
corresponding with Americans such as the botanist Dr. Edwin James,
the Philadelphia museum director Titian Peale, and the ornithologist
Thomas Say, all of whom had reached the edge of the Rockies around
Pikes Peak with Major Stephen Long in 1820. St. Louis, it seemed,
was almost a German city these days, or so Maximilian was told by his
Thuringian friend Duke Bernhard of Saxe-Weimar, who had been feted
there in 1826. The young Rhineland physician Gottfried Duden had
farmed for three years on the Missouri near Dutzow, fifty miles west of
St. Louis. Maximilian had studied Duden's report, published in 1829,
which had inspired thousands of Rhinelanders to emigrate to the St.
Louis area. He had received still more information from Duke Paul
Wilhelm, whose family owned the duchy of Württemberg, centered on
Stuttgart and the Upper Rhine. In 1823, Duke Paul had called on
General Clark himself in his St. Louis mansion at Main and Vine to
enjoy his food and wine and to ask questions about the further West.
He had ascended the Missouri that summer in a keelboat as far as the
mouth of White River in today's South Dakota.

Prince Max sailed for America in mid-May, 1832, and arrived in
Boston harbor on Independence Day, with guns booming on Beacon
Hill. Two men comprised his scientific and domestic staff. One was
the extraordinary manservant David Dreidoppel, sturdy, self-effacing
and ingenious, who had been with the prince in Brazil and was far more
than a valet, having come to function almost as one of Max's vital or-
gans. The prince called him "King David."

His second companion was the promising Swiss-German artist, Karl Bodmer — "an able draughtsman," in Max's opinion. Bodmer was born in Zurich in 1809 and had studied in Paris under Sebastien Cornu while Alfred Jacob Miller was copying old masters at the Louvre. His inspiration was the Byronic violence and color of Delacroix in his Greek massacre scenes. He hoped to make a reputation of his own portraying a similar exoticism about the American wilds. Dreidoppel and Bodmer were tall handsome dudes with exquisite manners, and dressed in the height of Bavarian fashion. By utter contrast, their employer was an unstylish snapping turtle of a man, blinking, waddling, sniffing, staring, fearless and pugnacious. He was all of five feet four inches tall, with small wary blue eyes and a blond beard.

Major Alexander Culbertson, an American Fur Company factor, described him (somewhat incorrectly) some months later:

> The Prince was at that time nearly seventy years of age, but well preserved and able to endure considerable fatigue. He was of medium height, rather slender, sans teeth, passionately fond of his pipe, unostentatious, and speaking very broken English. His favorite dress was a white slouch hat, a black velvet coat, and probably the greasiest pair of trousers that ever encased princely legs. The Prince was a bachelor and a man of science, and it was in this latter capacity that he had roamed so far from his ancestral home on the Rhine. He was accompanied by an artist named Boadman and a servant whose name was, as nearly as the author has been able to ascertain its spelling, Tritripel, both of whom seemed gifted to a high degree with the faculty of putting their princely employer into a frequent passion.

Culbertson could have mentioned also Maximilian's long sideburns curving forward, his pursing mouth, hard round hat and long leggins fastened with fifteen buttons on each side.

The prince waddled his way slowly from Boston toward St. Louis, infinitely intrigued by the East and filling his notebooks with sharp observations in tiny cramped script. By mid-July of 1832, he and his entourage of two were in New York — "the city is extremely animated." He found that the inns there were unclean, the rooms too small, the newspapers too big and the mint juleps insupportably full of ice. Also, New York men ate too fast, though the women were elegant. The flies bothered him in Philadelphia but he admired the settle-

Prince Maximilian had not meant to winter in New Harmony, Indiana, but he fell sick there and stayed from October, 1832, until March, 1833. The town was in the doldrums after two decades of Utopia under German Harmonists and the English Socialist, Robert Owen. Thomas Say, the artist-naturalist, lived in New Harmony and told Max of his experiences up the Missouri and west to Pikes Peak with the Stephen Long expeditions of 1819-1820.*

ment of Moravians at Bethlehem, Pennsylvania, some of whom had been born in Neuwied. He was fascinated by the yellow covered bridge at Easton and flew into a rage at Delaware Water Gap when Bodmer confessed that he had left all his drawing equipment back in Bethlehem. As he staged his way west through Allentown and Harris-

*All reproductions of watercolors, lithographs and drawings in the chapter are by Karl Bodmer and are presented with the permission of the Northern Natural Gas Company, owner of the superb Maximilian-Bodmer Collection, Miss Mildred Goosman, curator, at the Joslyn Art Museum, Omaha, Nebraska.

burg, he saw Poland China and Duroc-Jersey hogs in the big red Pennsylvania Dutch barns, just as tourists see them on U.S. 22 today. On the Ohio below Pittsburgh, he paused at the communistic town of Economy, founded by Swabian rebels from Duke Paul's Württemberg. They called themselves the Harmony Society but he found them in disharmony over the issue of whether to be, or not to be, celibate.

He moved by steamer down the Ohio, complained of the armies of cockroaches and confided to his notebook that American conceit "is to be attributed partly to their excessive patriotism, and partly to their ignorance, and want of acquaintance with other countries." Louisville, Kentucky, was "a spot which is intended for horse-races, an institution quite new in the United States." Karl Bodmer continued alone downstream to New Orleans when Maximilian decided to call on the great bird man, Thomas Say, who was living at New Harmony, Indiana, on the Wabash, another Harmony Society colony. It was October now. The prince could not get over the sight of the gorgeous fall foliage — blazing catalpas and pawpaws, walnut and cherry, hickory and maple and buckeye. Europe, he wrote, had nothing remotely like it. He had not planned to stay long on the Wabash but came down with a persistent fever which could have been cholera. Dreidoppel spent much of that winter nursing him. Bodmer rejoined him at New Harmony and it was mid-March of 1833 before he was well enough to take a boat down the Ohio, and so up the beautiful Mississippi to St. Louis.

The town's Franco-American high society received the three men ecstatically, being fooled not a bit when Max pretended at first to be merely a Baron Braunsberg. The ladies had been keeping Captain Stewart busy all winter with gumbo cotillions, and now they had a bachelor prince as well as a Waterloo veteran to lionize and lubricate with apple toddy and rum punch. Maximilian declined some of the balls on the grounds that he had come to the frontier to study aborigines, not Paris fashions. The super-valet Dreidoppel stood in for him at the toddy tables while he and Bodmer interviewed Sauk and Fox Indians at General Clark's home and visited their tragic little old Chief Black Hawk, who was jailed in Jefferson Barracks for opposing white poaching on his Illinois lands.

Prince Max's immediate problem was where to go from here, and how. A rivalry for his favor arose at the start. Captain Stewart, General Ashley and the Rocky Mountain Fur Company men thought he should go West with their pack train, up the Platte to the Green River country. General Clark, his nephew Major Benjamin O'Fallon, and Pierre Chouteau, Jr., head of the American Fur Company, recommended the trip north up the Missouri, past the string of AFC posts on the AFC steamer *Yellowstone*. O'Fallon was particularly persuasive. He entertained Max and Karl Bodmer lavishly at his country place and showed them paintings of Missouri scenes which the Philadelphia artist George Catlin had made the year before when he journeyed on the *Yellowstone* to the AFC's Fort Union. And he gave Max a manuscript copy of the map Lewis and Clark had drawn of their Missouri-Columbia route to the Pacific. He stressed the viciousness of the Indians who attended rendezvous on Green River, and he suggested that the Ashley crowd was a rather low assortment of "individuals and small associations" which "have since made frequent attempts to carry on the trade in the Indian Territory and the Rocky Mountains, but have always been obliged to give way to the powerful and wealthy company" — the AFC, of course.

Of his final decision Maximilian wrote:

> Captain Stewart (of Grand Tully), an English traveller, with whom I had become acquainted at St. Louis, was on the point of setting out by land by the caravan, and it would have been agreeable to me to travel in his company; but after I had consulted many persons well acquainted with the country, the plan of following the course of the Missouri seemed to be the most suitable for my purposes; for, first, I should not be able to observe any Indians on the land journey; for if you happen to meet them, you must fight them; and, secondly, it is extremely difficult, nay impossible, to make considerable collections of natural history on such a journey. These reasons were decisive: I hoped, therefore, to obtain from the gentlemen of the American Fur Company, a passage up the Missouri in their steamboat, the Yellow Stone, which was daily expected to return from New Orleans.

PRINCE MAX boarded the S.S. *Yellowstone* at St. Louis on April 10, 1833, scorning the risks of his advanced years and brimming with joy at the thought of finding species no scientist had reported before. The sidewheeler was a jaunty little craft of less than forty tons. Pierre Chouteau, Jr., had her built for the American Fur Company at Louisville, Kentucky, during the winter of 1830-1831. On her maiden voyage in the spring of 1831, she had pushed up the five-mile-an-hour tawny

The gallant little steamer Yellowstone *had much to do with developing the Upper Missouri but it always had trouble getting upstream. It is shown grounded here on April 19, 1833, below Fort Leavenworth. Men are lightening it by moving cargo to shore on a lighter. Note cargo baskets in foreground. Bodmer's birds look like great blue herons.*

current of the Missouri, shaking with effort, her foredeck awash, her twin stacks belching wood smoke furiously. While river men had ridiculed that first attempt to send a steamer so far up such an angry stream, the boat somehow had reached Fort Tecumseh — soon to be replaced by the AFC's Fort Pierre (present Pierre, South Dakota). That was fifteen hundred miles west and north of St. Louis. A year later, as we have seen, the *Yellowstone* had carried George Catlin two thousand miles — all the way to Fort Union and near the mouth of the river for which she had been named. The feat had encouraged Pierre Chouteau, Jr., to order in Cincinnati a second, larger AFC steamer, the single-engined *Assiniboine,* drawing less water. This boat, Max learned, was somewhere up ahead on *her* maiden voyage. The *Yellowstone* would not try again to reach Fort Union. She would take the royal party only to Fort Pierre. In the five hundred miles of shallower river from there to Fort Union, Max would ride the *Assiniboine.*

Swarms of St. Louis swells, Indians and riverfront bums cheered, and two clarinetists piped "Yankee Doodle" as the *Yellowstone* left the docks and moved up the Mississippi to enter the Missouri on her third voyage. Her decks were crammed with the trade goods Indians loved, with coops of live chickens, and with eighty French-Canadian employees — oarsmen, steersmen, towers and so on. Prince Max had a small cabin of his own. Another was reserved for AFC officials and Indian agents, half of whom seemed related in some way to Pierre Chouteau, Jr. Max was taken especially with the wily, reserved and implacable Scot, Kenneth McKenzie, aged thirty-two — a relative of the immortal Alexander Mackenzie who had crossed Canada to the Pacific in 1793. Kenneth McKenzie's talents as AFC factor at Fort Union were bent presently toward bankrupting Captain Stewart's friends, Bill Sublette and Robert Campbell, in the Upper Missouri trade area. McKenzie confided to the prince that he had married a pretty Cree girl recently because Cree girls seemed to put out more heat in bed than others he had tested, and heat was what he needed during bitter winter nights at his Fort Union post.

The days slipped by on wings of happiness for Prince Max with his flora and fauna collecting, for Bodmer with his sketching, and for Dreidoppel, an enthusiastic hunter. They had the bursting spring to enchant them — bursting with color and songs of new kinds of birds, in

Fort Pierre, just a year old, was a model trading post of the American Fur Company when Maximilian stopped there in June of 1833. It served the Sioux Indians. Max liked them, especially the women for their beauty and the elegance of their dress. The Yellowstone had learned from experience not to go farther up the Missouri than Fort Pierre. The S.S. Assiniboine, drawing less water, kept on to Fort Clark and to Fort Union.

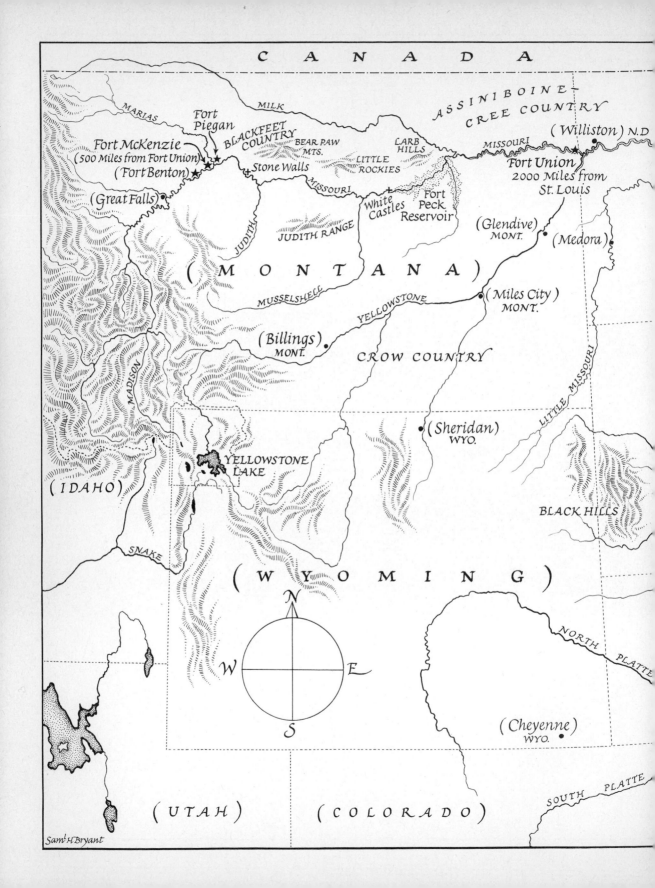

C A N A D A

MARIAS

MILK

Fort
Piegan

BLACKFEET
COUNTRY

ASSINIBOINE-
CREE COUNTRY

Fort McKenzie
(500 Miles from Fort Union)

BEAR PAW
MTS.

LARB
HILLS

MISSOURI

(Williston) N.D.

(Fort Benton)

Stone Walls

LITTLE
ROCKIES

Fort Union
2000 Miles from
St. Louis

(Great Falls)

MISSOURI

White
Castles

Fort
Peck
Reservoir

(Glendive)
MONT.

(Medora)

JUDITH

JUDITH RANGE

(M O N T A N A)

MUSSELSHELL

YELLOWSTONE

(Miles City)
MONT.

LITTLE MISSOURI

MADISON

(Billings)
MONT.

CROW COUNTRY

(Sheridan)
WYO.

YELLOWSTONE
LAKE

(IDAHO)

BLACK HILLS

SNAKE

(W Y O M I N G)

N

W   E

S

NORTH PLATTE

(Cheyenne)
WYO.

Sam¹ H Bryant

(U T A H)

(C O L O R A D O)

SOUTH PLATTE

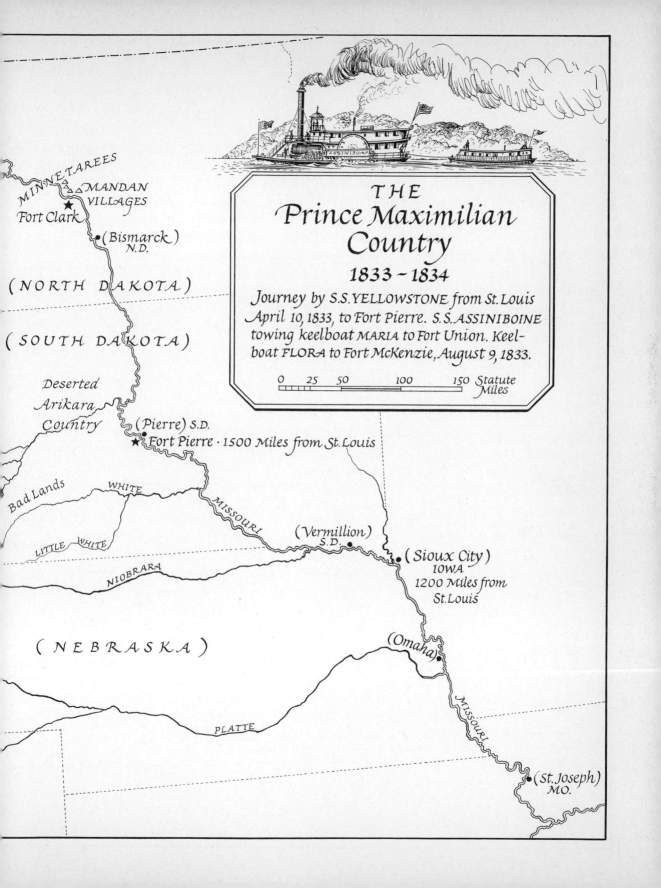

THE
Prince Maximilian Country
1833 ~ 1834

Journey by S.S. YELLOWSTONE from St. Louis April 10, 1833, to Fort Pierre. S.S. ASSINIBOINE towing keelboat MARIA to Fort Union. Keelboat FLORA to Fort McKenzie, August 9, 1833.

0   25   50   100   150 Statute
                                  Miles

MINNETAREES

△△ MANDAN
△△ VILLAGES

★ Fort Clark

● (Bismarck) N.D.

(NORTH DAKOTA)

(SOUTH DAKOTA)

Deserted Arikara Country

(Pierre) S.D.
★ Fort Pierre · 1500 Miles from St. Louis

Bad Lands

WHITE

MISSOURI

LITTLE WHITE

NIOBRARA

(Vermillion) S.D. ●

● (Sioux City)
IOWA
1200 Miles from
St. Louis

(NEBRASKA)

(Omaha) ●

MISSOURI

PLATTE

● (St. Joseph) MO.

the marshes and fields and verdant woods of Missouri, and then on the lovely low grassy hills as the steamer approached present Nebraska. At Fort Leavenworth (just promoted from a cantonment) Max had a choleric fit when Major Riley seized the cask of brandy which he had brought to preserve his specimens. Riley seized thirty barrels of McKenzie's Fort Union whiskey too, since liquor for drinking was supposed to be banned in the Indian country. Riley kept the brandy cask until Max convinced him of its scientific purpose by pushing a live black snake into it. Meanwhile Karl Bodmer, a tenderhearted youth, learned a lesson about Plains Indians. Word came to the steamer that some Iowas had raided the Omahas nearby, and had brutally kidnapped a woman and her child to sell into slavery. The gallant artist went forth with the posse rushing to their rescue. They found them, but both the kidnappers and the kidnapped had drunk so much whiskey to celebrate the crime that nobody could walk. Rescue was out of the question.

The *Yellowstone* passed small trading posts often (they would be city sites in two short decades — St. Joe, Omaha, Council Bluffs, Sioux City, Vermillion). A succession of Indian tribes watched the white man's "hissing machine" from the yellow riverbanks. They watched in eerie silence, thinking perhaps of attacking the boat, but Max let the other passengers worry about that danger. He was too preoccupied with the anthropological appearance of the enemy to worry about getting scalped. He noticed many similarities between them and the Tapuyan tribes which he had studied in the highlands of eastern Brazil. He decided that the Omahas were lazy, ugly and unintelligent, the Ponchas quite the opposite, and the Dakota Sioux surprisingly sophisticated in dress, and generally well-to-do. He was not afraid of any of them — and still he was shocked on May 14 when some French-Canadians, canoeing downstream, reported to Kenneth McKenzie that the bloodthirsty Arikaras of the neighborhood had just murdered three white men. One of them was that coming creature of folklore, Hugh Glass, who had led a charmed life as New Orleans pirate, slave of the Pawnee Indians, lone Rockies trapper and bare-handed battler of enraged grizzlies. The canoemen added that the Blackfeet Indians were being discourteous too. They had killed thirteen white boatmen up the Missouri, near the Rockies far above Fort Union.

The Minnetarees, wearing their best, called on the prince at Fort Clark from their village upstream. Here Max's interpreter, Toussaint Charbonneau, points out Max to the head chief and the bowing horse, fearing perhaps that the company would pick the distinguished-looking Bodmer (top hat) as the guest of honor. Charbonneau, you recall, was Sacajawea's husband.

Disturbing news, since Max himself hoped to visit the Rockies by way of the Missouri. And yet he suspected that the steamer *Yellowstone* was a much greater threat to his life than these interesting aborigines. Every inch of her advance was a desperate flailing of paddle wheels, of poling at the stern, or men on the banks towing regardless of obstacles in their path — willows, boulders, collapsing banks. Some navigational catastrophe occurred hourly. A cabin chimney would catch fire, threatening to touch off barrels of gunpowder stored near it. The wide river's current carried along whole forests of dead trees, the underwater snags of which had to be divined by Captain Bennett's extrasensory perception. As Max slept early one morning, a large tree branch forced its way into his cabin, "carried away part of the door case, and then broke off, and was left on the floor . . . when one might have been crushed in bed." The *Yellowstone* could not float in less than five feet of water. During one grounding:

. . . we landed twenty men on a sand bank, to tow the steamer, but their efforts broke the rope, and they all tumbled one upon another, to the great amusement of those on board. By way of precaution, our vessel was fastened to a large tree, which proved our safety, for the rudder was soon afterward deranged, and rendered unserviceable. It was repaired about two o'clock, but we soon ran aground on a sand bar where we were obliged to remain all night, in a rather unsafe situation. On the morning of the 19th a flat boat was procured to lighten our vessel, by landing a part of the cargo, which was piled up in the wood, on the bank, and covered with cloths. . . . Mr. Bodmer made a faithful sketch of this scene.

The grounding crises reached a climax some weeks later:

At the mouth of the Little Nemehaw River, the Missouri was very shallow. We ran aground about noon, on a sand bank, and were obliged to put out a boat to take a sounding, but the wind, which blew with increasing violence from the open prairie in the south-west, drove us further into the sand bank. Every moment it became more furious; our vessel lay almost on her side, which the people endeavored to counteract by fastening her with strong cables to the trees lying in the water. After dinner several of our hunters went on shore, but the boat had scarcely returned, when the storm suddenly increased to such a degree that the vessel appeared to be in imminent peril. One of our chimneys was thrown down, and the foredeck was considered in danger; the large coops, which contained a number of fowls, were blown overboard, and nearly all of them drowned. As they got upon the sand banks they were afterwards taken up, with other things which we had been obliged to throw overboard; our cables had, happily, held fast, and, as the wind abated a little, Captain Bennett hoped to lay the vessel close to the bank, which was twenty feet high, where it would be safe, but the storm again arose, and we got deeper and deeper into the sands. Some of our hunters and Mr. Bodmer appeared on the bank, and wanted to be taken on board, but the boat could not be sent, and they were obliged to seek shelter from the storm in the neighboring forests. . . . On the following day we were obliged to lighten the ship before we could proceed, by landing the wood which we had taken in the previous day, and many other articles. Our vessel, however, soon ran aground again, and as we could not proceed, we made the vessel go backwards to the right bank, where we passed the night. In the preceding year the Yellow Stone had been detained five days at this place.

And still the little boat endured, and even progressed upstream at an average of twenty miles a day (trees floating downstream made six times as much). Six weeks after leaving St. Louis, she entered the prairie dog country north of the Niobrara River, with chains of low sand hills and odd rock shapes rising from the tablelands. On June 2, the fifty-first day of the voyage, the prince, Bodmer and Dreidoppel left the *Yellowstone* for good at the Sioux-serving AFC trading post of Fort Pierre — blockhouses, residences, warehouses and a population of a hundred clerks, interpreters and hangers-on. Around the fort Max saw fertile fields filled with cattle and horses, and hundreds of Sioux tipis made of buffalo skins. Beyond them were the Indian burial stages, supported on long cottonwood poles holding corpses wrapped in skins. If the wind was right there was an odor, though Max did not find it morbidly unpleasant. The S.S. *Assiniboine* had reached the fort some hours before. The royal party shifted gladly to her roomier, more comfortable cabins fore and aft. A large area between decks was reserved for the French-Canadian crew.

On June 5, the *Yellowstone,* loaded with eight thousand buffalo skins, paddled off downstream toward St. Louis without a care in the world. The *Assiniboine* resumed her grim upstream battle through "hills of clammy, greasy, sterile clay." She carried sixty people and she was towing the keelboat *Maria.* Kenneth McKenzie told the prince the ominous origin of the name. In 1805, Meriwether Lewis had honored his girl back East, Maria Wood, by giving her name to the river which entered the Missouri five hundred miles above Fort Union (short of present Great Falls, Montana). A year later, as the Lewis and

Clark expedition was returning from the Pacific, Lewis shot a Black-
foot Indian who was stealing his horse, on a branch of this Marias
River. His companion, Reuben Fields, stabbed another Indian to
death for stealing guns. The Blackfeet swore vengeance. They made
the region off limits to white men, until 1831 when McKenzie was completing Fort Union. He came to trading terms with them, more or
less. The result was the construction of the loneliest and most dangerous post in all the Western fur country near the mouth of the
Marias — the AFC's Fort Piegan first, and then the larger Fort Mc-
Kenzie close by, built in 1832. ·

The clammy hills continued as the *Assiniboine* struggled past villages abandoned in late years by the Arikara Indians under pressure
of the Sioux. Soon she entered Mandan territory, reaching Fort Clark
in its setting of blue hills on June 18. Hundreds of Indians of all ages
and their snarling dogs greeted the travelers — Yankton Sioux and
"remarkably tall and handsome Minnetarees" and even Crows from
far up the Yellowstone. Max met old Toussaint Charbonneau, the husband of the Lewis and Clark heroine, Sacajawea, and hired him as his
interpreter. Charbonneau escorted him through one of the Mandan
villages and arranged portrait sittings for Karl Bodmer with several
Mandan chiefs. It was all an anthropological heaven for the prince,
who was only mildly annoyed when "a young warrior took hold of my
pocket compass which I wore suspended by a ribbon, and attempted to
take it by force. . . . I refused his request, but the more I insisted in
my refusal, the more importunate he became. He offered me a handsome horse for my compass, and then all his handsome clothes and
arms into the bargain, and as I still refused, he became angry, and it
was only by the assistance of old Charbonneau, that I escaped a dis-
agreeable and, perhaps, violent scene." Max was fascinated by "the
haughty Crows riding on beautiful panther skins, with red cloth under
them." He was astonished by their horsemanship, and by the beautiful
embroidery of the Crow women. He observed, as Captain Stewart had
observed on Green River, that "they have many bardashes, or her-
maphrodites, among them, and exceed all the other tribes in unnatural
practices. Of the female sex, it is said of the Crows that they, with
the women of the Arikkaras, are the most dissolute of all the tribes of
the Missouri."

Good Book

Prince Max found a Mandan Indian village three miles above the American Fur Company's Fort Clark and was charmed when the residents staged this buffalo dance for him. The variety of action would seem to compare with the best of movie spectaculars. Max noted that the spherical clay huts of the Mandans resembled the "hippahs" of aboriginal New Zealand.

Next day the *Assiniboine* thrashed on. Max began seeing antelope and bighorn sheep but, oddly, no buffalo. On the serene windless afternoon of June 24, the boat reached the mouth of the Yellowstone, a full, dark-blue stream issuing from soft gray slopes. It was the prince's seventy-fifth day of travel out of St. Louis. From that point (barely inside today's North Dakota) he saw, at a distance of two miles, the blockhouses of Fort Union on the north bank of the Missouri. But the river took a twist, and the steamer had to go five miles to get there. The fort's quadrangle sat near the river just inside present Montana, in splendid grasslands backed by handsome hills. As the boat approached at sunset, everything glowed warmly golden beneath an azure sky — the clustered log buildings, the tipis of the Indians, the large horse herd, the limpid river. The fort's several cannon boomed welcome and a hundred employees on the bank shouted greetings which Max recognized to be in English and German, in French and Spanish, Russian and Italian. At the head of this noisy delegation was the fort's bookkeeper, the distinguished, graying James Archdale Hamilton. His real name, Max learned from McKenzie, was Lord Archibald Palmer; he was said to have fled England to escape scandalous difficulties. It was he who escorted the prince, Bodmer and Dreidoppel to pleasant quarters in McKenzie's rambling one-story home within the quadrangle. He was as punctilious in manner and as fastidiously garbed as any of His Majesty's Britannic diplomats.

MAXIMILIAN SPENT TWELVE DAYS at Fort Union studying details of its operation and observing its clients, the Assiniboines, a rather impoverished breed of Sioux. Crees were present also, in smaller numbers. The two tribes occupied the same lands along the Canadian border and shared a hatred of the Piegan branch of Blackfeet around Fort McKenzie. As time passed, Max nourished a strong desire to go to Fort McKenzie and to spend the winter there. He talked it over with the factor of that trading post, David Mitchell, an experienced AFC official who was about to return to McKenzie from Fort Union on the keelboat *Flora*. Mitchell advised him not to go. The month-long journey of five hundred miles was itself perilous. Mitchell had started up the Missouri the summer before, got caught in a storm, and lost his thirty-thousand-dollar cargo, keelboat and three crewmen. The thousands of

When Kenneth McKenzie built Fort Union in the late 1820's barely inside the present border of Montana, he picked an Upper Missouri site of spacious beauty. It was salubrious, too. "We have no disease here," Max was told. In Bodmer's painting, the Missouri is hidden by cottonwood groves, with tawny bluffs showing above its south bank. The Yellowstone River comes in just out of range to the left. Fort Union attracted all sorts of Indians to trade — Assiniboines, Crees, Gros Ventres, Crows, Blackfeet.

Piegans and others around Fort McKenzie still seemed to detest white men, for all their pretense of friendship after the trading truce of 1831 with the AFC. They could have murdered the fort's handful of inmates at any time and months would pass before anyone heard about it.

The prince was not persuaded. He remarked that he had not seen even a herd of buffalo yet. He envied Captain Stewart, who must have reached the Rockies by now, and if Stewart could make his way to them, Maximilian of Wied-Neuwied could too. And so Kenneth McKenzie gave him reluctant permission to board the *Flora* on July 6. Bodmer and Dreidoppel came along loyally. The prince and Mitchell shared the small stern cabin. Bodmer and Dreidoppel laid out their blankets on deck with the other forty-eight passengers and crew. Major Alexander Culbertson was on hand — a large, placid man who had emigrated from Florida in 1832 to complete Fort McKenzie for Mitchell. The *Flora* was an exasperating craft, sixty feet long and sixteen wide, with mast and sail. A force of twenty-six nearly naked voyagers towed her most of the time, sloshing through the shallow water of the Upper Missouri while five men rowed and poled. Max had hardly got his sea legs when "an immense tree swept our deck, as the people who were towing did not hear us call to them, and broke the stays, by which I received a severe blow, which might have proved dangerous." The barren land of what would be eastern Montana grew more and more dreary. Max thought of his lush tropical Brazil and missed the racket of parrots and macaws and monkeys. Buffalo appeared, but their bellowing was occasional and melancholy, as was the howling of wolves, screaming of elk and cawing of crows. A pall of depression enveloped the keelboat as it lurched through the badlands near today's Fort Peck Reservoir. Trail travelers avoided this desert section then, just as they do now, passing instead sixty miles to the north along the present course of U.S. 2 and Milk River. David Mitchell spoke darkly of Fort McKenzie, wondering if his twenty-seven employees had been allowed to survive during his absence. Hints of Rocky Mountains were beginning to show ahead — Larb Hills, Little Rockies, Bearpaws, Judith Range. Bodmer made sketches of the ghostly hill strata known as the White Castles. They passed the mouth of Musselshell River on July 28, and the *Flora* moved more easily because the Missouri became straighter and free of floating trees.

In the beautiful Stone Walls area above the mouth of Judith River, the landscape swarmed suddenly with Indians — Gros Ventres of the prairies. Dozens of them scrambled on the *Flora* demanding brandy, gunpowder and lead. Mitchell managed to control them and told the prince that they were harmless beggars, adding in the next breath that they had massacred the staff of a Canadian post lately, and had killed five white trappers at the Battle of Pierre's Hole in 1832. On the evening of August 8, the *Flora* passed the mouth of the Marias, and was tied up for the night near the charred remains of Fort Piegan. The next morning, the thirty-fourth day out of Fort Union, Mitchell was up at dawn expecting trouble ahead. The worried passengers prepared for it as the *Flora* was towed upstream thirteen miles further, to Fort McKenzie on the north bank. But no trouble developed. The fort's garrison *had* survived Mitchell's absence, and rode forward to greet the arrivals. The American flag waved languidly on the fort's fifty-foot staff. Max could see a thousand Piegan and Blood Indians waiting for them along the mile of prairie around the fort. Their chiefs were in a warm, welcoming mood, resplendent in "red and blue uniforms, trimmed with lace, and wearing round hats with plumes and feathers." These chiefs and the employees formed a double receiving line at the boat landing. Mitchell and the prince stepped from the *Flora* first, and walked two hundred feet to "the most dangerous post in the fur country." Perhaps it was. But as Maximilian moved between the lines to the fort, bowing and shaking hands with the chiefs, he felt that royal protocol could not have been more genteelly observed anywhere in Europe.

The hastily built fort sat in a two-hundred-foot-square compound, enclosed by cottonwood pickets fifteen feet high and with bastions at two corners. Max, Bodmer and Dreidoppel were quartered in the factor's log house which was twenty feet wide and seventy-five feet long. Near it were cabins for the clerks, the kitchen, the mess, and for trading conferences with the Indians. There was stable space for thirty to forty horses. From a bastion, Max could see the high, black-clay south bank of the Missouri with the Highwood Mountains behind, rising to seven thousand feet above sea level. Northward was a range of hills. Max learned that the Great Falls of the Missouri were forty-five miles further upstream, and the actual Rockies, which he wanted so much to visit, were sixty miles west of the Falls.

THE FRIENDLY ATMOSPHERE which had prevailed at the *Flora*'s arrival lasted only a few hours. It was followed by three weeks of confused turmoil and threats of turmoil inspired by half a dozen varieties of Indians. Max and Bodmer and Dreidoppel would have been entertained by it all if their lives hadn't been in constant danger. The turbulence started when David Mitchell called in Chief Ninoch-Kiaui, of the Piegan branch of Blackfeet, and gave him a new uniform which the AFC had bought in St. Louis at a cost of a hundred and fifty dollars. It was a stunning affair, half red and half green, with red and green facings and trimmed with silver lace. It reminded the prince of the convict uniforms he had seen at London's Bridewell.

Mitchell told Ninoch-Kiaui, an ugly old martinet, that the uniform was his reward for refusing to trade with the Hudson's Bay Company at its Canadian posts to the north. Ninoch-Kiaui celebrated with much brandy that night and boasted of his uniform to several chiefs of the smaller Blood Indian branch of the Blackfeet. The Bloods were deeply offended by Mitchell's favoritism, stole three Piegan horses and threatened to attack the fort and murder Mitchell and everybody else. They did kill one white employee (by accident, they said later) and Ninoch-Kiaui's nephew, "a quiet, well-disposed young man." In retaliation, the Piegans gathered in front of the fort on August 17 and went forth to destroy the Bloods who were camped nearby. Some Gros Ventres, Sarsis and Kootenais watched, undecided whom to support. The Bloods retreated far downstream toward Fort Union, perhaps to discuss the situation with the Piegans' enemies, the Assiniboines. Meanwhile Ninoch-Kiaui presented the corpse of his nephew to Mitchell as a mark of his esteem, and also the corpses of the nephew's brother and a Piegan child, who happened to die at the same time. So Prince Max had three corpses for scientific study close at hand in the factor's house.

Ten days of extreme unrest followed, during which Mitchell and Major Culbertson tried to carry on trading with the Piegans and to bale furs for shipment to St. Louis. Then, on August 28, came the explosion. As dawn broke, Prince Max was awakened by a wild singing — a sort of musical yowl of abrupt broken tones which reminded him of the war song of Russian soldiers which he had heard in France in 1814. He jumped from bed and joined the seventy employees who were

In the pleasant heat of a Montana mid-summer, the prince's party moved by keelboat from Fort Union up the river in the five-hundred-mile run to the last AFC post, Fort McKenzie. Around the mouth of Milk River where Fort Peck Dam stands now, the men found immense quantities of game. Here Max's valet, "King David" Dreidoppel, stalks Ursus horribilis, watched by attentive black vultures.

at the bastions defending the fort. The prairie along the river was alive with Assiniboines (and some Crees) — six hundred of them mounted and on foot. As Culbertson wrote later, Max merely meant to observe, but became imbued with war fever and the savagery of this exotic environment. He seized his gun and manned a porthole. Though the gun was loaded already, he rammed down a second big charge and fired at an Assiniboine. The gun's recoil was tremendous and the five-foot-four-inch royal warrior "proceeded to revolve with great rapidity across the bastion till he came in severe contact with the opposite wall and fell stunned to the floor."

He recovered soon, and it was clear then that the Assiniboine objective was not the fort but the nearby huddle of twenty tipis containing Piegan celebrants sleeping off a drunk after completing their trading. Most of these Piegans left the riddled tipis and staggered into the fort. But four women and several children, burdened with saddles and skins which they were trying to save, moved too slowly and were shot down at the fort's entrance. An Assiniboine male lay dead among them. Max and Karl Bodmer, who was sketching, saw the start of a counterattack by a force of Piegans and AFC employees. The Assiniboines retreated slowly downstream toward the Marias. As they did so, Piegan men sent many bullets into the dead Assiniboine. Their women and children beat the scalped body with clubs and stones and, as Max put it, "the fury of the latter was particularly directed against the privy parts." To the prince's dismay, the man's skull was shattered and the pieces scattered. He had wanted the skull for his collection, and felt he should have had it, being sure that this was the Assiniboine he himself had shot.

By one o'clock that afternoon, the strange battle, or game, or whatever it was, ended. The defeated Assiniboines were moving out of the region northeastward toward the Bearpaw Mountains and Canada. Old Chief Ninoch-Kiaui, whose gaudy uniform seemed to be the issue, expressed gratitude to the prince, declaring that "no ball had touched him; doubtless because Mr. Bodmer had taken his portrait a few days before." On August 29, Ninoch-Kiaui led his people in a noisy victory celebration around the fort. It was watched dourly by the Bloods on the high bluff across the river, and a few shots were exchanged. Max thought that another battle impended. But the shots turned out to be

At Fort McKenzie, terminal point of the prince's trip, he had the good luck to witness a wild battle between a Piegan band of Blackfeet and some Assiniboines and Crees from Fort Union. It occurred just outside the stockade. Inside, Max succumbed to the general excitement, grabbed a gun and plugged a redskin or two himself.

mere preliminaries for a peace treaty which was concluded between the Bloods and Piegans in a few days.

Now THE AIR at Fort McKenzie had the crisping feel of fall. The pause of early autumn, brooding and wistful, was upon them. The birds were flocking before starting south. The prince, Bodmer and Dreidoppel were weary from the tensions of August. The trail to the Rockies a hundred miles upstream was infested with Indians of uncertain disposition. Max decided to forego that trip. Furthermore, the thought of spending the winter in Mitchell's drafty house at that parlous world's end was not alluring. So he asked the factor to have a boat built for the return of his party to Fort Union — a flat-bottomed, square-sterned Mackinaw. The boat was put in the river on September 11, and loaded with the prince's specimen cases and with the large cages for the two live grizzly bears which had been captured for him.

Three days later, Max, Bodmer and Dreidoppel said good-bye to all their white and red friends and floated off downstream with their crew of four men. The bears groaned and moaned day and night, the boat leaked, Max's pet chipmunk drowned in a storm and many specimens were ruined by mildew. But they got through the Montana badlands safely and arrived on September 29 at Fort Union with its withered prairie and orange-colored woods. Here they passed a comfortable month with Lord Palmer and his clerk, J. E. Brazeau. Then they continued in a larger Mackinaw to Fort Clark, disembarking there on November 8 to spend the winter.

The Fort Clark sojourn was a trial. Kenneth McKenzie had built a log cabin for the three scientists. It had — miracle of miracles! — glass windows, but the wind whistled through cracks in the mortar, rats gamboled over them at night, and there was not enough firewood to cope with temperatures of twenty-five degrees below zero. Bodmer's paints and the prince's inks froze solid. The fort's winter diet was corn almost entirely. Max came down with a mysterious disease on March 11 which brought on a terrible swelling of one leg, extreme weakness and high fever. He noted that "at the beginning of April, I was still in a hopeless condition, and so very ill that the people who visited me did not think that my life would be prolonged beyond three, or, at the most, four days." At this crucial point, the fort's Negro cook, a St. Louisan, stepped into the case. He told Max that he suffered from scurvy, due to the lack of fresh vegetables. He put a group of Indian children to work gathering wild onions, boiled them into a spinach-like dish, and ordered the prince to consume them in quantity. Within hours, the patient was feeling better. By April 5, he was well.

During the winter of 1833-1834 at Fort Clark, Max nearly died of scurvy. But he was well by mid-May as he floated down the Missouri in this version of a Mackinaw boat. Bodmer's lithograph shows Max standing in the boat while the artist and Dreidoppel stand on shore.

Maximilian passed those winter months organizing the mass of scientific material in his notebooks and completing his study of Mandan and Minnetaree Indians, with Toussaint Charbonneau's help. He continued to find similarities between the Upper Missouri River people and the Brazilians he had met in 1817. He observed, for example, that the Piegans and Bloods had small hands and feet "with prominent veins, exactly like the Botocudos and other Brazilians. . . . Children, as in Brazil, have in general, prominent bellies and thin limbs, and often the navel large and swollen. . . . Their mode of swimming was not like the Europeans, but perfectly resembled that of the Brazilians." He added, though, "that there are more cripples among the North American Indians than in Brazil. A dwarfish Assiniboin [*sic*] frequently visited Fort Union, who was, at the most, between three and four feet high. . . . I met with several Indian dwarfs; but not a single instance among the many Brazilians I have seen."

His conclusions were startling in 1834, and remain startling now. North American Indians, he suggested, were not savages. They were as civilized as Caucasians, in terms of their environment. They were as intelligent as whites, as moral, and at least as peaceful as Europe's constantly warring people. They were as honest, as generous, as hospitable, and cleaner on the whole. They had a subtle sense of humor. Artistically, their taste in color and composition was remarkably good. Their leathercraft compared well with that of Hungarian specialists. The long skirts of the women were as gracefully designed as similar skirts Max had seen in Poland. Their cuisine could be superb in the use of herbs. Their perfume, made from a foreskin secretion of the beaver, was quite as pleasant as French perfume based on an ingredient of whale blubber. They had charming social customs, such as flicking brandy into the air with a finger before drinking it, as a gesture of love and remembrance to deceased friends and relatives. Instead of buying drinks for friends, as Europeans did, they spat brandy into each other's mouths. They were never morbid about death. An Assiniboine father was delighted when Dreidoppel, who had been studying burial stages, told him that he had found a mouse nesting in the skull of his departed son.

As a naturalist, the prince was more than a mere reporter. He was thrilled by everything he saw and tried to communicate his ex-

The travelers found fairy castles inhabited by bighorn sheep in a twelve-mile stretch of the Missouri above Judith River. These white sandstone formations were called the Stone Walls and they reminded Max of Harz Mountain scenes in Germany. Bodmer painted in a whooping crane. Tourists today see the enchanting area in rubber boats floating down from Fort Benton, Montana.

citement. "The cry of the male elk in the rutting season," he wrote, "is very singular, and seems to be in no due proportion to the large, heavy animals. It is a shrill whistle, which, for the most part, runs regularly up the scale, and then suddenly falls to a low, guttural note. The notes perfectly resemble a run upwards on the flageolet."

Modern bird students can understand what joy Max knew out there, seeing white pelicans and great blue herons and whooping cranes and hawks and swans and Bohemian waxwings. He gave many birds interesting names of European derivation. By "blue-crested roller" he meant the blue jay. His "sea pheasant" was a pin-tail duck, and his "beautiful bluefinch" was the lazuli bunting. The "blue-gray butcher bird" was a loggerhead shrike and his "black water-hen" was a coot. His "starling" was a western meadowlark. His "goat-sucker" or "manger des maringouins" was the nighthawk and his "black and white bunting" was the lark bunting. "Yellow-headed oriole" referred to the Bullock's oriole. He took a specimen of the ubiquitous magpie "which in appearance much resembles that of Europe; but differs considerably in its note and manners."

Max's last act at Fort Clark was to prepare his precious collection of Upper Missouri material for shipment downstream later on the S.S. *Assiniboine*. The three men and the grizzly bears left the place on April 18 in the Mackinaw boat. They stopped briefly at Fort Pierre so that the prince could get some skulls from graves in the deserted Arikara village to make up for the Assiniboine skull he had failed to get at Fort McKenzie. Food was scarce at Pierre. But the factor wanted to feed his distinguished guests well and paid twelve dollars for a dog which, Max wrote, "was very fat, about the colour of mutton, and the taste was really so excellent that we speedily surmounted our prejudice and antipathy." On May 18, the travelers in the Mackinaw floated past Fort Leavenworth and reached the American Hotel at St. Louis ten days later. Prince Max resumed calling himself Baron Braunsberg. After a week's rest, the three continued by steamer and stage to New Harmony, Cincinnati and Portsmouth, Ohio. They took a canalboat then on the Ohio and Erie Canal to Lake Erie, and on by steamer to Buffalo and the Erie Canal. Here they boarded a canalboat again and arrived in Albany, New York, on July 4, 1834 — exactly two years since their arrival in North America. The bears caused great excitement everywhere along the marvelously comfortable, rapid and

Maximilian returned to his castle on the Rhine in August, 1834, and toiled for three years writing his report of his Upper Missouri adventure. This later portrait shows him as a retired soldier, scientist and explorer.

scenic canal routes. Max and Bodmer were stirred especially by "the violent commotion" of Niagara Falls. But they found the greatest beauty of all in the steamer trip down the Hudson River past the Catskills, High Tor, and Sing Sing Prison to New York City. On July 16, they left America on a sailing ship bound for Le Havre.

MAXIMILIAN, PRINCE OF WIED-NEUWIED, spent the next few years writing one of the greatest works of the West, titled in German *Reise in das Innere Nord-America in den Jahren 1832 bis 1834.* It was published in 1839–1841 at Koblenz in two quarto volumes, with an atlas containing eighty-one of Bodmer's magnificent watercolors. The prince had hoped to support his observations with his collection of Upper Missouri flora and fauna, which he had left at Fort Clark. Room for the collection cases was not found on the *Assiniboine* until the spring of 1835. Then, as she was descending the Missouri near present Bismarck, North Dakota, sparks from her cabin stovepipe set her afire at the head of Sibley Island. The collection was destroyed, along with 1,185 packs of AFC buffalo robes and beaver pelts. Four captive buffalo consigned to St. Louis abandoned ship and swam ashore to freedom. The collection's loss was a tragedy. Max was not consoled much by Dreidoppel's success in getting the Arikara skulls to Germany. One of them went to the Anatomical Museum at the University of Bonn, and the others to the University of Göttingen.

After publishing his book, the prince settled down in his schloss on the Rhine to enjoy a long and honorable retirement. He died at Neuwied in 1867 at the age of eighty-five. In the world of science, he would have been immortal for his pioneer studies in Brazil alone. The significance of his American work was heightened by the terrible smallpox epidemic which struck the Upper Missouri in 1837-1838, killing at least fifteen thousand Indians. The Mandans were wiped out totally. Two-thirds of the Assiniboines, Minnetarees, Blackfeet, Arikaras and Gros Ventres died. Their civilization was destroyed. Maximilian's material on their technology, symbolism and legends remains a primary source of information, complementing the studies of George Catlin.

For Karl Bodmer, his dude trip West was merely the start of his artistic career — interesting but incidental. Back in Europe, he resumed his Paris studies and then made his home at Barbizon near Fontainebleau. Here he became an early member of the "Barbizon school" of romantic landscapists. By the time of his death in 1893, the Bodmer engravings in Maximilian's atlas were as forgotten as the watercolors which Alfred Jacob Miller had done in 1837 for William Drummond Stewart. Bodmer would have been pleased if he could have foreseen how today's art critics would resurrect his Upper Missouri scenes and compare their draftsmanship and melodrama with Miller's naive excitement and George Catlin's powerful realism.

The two dudes Lord Milton and Dr. Cheadle built Fort Milton with their own hands and survived the hard Canadian winter of 1862-1863 within its log dimensions of fifteen by thirteen feet. It stood in present Saskatchewan, near Prince Albert National Park.*

*All sketches in this chapter are by J. Cooper, R. P. Leitch and T. W. Wilson, and are copied from illustrations in *The North West Passage by Land* by Viscount Milton and Dr. W. B. Cheadle, sixth edition (Cassell, Petter and Galpin, London, undated). The reproductions have been obtained through the kindness of Denver Public Library Western Collection.

3

ORDEAL OVER YELLOWHEAD

DURING THE TWENTY YEARS after Sir William Drummond Stewart's visit to Yellowstone in 1843, the volume of westering dudes increased hugely. The old appeals of big game hunting and scientific discovery brought many of them. Others were lured by the excitement of American emigration to Oregon, and by the Mexican War in the 1840's and, in the 1850's, by the gold rush — to California, and up the Fraser River of British Columbia, all the way to the Cariboo diggings short of Yellowhead Pass.

We are now tracing events leading to the Cariboo trek of the heroes of this chapter, Walter Butler Cheadle, whose father was vicar of the charming English village of Bingley in Yorkshire, and his friend William, Viscount Milton, also a Yorkshireman, of the great Fitzwilliam line of English peers. Young Cheadle was the typical sturdy son of Old England, upright, modest, judicious and resolute. He was a big ruddy-cheeked man weighing thirteen stone (182 pounds) and he loved every kind of athletics. In 1859 a family bereavement prevented him from rowing on the Cambridge eight in the race against Oxford and securing his full blue. Lord Milton, born in 1839, was four years his junior and met him while both were at Cambridge. Milton was Cheadle's exact opposite — slight, gay, irresponsible and soft-hearted, with a fondness for good rum and for pretty women not necessarily good. He was far from robust, being subject to fits now and then.

Lord Milton's father was William Thomas Spencer Wentworth Fitzwilliam, soon to be the sixth Earl Fitzwilliam, Knight of the Garter and aide-de-camp of Queen Victoria. While touring America in the mid-1850's, Lord Fitzwilliam spent some time out of St. Louis with the celebrated sport from Sligo, Ireland, Sir St. George Gore, eighth Baronet, who planned three years of hunting in Texas, present Colorado, Wyoming and Montana. Gore's retinue seems to have been even more elaborate than that of Sir William Drummond Stewart. It consisted of forty-odd employees, twenty-one carts, one hundred and twelve horses, eighteen oxen, three milk cows and fifty Irish staghounds and greyhounds. Inspired by Gore, Lord Fitzwilliam developed an interest in the West which was shared by his wife, the former Lady Frances Harriet Douglas, of the Scottish clan. One of her late relatives, Thomas Douglas, fifth Earl of Selkirk, had gone to western Canada at the turn of the nineteenth century, got control of Hudson's Bay Company, had the Selkirk Mountains named for him, and founded Red River Settlement which grew around the HBC post of Fort Garry (present Winnipeg). Another Scotch connection was James Carnegie, ninth Earl of Southesk, who spent the summer of 1859 exploring west from Fort Garry and Fort Edmonton almost to Yellowhead Pass, through parts of present Jasper and Banff Parks.

Southesk's trip was the main factor in Lord and Lady Fitzwilliam's sending their son to Fort Garry two summers later. Young Milton's first stay was brief, but when he returned to Yorkshire he dreamed of traveling further west if he could hire a suitable companion to help him through his occasional fits. Lady Fitzwilliam encouraged the dream just as Walter Butler Cheadle was finishing medical studies at Cambridge and winning the title of doctor. Cheadle and Milton got to discussing the "further west" idea and evolved it into a fantastically bold objective — the aforementioned Cariboo diggings in British Columbia. The main Cariboo camp, to which thousands were flocking in 1862, was a wild boom town called Barkerville. The standard route to it was easterly from the Pacific — from Victoria and New Westminster six hundred miles up Fraser River by steamer and stage. Our dudes proposed to pioneer a unique westward approach — from Fort Garry to the HBC's Jasper House, and on over Yellowhead Pass to the Upper Fraser. From there they hoped to find a way to the Cariboo.

EVEN AS LATE AS 1862, the vast hinterland of western Canada was far behind the U.S. West in frontier development. The name Canada meant the upper and lower eastern provinces (present Ontario and Quebec). British Columbia west of Yellowhead had only just become a Crown colony because of the Fraser River gold rush. The two thousand miles of prairie and forest in between (present Manitoba, Saskatchewan and Alberta) were still the preserve of Hudson's Bay Company and its small band of white and half-breed employees. The region west of Fort Garry was as remote and mysterious as Tibet to the twenty-six-year-old Cheadle and his frail patient of ancient lineage, aged twenty-two.

They sailed from Liverpool on the steamer *Anglo-Saxon* on June 19, 1862, and Cheadle began his daily log on everything and everybody — waspish, perceptive and self-revealing. He wrote of the "Romish round fat oily man of God" on the boat, of "the shovel-board, very slow game & most of us dreadfully bored," of the joys of pipe-smoking, of how he badgered the Yankee, Mr. Gray, "about the slave question & the present condition of the Cession . . . had at him about General Butler's villainous proclamation to the women at New Orleans." He worried for fear Lord Milton would "get screwed" (intoxicated) on mint juleps and brandy squash, and he was embarrassed when his patient declared noisily at the captain's table "that American women are the most beautiful in the world." Cheadle met Mr. Messiter, also Fort Garry-bound, "a tall fine young fellow, Etonian & Oxonian . . . on his way to hunting the buffalo & grisly bear. . . . He goes out prepared with arms & ingenious appliances of all kinds to alleviate the discomforts of wild life. 5 rifles, 3 revolvers & a gun! Gloves! Musquito nets, strychnine, rifle shells for the 'grislys,' etc., etc. What he will do with all his fixins I can't imagine."

The voyage was rough but they arrived safely up the St. Lawrence at Montreal on July 4, and on to Toronto, Niagara Falls ("disappointing"), Detroit ("a large, straggling place") and Chicago by lake steamer and rail. The Milton party numbered three now, Messiter of Oxford having joined the Cambridge pair. Cheadle found that his forebodings about Americans were correct: "Sallow faces . . . nasal twang, 'I guess' used universally for 'I suppose' . . . general rudeness of people; push past without begging pardon, etc. Shopmen serve you as if they were doing a favour." He despised them for fawning

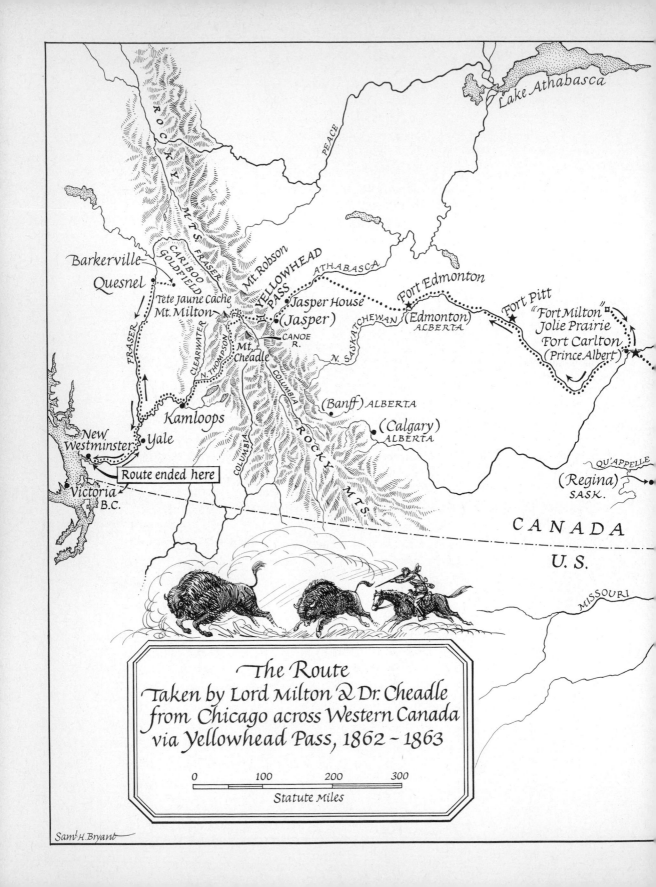

The Route
Taken by Lord Milton & Dr. Cheadle
from Chicago across Western Canada
via Yellowhead Pass, 1862 ~ 1863

0   100   200   300
Statute Miles

Sam.ᴵ H. Bryant

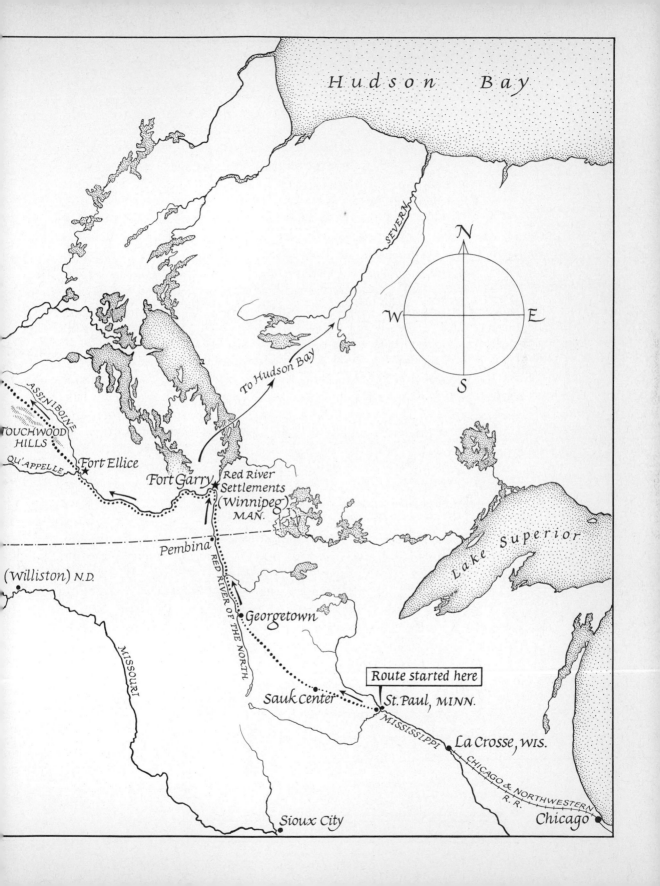

Hudson Bay

SEVERN

N
W E
S

To Hudson Bay

ASSINIBOINE

TOUCHWOOD
HILLS

QU'APPELLE

Fort Ellice

Fort Garry

Red River
Settlements
(Winnipeg)
MAN.

Pembina

(Williston) N.D.

RED RIVER OF THE NORTH

MISSOURI

Georgetown

Lake Superior

Sauk Center

Route started here

St. Paul, MINN.

La Crosse, WIS.

MISSISSIPPI

CHICAGO & NORTHWESTERN R. R.

Sioux City

Chicago

on Lord Milton and he deplored American sleeping-car etiquette. "Ladies and gentlemen very promiscuous. Ladies don't keep their division curtain down but watch the gentlemen dressing with great satisfaction." They rode the Chicago and Northwestern Railroad to the Mississippi at La Crosse, Wisconsin ("the prettiest state we have seen") and journeyed on up the Mississippi by steamboat to St. Paul. A spring wagon carried them westward to Red River through Sauk Center where Milton bought for twenty dollars "a dapper-looking, smooth-haired dog the size of a beagle . . . how faithfully Rover served us!" At Georgetown, Minnesota, on Red River, they rented one birchbark canoe and bought another for six dollars.

And so at last they faced the hard facts of exploration. Fort Garry was three hundred miles northward downstream, across the Canadian border beyond the last U.S. outpost, Pembina. Their soft hands blistered as they learned how to paddle. Their store food spoiled at once. They survived on frogs, small fish called mooneyes, and the lovely passenger pigeons and plover which Rover retrieved for them. Messiter almost shot Rover with one of his expensive guns, thinking he was a hostile Sioux. The canoes leaked abominably. Constant rain kept them soaked and miserable. The muggy days were hot and they traveled often at night, steering by lightning flashes. They broke the handles of their axe and frying pan. Messiter had the only watch and it stopped. Their matches would not light. The Georgetown-Fort Garry steamboat *International* almost ran them down in the Red River rapids.

To Cheadle, always a forthright and reasonable man, the worst thing was having to listen to the violent and constant bickering over bootless issues between Milton of Cambridge and Messiter of Oxford. Any issue would do. What time it was. The use of "damn it" in polite society. Whether Indians were worth saving and whether Rover weighed three stone. More than once Cheadle dreamed of being back in Bingley's sweet vicarage taking care of his recently widowed mother instead of these spoiled adolescents.

But they made it to the stone-wall enclosure and round towers of Fort Garry on August 7, 1862, ravenously hungry and covered with a multitude of boils and insect bites.

DUE TO MILTON'S TENDENCY to dawdle, they stayed a fortnight instead of a few days at the fort's busy Red River Settlement of whitewashed shacks. The time was passed outfitting for the winter, which they would spend further west, beyond HBC's Fort Carlton and the forks of the Saskatchewan. Milton hired three guides, including La Ronde, the alcoholic French half-breed whom he had met and felt sorry for on his previous visit. Cheadle paid twenty pounds for "a most extraordinary animal," which he named Bucephalus after Alexander the Great's favorite horse. "Bucephalus," Cheadle wrote, "stood about fifteen hands, was straight in the shoulder, one of his legs was malformed and crooked, his head was very large and tail very long . . . but warranted sound & to go up to buffalo well & stand fire." Milton developed a whitlow (inflammation) on his thumb. He caused Cheadle further anxiety by being weeks behind on the diary he was trying to keep for Lady Fitzwilliam, and by staying up until 1 A.M. one night with La Ronde's sister, probably making love to her, but telling Cheadle that she took that long to make his hunting shirt.

It was August 23 when they set out finally, up the lovely Assiniboine valley toward Fort Carlton five hundred miles further west, Rover leading, Milton and Messiter behind in perpetual heated debate, and then Cheadle and the guides. They dawdled two days later so that Milton could attend a country wedding and dance the double shuffle with the "very pretty, pensive-looking" bride. Messiter ate too many mushrooms one night and ruined the party's rest by having a nightmare and screaming for help because the Sioux were hostile again. One guide quit next day. Then Cheadle was summoned off their route by Lord Southesk's brother-in-law, Lord Dunmore, whose messenger said he was dying of jaundice. After two days of fatiguing forced march, Cheadle reached Fort Ellice, near the junction of Assiniboine and Qu'Appelle Rivers, to be told that his lordship felt very much better and was off hunting buffalo.

The September nights were growing cold. Milton's nose bled frequently, and Bucephalus was beginning to wear out. Both Messiter and Cheadle had caught a strange itch from one of the guides. But they passed the Touchwood Hills and reached Fort Carlton (near present Prince Albert, Saskatchewan) on September 26. The delicious buffalo steaks at the fort and glowing talk with the local Cree Indians about the fine buffalo hunting restored them all rapidly to physical and mental health. In 1862 the chance of experiencing a real buffalo hunt was still the ideal of every true sportsman the world over. Even Cheadle discarded all controls on his emotions and let himself go as he set out from the fort on October 1 with Milton, Messiter, La Ronde and the new guide, Zear. The entry he wrote for that day is the longest and most expressive in his whole journal:

Set out at 8. Somewhat excited, expecting to see bulls every moment. I ride the little roan mare again, Bucephalus being still unfit. After some 3 miles the carts which were in advance pulled up as they saw "les boeufs" in the distance; we rode up & saw 8 or 9 feeding about a couple of miles off, & presently several more herds at small distances from each other; 30 or 40 in all; girths were forthwith tightened, arms prepared. Messiter & I taking loose powder & charger, leaving our flasks behind. On went Milton a good deal excited, I feeling much as if I was in for something rather desperate, being however more afraid of not killing than of any danger. At a foot's pace in line, I on the right, Milton next, then La Ronde with Messiter on the left. When we got within ½ mile of the largest herd, La Ronde began to low, the other groups then looked up from grazing & then trotted off to join the main body. La Ronde then gave the word, & we broke into a canter, the large herd only looking round at us, & walking slowly forward, until joined by all the rest, when they began a slow lumbering canter; we quickened our pace a little & kept on the same so that we soon got within 200 yards. Then La Ronde cried "allez allez" & away we went, helter skelter, Milton leading on the Old Red by a couple of lengths, La Ronde next on the Grand Rouge, Messiter after on the Grey, I bringing up the rear on the little roan who did not go so freely as after the wolf the day before being, I fancy, rather the worse for her severe course. Then whip, whip, both heels hammering our horses' ribs, arms flying, guns brandishing & yelling in true half-breed fashion.

As Milton nears them the band divides, the larger half bending to the right nearer me, giving me a chance to get pretty well in; ½ miles & I am within 20 yards; another ½ I get within 7 or 8, my horse gaining very slowly; a comical appearance they presented, with head and shoulders covered with long hair, & bare hind quarters, like shaved French poodles, their long beards of fringed dewlaps wagging about, as they went along at a rolling gallop apparently very slow really have a good pace. They looked venerable but dissipated & used up. When within 10 yards of the herd I fired both barrels at one & two separated. My horse made a vigorous effort to cut them off, & succeeded in separating one after whom I kept on, dropping into a canter to reload, soon came up to him again, fired one barrel of my gun & then 3 of revolver without any effect; knowing that I should lose ground if I reloaded & that he would probably stop before long, I kept on with my one barrel loaded, & in about 200 yards, up went his tail with the tuft at the end waffing about, & he turned round & faced me with head down, & looking very vicious indeed. Just as he turned his broadside & before he got under way to charge I fired, aiming behind the shoulder. He turned again away from me, walked two or three yards, then, stretched his legs & died. I felt highly elated at having succeeded in slaying my first buffalo, & had been highly excited during the run, screaming & shouting & like a madman. I went up to him, feeling afraid he might not be quite dead & get up and charge, dismounted however & looked for my shot. Found it exactly in the right place just behind the shoulder, nothing wonderful at ten yards, but good for a quick shot. I took out the tongue & cut off his tail as a trophy. I hung them on to my saddle, marked the place & trotted off to rejoin the carts, after a mile & half descried the carts of Milton & La Ronde in the distance. La Ronde & Messiter each claimed to have killed two. Milton however found that one Messiter stated to be his was the one he had killed. A hot dispute. Evidence in favour of former — Messiter reluctantly gives up. Cheadle went back to his dead buffalo — wolves already had eaten entrails. Cheadle cut out marrow bones. . . . Presently saw Messiter in the distance in full career after a herd of bulls & then Zear cried out excitely "Voila, voila les boeufs," & I saw 9 bulls galloping straight toward us over the hill 3 or 400 yards off. I dropped my knife, seized my gun & loaded, ran forward to get as near as possible when they passed, fired at the leader, heard the 'thud' of the ball; he dropped behind the rest & I gave him the other barrel, he staggered on a few yards & dropped dead. We ran up, I excited & delighted. Found one ball behind the ribs, the other just in the right place behind the shoulder. Measured the distance & found it 105 of the longest strides I could take. Not bad practice with a smooth bore on an animal at the run.

Cheadle and Milton shed the contentious Messiter at Fort Carlton in mid-October, though the compassionate Milton was upset about it. The young adventurers spent that winter of 1862-1863 in a log cabin fifteen by thirteen feet which they built themselves, as directed by La Ronde and a trapper named Athanese Bruneau. The cabin sat in a sheltered glade on a lake eighty miles northwest of Fort Carlton, near present Prince Albert National Park. The spot was transitional, rolling Canadian prairie becoming northern forest. An attraction was its chalybeate and sulphur springs, which Cheadle compared to those at Harrogate in Yorkshire. They called it Jolie Prairie and named the cabin Fort Milton.

Their neighbors were charming, docile Wood Crees led by a chief whom Cheadle called Old Boy. The Crees, male and female, doted on Milton because he brought along from Fort Carlton three barrels of rum and distributed it generously — too generously, Cheadle felt. Old Boy appointed himself a sort of arranger for the two dudes. They had barely got settled at Fort Milton when Old Boy offered them his prettiest daughter as a joint project for a nominal sum. He had sold her to an Indian for a horse a week earlier and had reclaimed her when the husband stole the horse. "We declined the offer," Cheadle wrote on November 4, and added reflectively, "Not bad looking though." Whether Milton declined to possess her on his own part is a moot point. For weeks thereafter, Cheadle confided to his journal that Milton spent too much time with a girl guardedly designated as "Delilah" or "La Petite Sauvagesse." Cheadle was particularly wroth on November 29 when he found himself having to sleep outside Fort Milton, just as poor Holmes had had to do when Captain Stewart was conducting research with "the ductile Idalie" — also a Cree maiden from Saskatchewan, you may recall.

It was a winter of trapping, and Cheadle at last plunged into this exacting craft with characteristic thoroughness. While Milton usually stayed home smoking and loafing, Cheadle endured the awful cold of his traps circuit, learned how to snowshoe, and how to keep sane while handling a dog team ("Verily I believe driving a heavily-laden dog sled in hilly country would spoil the temper of a saint"). He relished the expectation of approaching a trap which might hold a priceless silver fox or perhaps only a fisher or marten or otter. Or it might hold nothing, having been robbed of its bait by the incredibly ingenious wolverines. He loved hunting moose and found the meat "extremely tender — a cross between venison and mutton." His relation to Milton was more and more that of a not unfond father, at once exasperated and entertained. Both men learned to speak some Cree and came to admire the Old Boy and his band. "The perceptions of an Indian," Cheadle remarked, "are so nice." The Fort Milton cabin became so filthy even the viscount got to work on it. Cheadle wrote in February, "I nearly died with laughter at Milton on hands & knees grubbing dirt

At the pemmican center of Fort Pitt, halfway between Fort Carlton and Fort Edmonton, Lord Milton hired Louis Battenotte ("the Assiniboine"), his wife and thirteen-year-old son to guide him and Dr. Cheadle over Yellowhead Pass. J. Cooper's sketch from a photo shows the doctor in the center with Lord Milton on his right.

from under the bedsteads with his hands." Milton showed unexpected skill as a chef and made a delicious plum pudding, despite its odd flavor of gunpowder, tobacco, shot caps and soap, since the currants and raisins had been stored with these items.

They packed up and left Fort Milton on April 3, 1863, "without a tear but feeling regret," hired the half-breed Baptiste Supernat at Fort Carlton as guide, paid off La Ronde and Athanese Bruneau and gave Rover to them. They spent five weeks moving four hundred miles up the North Saskatchewan to Fort Edmonton by way of the small Fort Pitt, near today's Saskatchewan-Alberta border (Frenchman Butte, Saskatchewan). At Fort Pitt, a pemmican supply center, Milton hired for general purposes a French half-breed, Louis Battenotte, aged about forty, his sturdy wife and his young son of thirteen years ("the boy"). Cheadle always referred to Battenotte as "the Assiniboine," since he had grown up in that tribe. He was middle-sized, soft-voiced and had only one usable hand, the left having been shattered in a gun mishap. Cheadle wrote of him, "Although his countenance beamed forth benevolence, and he cooed softly as any dove when at peace, yet when angry and excited, his aspect became perfectly fiendish. . . . we learnt subsequently that he had killed another half-breed in a drunken squabble."

At Fort Pitt, Cheadle began worrying about Milton who was drinking too much rum and showing the first symptoms since leaving England of his tendency to throw fits. In mid-May, as they neared Fort Edmonton on its picturesque cliff above the broad Saskatchewan's wooded banks, Cheadle wondered how long his high sense of honor would hold him to his duty toward his wayward patient. But at the fort a problem arose so vexing and insoluble as to put all thought of Milton's foibles out of Cheadle's chivalrous mind. The problem took the form of an Irishman in his late forties named O'Byrne who, one fateful May afternoon, presented himself to Cheadle and Milton as a graduate of Clare Hall at Cambridge. Cheadle described this personage with obvious, if paradoxical, amusement:

> His face was long and its features large, and a retreating mouth almost destitute of teeth gave a greater prominence to his rather elongated nose. He was dressed in a long coat of alpaca, of ecclesiastical cut, and wore a black wide-awake [soft felt hat], which ill accorded with the week's stubble on his chin, fustian trousers, and highlows [ankle-boots] tied with string. He carried an enormous stick, and altogether his appearance showed a curious mixture of the clerical with the rustic. . . . He crammed birth & aristocracy down my throat in nauseating doses — had studied law after Cambridge, became connected with the press. After that private tutor to different swells' sons. Been in India without bettering himself (I could not discover in what capacity). Returned to England. Did well till prosperous friend failed. After that engaged by planter at $2,000 & lived until [Civil] war broke out. One day confounded by planter coming up & congratulating him upon being elected Captain of the [Louisiana] home guard.
>
> As he is tremendous coward he was horror struck & decided that the only thing to be done was to escape at once . . . classical professor at

It was at Fort Edmonton on the North Saskatchewan, where Edmonton flourishes now, that the Milton-Cheadle party met its greatest problem — an Irish deadhead named O'Byrne.

northern college, St. Paul, Fort Garry to start a school, classics were however at a discount amongst the half-breeds, the academy failed to get started, so being sent to the Pacific by Archdeacon Cockran . . . to Fort Edmonton and Wolsey the Methodist Minister took pity on him during winter & in spring he came back here & lived in miner's shanty. He is a great talker & I fancy a great humbug & 'ne'er do well' who has been a dead weight on his friends throughout. Seems a well-informed fellow, however, & nearly knocked my head off with Latin quotations. Horribly afraid of bears & even wolves. . . . He wishes to go with us. . . . Poor fellow I wish we were not so short of carts. . . .

WHEN THEY LEFT FORT EDMONTON for the Cariboo goldfield in early June "the great humbug" was with them, due to Milton's soft heart. O'Byrne almost funked out at the last minute because the Assiniboine, knowing of his foolish fears about grizzlies, hid in the bushes and growled at him. Cheadle restored his morale with a huge dose of rhubarb and magnesia. Milton bought a gentle horse for him which he refused to approach to pack, believing he would be at least kicked and bitten. There were seven in the party, counting the Assiniboine family of three and the guide, Baptiste Supernat, who faded away in a few days because he disliked the company. The Assiniboine knew the trail as far as Jasper House on the Athabasca, where Milton would hire somebody to take them over Yellowhead Pass to the Shushwap Indian camp, Tete Jaune Cache, on the Upper Fraser. From there they hoped to cross the divide southward to North Thompson River, a Fraser tributary, rather than risk their lives on the Upper Fraser's rapids. They would follow the North Thompson down to Kamloops, British Columbia's most easterly outpost, and inquire there about reaching the Cariboo. The distance from Fort Edmonton to Jasper House was three hundred miles — another three hundred, reportedly, from Jasper to Kamloops. They had two hundred pounds of flour and three hundred pounds of pemmican which would last them fifty days, to July 24. That would put them in Kamloops at an easy rate of twelve miles a day. They had twelve horses all told, some of which could be eaten if necessary.

They reached the ridge of the Rockies — quite low and wooded at Yellowhead Pass — in a month, without much trail trouble, though the earnest Cheadle had his hands full coping with Milton's erysipelas and incipient fits and the Assiniboine's practical jokes at O'Byrne's expense. O'Byrne himself was Cheadle's worst trial. Each night he took a large axe to bed with him as protection against the Assiniboine's imaginary bears. He avoided his share of camp work by hiding behind rocks, where he steeped himself in William Paley's *Evidences of Christianity*. His skittish mind could not handle the slightest emergency. When camp embers started a small forest fire one night, he sat stunned until Cheadle had it all but out and then strode forth and poured a tin mug of water on it with a burst of Latin rhetoric.

He was forever lagging behind the party and crying piteously for help. When the men were building a raft to cross the Athabasca to

O'Byrne, seated left center, could not pull himself together enough to fight the forest fire with Lord Milton, Cheadle and the Assiniboine until it was all over.

Jasper House, Cheadle shamed him into carrying logs with Milton, though O'Byrne was careful to take the small ends. "O dear! O dear!" Cheadle heard him crying, "this is most painful. It's cutting my shoulder in two. Not so fast, my lord! Gently, gently. Steady, my lord, steady; I *must* stop. I'm carrying all the weight myself. I shall drop with exhaustion directly — *triste lignum te caducum."* Three days later, as the Assiniboine's wife led the way on her horse across the Miette, Cheadle had to force the terrified classicist onto his horse,

*R. P. Leitch may have stretched things a bit when he made this sketch of
Lord Milton leading Bucephalus up the trail with Cheadle prodding the
poor horse behind. Trails of such steepness would have been hard to find
in the Jasper area around Yellowhead Pass.*

which was following Milton's. O'Byrne clutched the horse's mane with
both hands, draped his lean form around its neck and pleaded, "Steady,
my lord, please, or I shall be swept off. Do speak to Mrs. Assiniboine,
my lord; she's leading us to destruction; what a reckless woman!
varium et mutabile semper femina! Mrs. Assiniboine! *Mrs. Assiniboine!* Oh, dear! Oh, dear! what an awful journey! I'm going! I'm
going! Narrow escape, that, my lord! very narrow escape indeed, doctor. We can't expect to be so lucky every time, you know."

"I never saw such an old woman in my life, or such a nuisance," Cheadle complained. But in spite of O'Byrne, the doctor had happy moments. He caught many trout on spinners and found these black-spotted, red-lined cutthroats "very like an English burn trout; they ate like our own fish." He bagged a mountain goat on a slope above the mouth of Lord Southesk's Rocky River, and picked "the marsh violet which Sarah & I found on the road to the beacon near Bolton Abbey." He liked the clean look of the little low-palinged Jasper House, twenty-five miles down the many-channeled Athabasca from today's Jasper town. He admired "Priests Rock" — present Pyramid Mountain, above Jasper Park Lodge.

The party left the Miette on July 9, crossed the imperceptible Yellowhead Pass to Pacific drainage of Fraser River, and camped on Buffalo Dung Lake (Yellowhead Lake these fastidious days). A cone-like terraced peak rose to the south, balanced on the north by a range of rugged rocks, "snow-clad with green slopes, & bright pines half way up." The Iroquois guide whom Milton had hired at Jasper House named the south peak Le Montagne de Milord, the north range Montagne de Docteur. Today's official Jasper Park map shows them as Mount Fitzwilliam (9538) and Bingley Mountain, for Cheadle's village. Fitzwilliam Creek flows from Mount Fitzwilliam into Yellowhead Lake. Cheadle's crooked-legged, big-headed, long-tailed horse is immortalized by Bucephalus Peak (9089) on the south side of Mount Fitzwilliam.

The summit just north of Bingley Mountain is called Mount O'Beirne, a variant spelling, perhaps, of O'Byrne. In any case, the name is pertinent, because the peak looked down on the party's struggle through muskeg and overflowing streams toward Moose Lake, and on the frantic O'Byrne's second horse crisis. "He still lagged behind," Cheadle reported, "and I again heard an awful shouting. I again went back, & found him leading his horse, which had the saddle under his belly, & in shirt sleeves & with a more lugubrious face than ever. The horse had fallen in a bog and rolled on him and he thought he was . . . 'very nearly killed, Doctor, this time. I thought it was all over. *Semel est calcanda via lethi.*' O'Byrne says he shall never forget the horrors of it. . . . He could not be persuaded to mount again."

Beyond Moose Lake and near Tete Jaune Cache, where their Iroquois guide left them to return to Jasper House, Cheadle gazed on Canada's highest Rocky Mountain, Robson Peak, "a giant among

The view up the Athabasca from near Jasper House (barely visible right of center) was as spectacularly beautiful in 1863 as it is today. The resort town of Jasper is twenty-five miles farther upstream from this point at the lower end of Jasper Lake.

giants and immeasurably supreme.'' It is 12,972 feet high and Cheadle's description of it by that name is one of the very earliest (if not the earliest) on record. The origin of the ''Robson'' is unclear. Some students believe it to be a corruption of Robertson. Colin Robertson was chief factor of Hudson's Bay Company around 1810 and plotted to snatch the Athabasca fur territory away from the rival North West Company.

The latest O'Byrne incident was the merest taste of infinitely

Beyond the Continental Divide, the Assiniboine showed tremendous courage by saving Bucephalus when the horse fell into flood-stage waters of the Fraser River. Today, Bucephalus Peak honors his memory near Yellowhead Pass.

worse troubles ahead, extending forty-four days and two hundred and fifty miles, until the party reached sanctuary at Kamloops. On July 15, harassed by the Fraser's high water, Cheadle lost his temper and berated Milton cruelly for his soft-hearted meddling with trail discipline. The Assiniboine threatened to go back to Fort Pitt if the dudes didn't stop quarreling. Soon after, he saved Bucephalus from drowning in the river by following him into the roaring deep current; caught under water beneath the horse's belly, he hung on heroically with his one good hand and worked the horse to shore. At Tete Jaune Cache, no Shushwap Indian wanted the job of guiding them south to

O'Byrne was afraid of everything, horses especially. He refused to ride his horse across Canoe River though he didn't mind hanging on to Bucephalus's tail as Cheadle rode across.

the North Thompson and Kamloops — a ten-day trip, they said. The Assiniboine was induced to try, and led them up the McLennan branch of the Fraser, over to Canoe River, and on south to its source at the present Canadian National Railway station of Albreda (a Fitzwilliam family name).

The six travelers attempted to cross the flood-stage Canoe River on a raft and, for once, O'Byrne was right in his predictions of catastrophe. As the raft bore down on a large, partly submerged pine tree, Cheadle, the Assiniboine and "the boy" leaped to shore. The raft rushed into the tree "through the branches of which the water was rushing & boiling like a mill stream at the wheel." The branches caught and held Milton and the Assiniboine's wife. But O'Byrne managed to stay on the raft, which flew on down the wild rapid. He sat quite still in the stern, calmly and placidly, as if steering. The Assiniboine chased

The Canoe River was flooding as badly as the Fraser. In trying to raft across it, Lord Milton and Mrs. Assiniboine were brushed by tree branches from the raft while O'Byrne floated calmly on through.

after him to stop the raft in a shallow. Cheadle sprang from shore into the pine tree to help Milton, who yelled, "Never mind me, help the woman." Then both Englishmen moved higher into the branches and grabbed Mrs. Assiniboine, who was pinned to the trunk by the tremendous water pressure, could not be budged, and appeared to be choking to death. At this point, Cheadle looked up and saw O'Byrne strolling toward them on the bank "with a face which betokened perfect imbecility. I shouted, 'For God's sake try & bring us a rope or the woman will be drowned!' but he only held up his hands in dismay. I shouted at him again & he sent his neckerchief by the boy. . . . Then the Assiniboine came and landed the woman safely.''

THEY WERE OUT OF RUM, tobacco, tea, coffee and sugar when they reached the North Thompson on July 26, with the Premier Group of magnificent icefield peaks behind them. Cheadle named a foothill of the group Mount Milton. The viscount chose a summit on the east side of the river and called it Mount Cheadle. The going so far had not been hard — and then suddenly it became desperately hard, as they entered a vast dense woods. Since all signs of game vanished in the gloom, they grew acutely aware that they had only ten pounds of pemmican left, and a little flour. The state of their despair was suggested by Cheadle's portrait of the scene:

> No one who has not seen a primeval forest where trees of gigantic size have grown and fallen undisturbed for ages, can form any idea of the impenetrable character of such a region. . . . The fallen trees lay piled around, forming barriers often six or eight feet high on every side . . . living trunks, dead trunks, rotten trunks, dry barkless trunks, and trunks moist and green with moss; bare trunks and trunks with branches — prostrate, reclining, horizontal, propped up at different angles; timbers of every size, in every stage of growth and decay, in every possible position, entangled in every possible combination. . . . horses almost impossible to drive, only 2 meals a day, doing 3 or 4 miles a day.

After a week at "3 or 4 miles a day" the pemmican was gone. Their fear of starvation was intensified when they came upon the seated headless rotting form of an Indian, plainly dead from hunger. Their clothes were in shreds, moccasins worn out. They had eight charges of gunpowder left. The North Thompson's rapids made it impossible for them to take to a raft, even if they could have fashioned one with O'Byrne's pocket knife, their only remaining tool. And yet — so often characteristic of the human species — their morale rose as their troubles increased. Milton astonished Cheadle by ceasing to dawdle and complain. He stopped having symptoms of fits. The Assiniboine was kind to O'Byrne. Even O'Byrne reformed somewhat and tried feebly to be of use.

Deep in the North Thompson wilderness, when starvation threatened,
Cheadle, Milton and the Assiniboine were not pleased to come upon a dead
Indian with the head missing.

On August 9, the group voted, with great reluctance, to let the
Assiniboine shoot the small thin horse Blackie, which produced thirty
pounds of meat. Three days later, as they entered a boiling chasm
called Porte d'Enfer Canyon, Cheadle feared that his own Bucephalus
might be the next victim. At Cheadle's request, O'Byrne was in the
rear leading the horse. Soon he ran up to the doctor minus Bucephalus.

"Where's the horse?" Cheadle asked.

"Oh, he's gone," O'Byrne said. "Gone, killed, tumbled over a
cliff. *Facilis descensus,* you see. It's not the slightest use going back, I

assure you, to look for him, for he's *commuted,* smashed to atoms, dashed to pieces! It's a dreadful thing, isn't it?''

Cheadle hurried back to the cliff and looked over. Bucephalus was there below all right, held astride a large tree, his long legs dangling helplessly, but very much alive. The doctor descended a hundred feet to him, removed his pack and rolled him off the tree trunk. He was not badly hurt.

A cruising crow announced their salvation, their emergence from the lifeless forest. They heard its caw on August 18 in the vicinity of the Canadian National's present Vavenby Station, British Columbia. They passed the mouth of Raft River (Milton named it Wentworth River, honoring part of his lineage) and the Clearwater's mouth, where a horse trail appeared. On August 24, as they ate the last bit of meat from their second butchered horse, they came upon a Shushwap squaw nursing her baby. She guided them to her family nearby, who stuffed them with fish and potatoes.

Four days later they arrived at the HBC's Kamloops post of three small buildings. They were a bit behind schedule. The six-hundred-mile trip from Fort Edmonton had taken eighty-five days instead of fifty. Bucephalus and the other nine horses were animate skeletons, stumbling along from weakness. The six humans were nearly naked, caked with dirt, their bodies covered with scratches and bruises, their long hair matted, hardly recognizable as people. The normally round-faced Cheadle was hatchet-faced now. He found that he had lost three stone (forty-two pounds). By odd contrast, the usually frail and slender Milton looked quite fat and robust. All six were bursting with good cheer and a jaunty pride in their achievement. That was their right. They were the second party of amateur travelers on record to get through Canada's western mountains by way of Yellowhead Pass.

Their first acts were to buy clothes, towels and soap, and to bathe in the North Thompson. "Then ah then," Cheadle wrote, "dinner — mutton chops, potatoes, fresh butter, delicious galette, rich pudding! Never shall I forget that delightful meal. Strong tea and plenty of sugar. Talk of intellectual enjoyment! Pooh! pooh! Your stomach is the door of true delight. No use in describing how we ate & drank."

The remaining months of their Canadian expedition were anticlimactic. Cheadle maneuvered a release from the O'Byrne problem by forcibly urging the man to remove his long face and Latin quotations

The insouciant Lord Milton seemed little the worse for wear when he had this picture taken in San Francisco during the Christmas holidays of 1863. His disposition remained sunny in spite of all he had endured from flood, famine and bitter cold, to say nothing of restrictions imposed by that model of righteousness, Dr. Cheadle. (Photo kindness of Provincial Archives, Victoria, British Columbia.)

from Kamloops by the next pack train bound for the Pacific. Cheadle and Milton followed a bit later — on September 8, 1863 — and proceeded to New Westminster by horseback as far as Yale on the Fraser, and then by steamer. Lord Milton insisted that the Assiniboine and his wife and son come along as a reward for their services. He showed them all the sights of Victoria — restaurants, hotels, shops, theaters. They were entranced by everything. Victoria's residents were entranced in turn by the presence of a genuine peer of their realm, and his curious aboriginals. At September's end, Milton sent his Indians on their way back to Kamloops, where they would pick up Bucephalus, Cheadle's gift, before returning to Fort Pitt.

The two dudes spent that fall reaching their objective, the Cariboo district, by steamer and stage up the Fraser. They took in the usual wild sights and sounds of a booming goldfield, but were happy to get back to Victoria in late November. After Christmas they landed in San Francisco, toured the Bay area, and attended a gala ball. "I danced several quadrilles & lancers," Cheadle wrote, "all much altered from English. A very pretty set of girls there, elegant figures, exceedingly pretty faces, beautifully transparent, delicate complexions, but nearly all with the usual failing of women of this continent, rather too flat chested & without that lovely roundness of form & limb so characteristic of *our* girls at home." They sailed from the Golden Gate in January and ended their great adventure six weeks later, March 7, 1864, at Liverpool, where it had begun.

The ordeal over Yellowhead was the high dramatic point of both their lives. Their careers thereafter were about what you would expect. Walter Butler Cheadle, the Cambridge oarsman and angler, became the distinguished specialist in children's diseases, Dr. Cheadle, M.A., M.D., Cantab., F.R.G.S., and Fellow of the Royal College of Physicians. He died in London on Good Friday, March 25, 1910, after a long and honorable life which included, of course, the hearty promotion of athletics. In 1866 he had married Anne Murgatroyd, a Yorkshire girl from near Bingley, who had won his approval, we can surmise, by her lovely roundness of form & limb. He outlived her, and his second wife too, Emily Mansel.

William, Viscount Milton, of the House Fitzwilliam, did not, after all, tarry on this earth too long. He married in 1867 and died of pneumonia on January 17, 1877, in Paris, where he had been living alone for some time seeking health. His death was before that of his father, and so he never became the seventh Earl Fitzwilliam. Eventually that title passed to his son. Lord Milton's poor health was his cross, but he was gay and kind to the end, and did his family duty as a somewhat dawdling member of the House of Lords. But to him life could not be considered a very serious matter. A pretty girl — European, American, Wood Cree or whatever — was indeed a melody and deserved his undivided attention more than, say, much of the foolishness in Parliament.

Finally, whatever happened to Mr. O'Byrne? Vanished. Disappeared. Dissolved in thin air. Gone with the wind. *Abiit cum vento!*

Mathew Brady caught the Romanoff glamour when Grand Duke Alexis stopped in his New York studio to have his picture taken. Here are the wavy hair, the manly face, the broad chest, the erect carriage, the intellectual forehead . . . (Mathew B. Brady photo courtesy of the Library of Congress.)

4

A GRAND DUKE FOR DENVER

In October of 1871, President Grant revealed that Grand Duke Alexis of Russia would make a goodwill tour of American cities. The news flamed across the land, though Alexis himself, aged twenty-one, was hardly in line for the succession. His father, Czar Alexander II, had four other living sons and two of these grand dukes, young Alexander and Vladimir, were ahead of Alexis. But Alexis would be the first genuine Romanoff to visit the United States, and that was excitement enough. Everybody knew that the Romanoffs were the most glamorous of all European royalty, even if they were upstarts dating back only to 1613.

Any freedom-loving American should have despised them, of course. They were absolutists, supreme egotists, contemptuous autocrats. They had been cruel beyond belief, building a great nation through the sufferings of their subjects. They were shudderingly immoral. Peter the Great had tortured and murdered his own son in the name of patriotism. Catherine the Great had had a stable of lovers, not out of sentiment, it seemed, but just for the exercise. Though Alexis's father was polite to his Czarina Marie, he spent his off-hours with his mistress, Princess Dolgoruki.

And still there was much about the Romanoffs for Americans to admire. They did as they pleased. They had great style. They seemed to move as actors in an exceedingly dangerous charade played in a framework of yachts, champagne, rock-sized jewels, caviar, and Europe's most beautiful women, lured to St. Petersburg by the Romanoff charm. Young Alexis had special merits. He was the handsomest of all the handsome grand dukes, a blond, square-set man six feet two inches tall, with huge hands and feet and a kindly manner. He had once rescued a child from drowning. He said his prayers each night. Though a clumsy dancer, he was good at wrestling and hunting. He was said to be seeking true love by carrying on with a commoner, the daughter of his father's old tutor.

His proposed goodwill tour had a strong political appeal. Americans had favored Russia against England and France in the Crimean War of the 1850's. The Abolitionists had applauded when Alexis's father took steps to free twenty million serfs in 1861. Lincoln's Civil War government was grateful to Alexander II for supporting the Union while England pulled strings to help the Confederates. Though Americans joked about the purchase from Russia of Alaska ("Seward's Folly"), the transaction increased the friendliness of relations between the two nations.

And so the residents of New York City, from the Battery to the

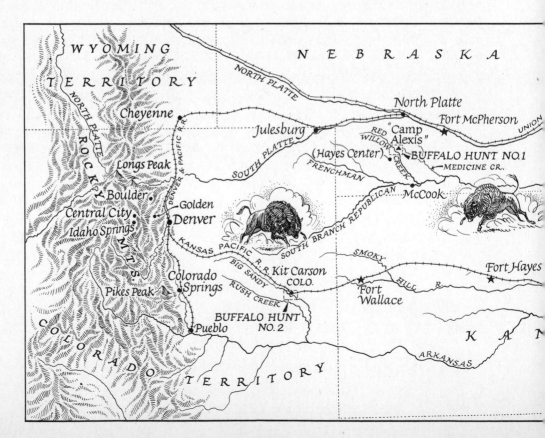

hinterlands north of Forty-second Street, were deeply thrilled as Alexis and his party of seventeen czarist diplomats sailed past Ambrose Light toward the Narrows on November 18, 1871. They rode the flagship of the Russian fleet, *Svetlana,* which was guarded by a Russian frigate and a corvette. The Atlantic voyage from Madeira had been so rough that the *Svetlana* had been unable to use her motors, and had sailed all the way — forty stormy days of it. The weather in the Narrows was still very bad, though the large U.S. Navy contingent sent by President Grant had fired twenty-one-gun salutes of welcome in the cold driving rain.

The bad weather persisted. The biggest reception in New York's history could not begin until the morning of November 21, when a boat carrying five hundred American officials and celebrities steamed down the bay to pick up the grand duke. He was dressed in naval costume and looked a bit green, having been seasick for more than a month. The greeters returned with him to the Battery and installed him in an open carriage drawn by four black horses with golden harness. Ten thousand U.S. troops and city police forced a path up Broadway through the cheering throngs as the carriage moved past Trinity

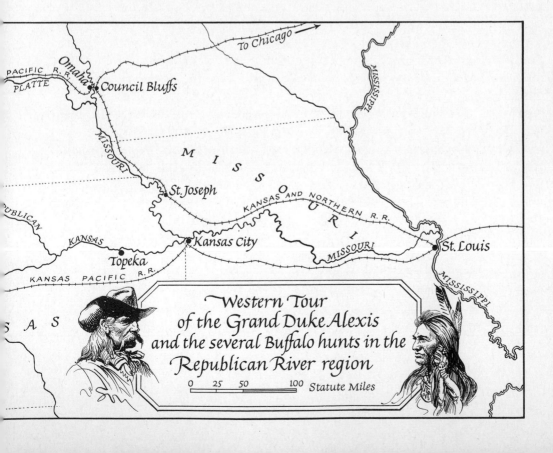

Western Tour of the Grand Duke Alexis and the several Buffalo hunts in the Republican River region

0   25   50   100   Statute Miles

Church, the bells of which chimed out the Russian national anthem, and then Grace Church, decked with American and Russian flags. The handsome Alexis was gay and smiling now, feeling much better on solid earth. He was particularly pleased when the carriage passed an Italian organ-grinder with a trained bear alleged to be Russian. The parade ended near Union Square at the Clarendon Hotel, which had been redecorated for Alexis's stay. A heated conservatory with a fountain in it had been built adjoining the ducal suite and a new Chickering piano had been placed in the parlor.

Two weeks of hectic festivity followed — balls for the grand duke at the Brooklyn Navy Yard and the Academy of Music, boat trips to Long Island and up the Hudson, and a night of grand opera to hear the Swedish prima donna Christine Nilsson. Letters by smitten ladies appeared in the papers. Mary Clemmer Ames, for example, saw Alexis entering Mathew Brady's gallery to have his photograph taken and wrote in the *Independent* of his "waving golden hair" and his "manly, thoughtfully earnest, erect carriage, breadth and depth of chest, intellectual forehead, and eyes deep blue, large and full. . . . If the Grand Duke can't dance well he can walk with a will. . . . His fair Romanoff face and magnificent head join the treasured pictures of memory."

On November 23, Alexis and the Russian ambassador, Count Catacazy, went to Washington to dine at the White House with President Grant, his Cabinet, and Lieutenant General Phil Sheridan, who was head of the Army's western division at Chicago. Some days later, Philadelphians greeted the grand duke at Independence Hall and he inspected the Baldwin works, where locomotives were being built for the Czar. In early December he went to Boston to attend a banquet in his honor, stopping on the way at Springfield to see Smith and Wesson pistols being made for his father's army. At the Boston banquet, Oliver Wendell Holmes eulogized him and James Russell Lowell delivered a pun about the American purchase of Alaska. "Our relations with Russia," he said, "are now of the most cordial and intimate kind, for the Emperor has made us the keeper of his *seals*." After Boston, Alexis visited Montreal, Niagara Falls, and, on January 5, 1872, Chicago, where he gave Mayor Medill five thousand dollars in gold for the relief of people made homeless by the October fire.

Chicago and Milwaukee were near the end of the scheduled goodwill tour, but something new had been added in November, during that dinner for Alexis at the White House. The grand duke, who spoke fluent English, had talked with President Grant and with General Sheridan about the American West. They had described for him its booming mines in the Colorado Rockies around Denver, and its millions of buffalo which were being slaughtered at a fantastic rate on the Great Plains. Sheridan told of the hunt he had organized recently in Nebraska for James Gordon Bennett, owner of the *New York Herald,* and other millionaires. The grand duke had remarked wistfully that hunting in Europe had become pretty tame and he hoped to shoot a buffalo some day.

The President seems to have given Sheridan some sort of nod or prod. Before Alexis had left the White House, the general had informed him that the War Department's entire western division was at his disposal. A visit to Denver by way of St. Louis and Omaha would be arranged for him. And there would be a buffalo hunt south of Fort McPherson and North Platte, Nebraska, in the Republican River region where the general had waged successful warfare against the Indians in the winter of 1868-1869.

LITTLE PHIL SHERIDAN, of the harsh features, short legs and overhung stomach, prepared for the hunt with characteristic flamboyance and zest. The great hero of the Shenandoah campaign was as revered as President Grant himself, and when he asked for things he got them. The Pennsylvania Railroad put together a five-car special train of new Pullmans for him. Alexis insisted on renting the special, though he accepted the offer of the carriers involved to haul the train free from St. Louis to Denver and back. While these arrangements were being made, Sheridan communicated by telegraph with that phenomenon of Western folklore, Buffalo Bill Cody, who was the first citizen of North Platte, Nebraska. Sheridan had admired Cody's scouting for the Army in the Republican River Indian wars, and hired him now to make sure that Alexis actually killed a buffalo. This was a reasonable assignment for the twenty-five-year-old Cody. The least of his feats since bagging an Indian at the age of eleven and riding for the pony express was the shooting of 4280 buffalo in a period of seventeen months.

Sheridan ordered Cody to find the famous Sioux chief, Spotted Tail, in his winter camp and to induce him to bring a thousand Indians, male and female, to the buffalo hunt as added entertainment for the grand duke. Buffalo Bill did find Spotted Tail on Frenchman River, a Republican River tributary a hundred miles or so southwest of North Platte town. The old chief promised to produce a show in exchange for a thousand pounds of tobacco. Meanwhile, another celebrity of the Republican River wars, Colonel George A. Forsyth, led troops and wagons from Fort McPherson, Nebraska, to set up "Camp Alexis" for Sheridan. The men followed the government road due south toward Fort Hayes, Kansas. This bleak terrain of snow-patched sandhills and grassy vales was the habitat of the Republican River herd of buffalo, and adjoined the habitat of the Arkansas River herd in the area of Fort Wallace, Kansas, and Kit Carson, Colorado. Forsyth's troops and train reached Medicine Creek in half a day and arrived that evening at the spot where the Fort Hayes road crossed Red Willow Creek, sixty miles south of North Platte. The men moved a mile up the east bank of Red Willow and laid out Camp Alexis next day in a handsome grove of cottonwoods at the foot of a small canyon. They erected two hospital tents for the royal meals, ten wall tents banked with earth for guests and generals, and a dormitory tent for orderlies and Russian servants. Sibley stoves were placed in all tents, firewood cut, a flagpole raised, privies dug, bonfires built and the tent interiors made luxurious with new bedding, carpets, chairs and tables which Phil Sheridan had forwarded from Chicago.

At noon on January 11, 1872, the special Pullman train left St. Louis for North Platte, bearing Sheridan and his exotic clutch of Russian nobility. The cars were olive-green — two sleeping cars, a diner, the luxurious parlor car *Adirondack,* and a refrigerator car filled with chickens, geese, turkeys, grouse, quail, eggs and butter, as well as Bass pale ale, Glenlivet Scotch, Holland gin, bourbon, rye, cognac and many cases of champagne. The train reached Omaha next day on tracks of the Kansas and Northern. It was switched to Union Pacific rails and was boarded by Army brass from the Department of the Platte, and also by General George A. Custer, the most colorful officer Sheridan could think of to be grand marshal of the hunt and the grand duke's escort. The histrionic Custer, with his fringed buckskin outfit, had caught the public fancy by his victory over the Cheyennes on the Washita in 1868. But he was on dull duty in Kentucky now, tending to his long locks and writing an appreciative book about his achievements, *My Life on the Plains*. He was thirty-two years old, his bitter fate at the Little Big Horn was still four years in the future.

Late that night of January 12, the special train ran past Fort McPherson and stopped on a siding at North Platte town, situated on fertile bottomland between low bluffs of the North and South Platte Rivers. The whole town turned out next morning to watch the ruddy Alexis as he left the train and climbed into one of five spring wagons. Generals Sheridan and Custer rode with him at the head of an extraordinary caravan numbering at least five hundred people — a hunting party infinitely more spectacular than Sir William Drummond Stewart's, or even Sir St. George Gore's. It included a whole pack of Department of the Platte generals, two companies of infantry in wagons, two of cavalry, the Second Cavalry's regimental band, outriders, night herders, couriers, cooks, trailing groups of Indians and sutlers, and three wagons of champagne and other royal spirits. Alexis's chef was along, too.

Buffalo Bill was on horseback at the grand duke's side, spouting tall tales, pointing out wolves and antelope, and explaining that this Fort Hayes road was still infested with hostile Indians. Cody, a six-footer plus, looked magnificent as always in buckskin coat trimmed with fur, black slouch hat and long hair hanging in ringlets over his shoulders. He described Alexis later as "a large, fine-looking young man, a democratic fellow, a jovial lively body." Cody's renowned Buckskin Joe was among the seventy-five trained buffalo horses in the remuda from Fort McPherson. The weather was mildly cold, but Alexis found it nothing like the severity of winter in St. Petersburg. The grand duke wore a jacket and trousers of heavy gray cloth trimmed with green, buttons with the Romanoff coat of arms, shiny spurred boots, and an astrakhan turban with cloth top. He carried a Cossack hunting knife and one of the engraved forty-four revolvers which Mr. Wesson of Smith and Wesson had given to him back in Massachusetts. The caravan stopped for lunch at Medicine Creek and moved into Camp Alexis on Red Willow Creek just before dark, as Forsyth's bonfires blazed and the band played "Hail to the Chief." Before bedtime, Chief Spotted Tail smoked the peace pipe with the grand duke and Cody coached him on buffalo-hunt technique.

General Custer got his hunters off in several parties at nine on Sunday morning, even though that January 14 was the grand duke's twenty-second birthday and time had to be taken for champagne toasts at breakfast. Custer's scouts had found buffalo some miles from Camp Alexis toward Medicine Creek. By mid-morning the hunters could see thousands of them covering several square miles of rolling terrain. Custer's hunt rules were simple. The Russian officials and American generals had to hang back until the grand duke, riding Cody's Buckskin Joe, made the first kill, aided by Cody and by two of Spotted Tail's men who carried bows and arrows. The two Sioux were a trifle annoyed when the grand duke asked them why they used "these absurd toys."

According to Cody's account, the wind was just right and the approach to the buffalo was easy. Buckskin Joe carried Alexis up to a bull and he began firing his engraved pistol as the animal lumbered away. His aim was bad, perhaps because of the birthday champagne. Cody wrote later: "He fired six shots from this weapon at buffaloes only twenty feet from him, but as he shot wildly, not one took effect." Buckskin Joe may have been part of the trouble. Cody had trained the horse to dart off toward another buffalo after one shot, since one shot was all Cody needed to kill. Bill continued: "I exchanged pistols with him. He again fired six shots without dropping a buffalo. Seeing that the animals were bound to make their escape without his killing one of them, unless he had a better weapon, I rode up to him, gave him my old reliable 'Lucretia' ["Lucretia" was Cody's "needle gun," a .50-caliber Springfield rifle converted to breech-loading] and told him to urge his horse close to the buffaloes, and I would give him word when to shoot. At the same time I gave old Buckskin Joe a blow with my whip, and with a few jumps the horse carried the grand duke to within about ten feet of a big buffalo bull. 'Now is your time,' said I. He fired, and down went the buffalo."

Alexis, usually so calm, seemed to be electrified by his kill. James A. Hadley has described the scene: "The Grand Duke leaped from the saddle in a transport of astonishment, turned the horse loose, threw the gun down, cut off the tail as a souvenir, and then, sitting down on the carcass, waved the dripping trophy and let out a series of howls and gurgles like the death-song of all the fog-horns and calliopes ever born. The Russians galloped up and he poured out excitement in a strange northern tongue, so steadily and so volubly that Cody reeled in his saddle. His countrymen embraced and hugged him. The gory

On February 3, 1872, Frank Leslie's Illustrated Newspaper *ran this sketch of how Alexis might have killed his first buffalo. It is not too far off base either, though Buffalo Bill is shown wearing eagle feathers. The men behind Bill are two Sioux Indians and a Russian official hurrying to congratulate the grand duke. (Denver Public Library Western Collection photo.)*

trophy went from hand to hand till all were plastered with blood and dirt." Servants appeared then with a basket of champagne — a bottle for each hunter.

Lunch was served in the field. The grand duke sat with Chief Spotted Tail and was startled to see a buffalo cow bearing down on them, driven by a howling Sioux on horseback. The Sioux — his name was Chief Two Lance — waved his "absurd" bow pointedly at Alexis, arched it fully and released an arrow just as the cow passed by the hunters. The arrow struck the kill point at the cow's shoulder with such tremendous force that it went completely through the hide and dropped free on the other side. Two Lance picked up the arrow from the ground while his horse was still on the run and presented it to Alexis.

The grand duke got his second buffalo in the afternoon, bringing down a cow with a remarkable pistol shot at thirty yards — by accident or design. That event caused more champagne to appear. Cody remarked, "I was in hopes that he would kill five or six more before we reached camp, especially if a basket of champagne was to be opened every time he dropped one."

That evening back at Camp Alexis some of Spotted Tail's thousand Sioux gave their show of sham fights, dances and lance throwing. While it went on, Custer was observed to be flirting strenuously with Spotted Tail's daughter. "The Grand Duke," James Hadley reported, "rounded up the dark-browed daughter of a greasy old villain named Scratching Dog." Hunting continued on January 15 — a general scramble this time with Indians and whites blazing away and dodging one another's bullets. Alexis shot six more buffalo but was not entirely pleased about it, particularly when Cody told him that the grand total of kills for the two days — fifty-six — was nothing special.

Next day the caravan had to return to the railroad so that Alexis could be produced in Denver according to Sheridan's plan. On the way to North Platte, Alexis had a final adventure. Don Russell tells the story in his book *The Lives and Legends of Buffalo Bill*:

> Alexis and General Sheridan rode in what Cody describes as "a heavy double-seated open carriage, or rather an Irish dogcart, and it was drawn by four spirited cavalry horses" not too much used to harness. The Grand Duke expressed admiration for the driving of Bill Reed, an Overland stage-coach driver who had brought the party to camp. When the General

Leslie's Newspaper *enjoyed poking fun at the Grand Duke's hunt in this page of cartoons appearing on February 10, 1872. (Denver Public Library Western Collection photo.)*

remarked that Cody was also a stagecoach driver, Alexis wanted a demonstration, and Bill took the reins. With Sheridan egging him on, Buffalo Bill let out the horses more than he had intended. There were no brakes on the carriage, and when they began descending a hill, he could not hold the horses in, so there was nothing to do but let them go. "Every once in awhile the hind wheels would strike a rut and take a bound, and not touch the ground again for fifteen or twenty feet," says Bill, who believed he made six miles in about three minutes.

When Alexis found himself safely back at North Platte he told Cody that he would "rather return to Russia by way of Alaska and swim Bering Strait than repeat that downhill ride." Still, he gave Bill valuable presents when they parted — a purse of gold and a diamond stickpin by one account; a Russian fur coat and jeweled cuff links and studs by another. Don Russell reports in his book that the Cody family still has the cuff links. "The presents," he wrote, "were the least valuable return Buffalo Bill received for this famous exhibition. He had put on his first Wild West Show, and he had made newspaper headlines."

PHIL SHERIDAN HAD WIRED his old friend John Evans in Denver from "Camp Alexis via North Platte" that the grand duke's train would reach Cheyenne on Wednesday morning, January 17. The patriarchal Evans was intensely Republican, and a man of great power. He had served Lincoln as Colorado's second territorial governor and had built the Denver Pacific Railroad south from the U.P. tracks at Cheyenne in 1870. He headed a benign Republican cabal which ran the Rockies. Among the cabalists were Grant's old battle comrade, Governor Edward McCook; William N. Byers, editor of the *Rocky Mountain News,* a brilliant booster of all things Coloradan — Republican things especially; and the Grant-appointed U.S. Marshal, Mark A. Shaffenburg, who had for adornment a beautiful wife, a beer garden and a $26,000 mansion on Denver's Curtis Street. John Evans sent one of his Denver Pacific locomotives and a carload of Republican office-holders to pick up the five Pullmans in Cheyenne, and to show Alexis Longs Peak and the even greater splendor of mountains further south on the hundred-mile D.P. run. It was clear that the grand duke was not going to meet any Democrats during his visit if the Denver Republicans could prevent it.

Half of Denver's ten thousand residents stood in the snow to greet Alexis at the station and to watch his party move to the American House at Sixteenth and Blake. The grand duke, in greatcoat and pearl-colored gloves, rode in Tom Smith's "clarence" — a glass-fronted closed carriage pulled by matched grays. The *News* reported next day that "from New York to the mountains Alexis has been glorified and adored, 'received' and danced to death" and described his boyish-looking sidewhiskers, his downy moustache, his light gold hair brushed straight back from his high forehead, his "elephantine" hands, and his feet — "simply immense." The *News* added defensively that Alexis represented an absolute monarchy, but "this will make no difference to our democratic natures."

If the grand duke expected a shack-town of pistol-packing men and hurdy-gurdy women, the Denver of 1872 must have surprised him. It bloomed with mining prosperity, which had tripled its population and wealth in two years. It was much more than the distributing point of an immense mountain West. Its spirit-lifting climate and its fertile setting beneath the snows of the Continental Divide in a valley fed by many streams attracted swarms of invalids — asthmatics, rheumatics, sufferers from consumption. The town was as cosmopolitan as Paris. Besides all sorts of Americans, high and low Europeans came to look, and often to stay. Many of them — Englishmen, Dutch, Germans — brought capital to invest.

The grand duke could have absorbed elements of Denver's modernity — a new horse-drawn streetcar line, public schools, Charpiot's fine French restaurant, roller-skating rink, circulating library, John Evans's Colorado Seminary. Large frame and brick homes, steam-heated and gas-lit, lined its streets. Though domestics were in short supply, the homes contained other forms of sophistication — oil paintings, chromos, exquisite china, and grand pianos. Not that Alexis found Denver everywhere refined. Vulgar capers were the rule downtown near the American House. In the saloons on Wazee and Blake Streets, gamblers and prostitutes entertained throngs of male visitors out for a good time — hunters and trappers in buckskin, tough teamsters, slumming dandies from the East. Mingling with them were gay Ute Indians — the men in silk hats, frock coats, epaulets and breech-clouts, the women in gingham dresses or flour sacks with corsets worn outside. If Alexis looked at the front page of Byers's *News* on Jan-

Many of the beauties at Denver's gala ball for the grand duke wore flounced skirts, bustles, and chaste chokers above not-so-chaste bodices. Alexis, towering over everybody, took it all calmly — but with a glint in his eye. This Dhem Brothers sketch of the American House dining room in 1872 ran in the Rocky Mountain Daily News *on November 13, 1897. (Denver Public Library Western Collection photo.)*

uary 17, he could have read this ad: "I, John Porter, of Erie city, Boulder County, will shoot any person in the Territory for from $100 to $500."

George Clark, McCook's territorial treasurer, installed Alexis in Parlor 25 — one of thirteen rooms reserved for the visiting Russians on the second floor of the American House. This four-story brick hotel was four years old and famous for its graceful stairway, glittering bar, portable bathtubs and a multitude of handsome coal-oil lamps. It was far more elegant than Sargent's Hotel, where Sheridan and Custer were staying. The Russians dined in their rooms and retired early. Next afternoon, relays of Republicans showed them Mayor Bates's brewery, the legislature in session, the U.S. Mint and the waterworks. But the tour was a dull prologue to the event of events — the ball for the grand duke which the ultra-social Pioneer Club was giving that Thursday night in the dining room of the American House. The ball had been planned for months as the club's leap-year party, with ladies inviting the gentlemen of their choice and escorting them to the hotel. This feature was retained for club members but the wife of the former Republican mayor of Denver, Judge Amos Steck, expanded the list to a total of four hundred guests, most of whom were conventionally escorted.

At nine o'clock the Four Hundred began arriving in the hotel's dining room, a handsome chamber with French windows and white square columns which gleamed in the soft light of four-lamp gas chandeliers. American flags hung from one chandelier, with a single Russian flag, which the seamstress of Governor McCook's wife had made by copying a picture in the dictionary. The grand duke, towering in full dress over his admirals and ambassadors, received the guests and passed them along smoothly. He said little and seemed unaware of the commotion he was causing. Hundreds of beautiful women clutched his great hand shyly, their complexions glowing with Magnolia Balm and the thought of what they would tell their grandchildren some day. Many wore bustles and skirts with four flounces, and chaste chokers above tight bodices. Some had clusters of "waterfall" curls tumbling forward out of hairnetted buns to fall down to their breasts. Two women only, the governor's wife and her sister Mrs. Charles Adams, dared to appear in the shocking new low-necked dresses, with their shoulders bare and their bosoms partly exposed. Mrs. McCook's eyes were shadowy from illness. She was at the ball against her doctor's orders.

Gilman Brothers Band struck up the grand march led by the grand duke and Mrs. McCook. The governor followed with the U.S. Marshal's pretty wife, Mrs. Shaffenburg, and then came General Sheridan and the wife of the lawyer Alfred C. Phelps. As the march ended, Mrs. McCook fainted dead away in Alexis's arms and had to be carried out. The grand duke took the crisis calmly and went on to lead the first quadrille. His partner was the wife of the Central City Republican leader, George E. Randolph. Alexis had trouble with the figures at first, complaining that they differed altogether from Russian figures. Before the ball ended, long after midnight, he was dancing passably if not nimbly. He was noticing things too, and even flirting a little with a Miss Monk (aged fifteen) and Miss Fleury of Golden, whom he declared to be the prettiest girl at the ball.

The people of Denver woke up Friday with a certainty that they would never forget their grand duke. The *News* listed a few tender souvenirs which it believed their owners would cherish always:

A Denver Belle's costly gauze which caught on the Ducal arm and seemed to reveal the beauties 'twas intended to conceal.

The stump of a cigar smoked so short it endangered the furze on the imperial lip. This was obtained by its adventurous female possessor from a spittoon in one of the corridors of the American House.

A glove which came in contact with the Duke's Number Nine kids. It is preserved in glass.

A piece of American House steak filched from the Ducal plate whose toughness rescued it from the imperial stomach and will preserve it for all time without embalming. It was stolen by a persevering blonde, but the proprietor of the American House can have no legal claim to it, as it was included in the $1,500 bill for two days entertainment for the Ducal party.

The train of a ball dress trodden on by the Number Eleven calf-skins of imperialism. It is preserved by a magnificent brunette honored by the Duke.

One hair filched from the Duke's comb and presumably his.

A white satin slipper that enclosed the tiny foot and favorite corn of a languishing blonde on which the Ducal boot fell quite heavily during the mazes of the Lancers.

A bit of velvet plush clipped from a chair in which His Highness was seated. A woman stole it.

Editor Byers expressed a general feeling about the ball when he wrote in Friday's *News*:

The Firemen's, the Masquerades, the Pioneer and Continental, the high-toned balls of the holidays and the recherche full dress parties which without contrast can stand the light of a strong comparison — all these must hide their heads forever; their terpsichorean fires are paled; their glory is departed, and they stand today amongst the disfigured, broken, insignificant things of the past. For we have had a ducal ball; we have had a live duke; the ladies have danced with him, and tried to talk with him. And the men have shaken his hand and gazed with wonder upon his im-

perial form. Everything of the past must be wiped out entirely, and the
leaders of fashion will take a fresh start upon the pathway of joyous dissi-
pation with the ducal ball as the initial mile post.

Years later, a Colorado cowboy musician named Chalkley McCarty
Beeson, who had played violin at the ball in the Gilman Brothers Band,
gave his reverent recollection of Alexis:

> It was not exactly condescension but you knew the minute you saw
> him that he did not belong to the common herd. The habit of command, the
> universal deference paid him, the easy way that he gave orders and ex-
> pected every one to wait on him was noticeable in that country and time
> the most democratic the world ever saw, where a scout was just as good a
> man as Phil Sheridan, and a cow-puncher as good as his millionaire boss.
> So, easy as Alexis was in his ways, not even a cow-puncher would have
> thought of taking liberties with him.

SOME COLORADO DEMOCRATS got to meet the Russians after all. On Friday morning, Alexis's party visited Golden town, W. A. H. Loveland's
Democratic stronghold at the foot of Clear Creek Canyon. The guests
were taken up the canyon on the roadbed of Loveland's Colorado Central Railroad, which was being built toward Central City and Idaho
Springs. At Huntsman's Ranch luncheon was served for them in a
tent, and there was a lot of drinking and singing. But Alexis's thoughts
were elsewhere. He was glad to get back to his five Pullmans and head
eastward that Friday night on the tracks of the Kansas Pacific.

What absorbed Alexis was an unexpected chance to shoot a lot
more buffalo. It seemed that during the ball General Custer had happened to mention to young C. M. Beeson, the fiddler in the Gilman band,
that the Nebraska hunt had been only so-so. Beeson had replied that he
knew where there was far better hunting — near his home town of Kit
Carson, Colorado, on the Kansas Pacific one hundred and fifty miles
southeast of Denver. The Arkansas River herd wintered in the area.
Beeson had added that five miles south of Kit Carson a man named
Duke Sherry had recently killed two hundred and fifty-nine of them
without moving from a three-foot hole.

Leaving Beeson, Custer had hurried with the news to Phil Sheridan, who had jumped into action as though a major war impended.
He had hired Beeson as guide and had wired Colonel D. Floyd Jones

at Fort Wallace, Kansas, seventy miles east of Kit Carson; Jones was to get troops, four six-mule teams, four spring wagons and two carloads of buffalo horses by rail to Kit Carson by early Saturday morning, January 20. Then Sheridan had wired Miguel Otero, the Kit Carson merchant, to set up a one-day camp between Big Sandy and Rush Creeks, and to stock it with a keg of whiskey and food and water for one hundred and fifty men.

The Kit Carson hunt turned out to have none of the spit and polish of the North Platte hunt. Though the train arrived in the little cow town on schedule, nothing else occurred as Sheridan had planned it. Alexis rode Beeson's good buffalo horse, but all the others were big untrained cavalry horses. When Sheridan opened his keg he found no whiskey in it. Otero's drivers had drunk it on the way to camp. The grand duke and Custer seemed to enjoy the lack of organization but it sent Sheridan into tantrums of profanity. Custer, more foppishly dramatic than usual, ignored every rule as marshal of the hunt. Beeson recalled that he did not divide the Russians, soldiers and Otero's drunken employees into parties. They advanced on the herd as a noisy mob. On the way, Custer gave Alexis a demonstration of knee-control horsemanship at a gallop, firing his pistol with accuracy both right- and left-handed. Alexis declared that the Cossacks couldn't do better. Just before topping the last rise, Custer conceived the notion of making a mock Indian battle of it. Beeson heard him announce loudly, "Boys, here's a chance for a great victory over that bunch of red skins the other side of the hill. Mayor Bates, you will take charge of the right flank. I will attend to the left. General Sheridan and the infantry will follow directly over the hill. Ready? Charge!"

The grand duke led at a gallop down the hill and into the herd, with Custer next and a hundred yelling soldiers and civilians behind Custer. General Sheridan and Beeson watched on foot from the top of the hill as the herd weaved and scattered. They saw Alexis bring down five buffalo in five minutes. Custer shot three. The inexperienced troopers fired at the animals every which way. Bullets whizzed over Sheridan's head and into the grass near him. He threw his short legs and fat body to the ground, telling himself perhaps that this fool charge was putting him in greater peril than he had known in the Battle of Winchester. Beeson heard him laying out Custer and the grand duke in paroxysms of new blasphemy until hunters and buffalo

At Topeka, Kansas, Grand Duke Alexis had his photo taken with his official escort, General George A. Custer. The studio canvas backdrop hardly suggests the Great Plains buffalo country. (Denver Public Library Western Collection photo.)

The politicians of Kansas hoped to give the grand duke at least as good a time in Topeka as he had had in Denver. At their banquet in his honor on January 23, 1872, thirteen kinds of wild game (from buffalo to squirrel) were served, plus fourteen varieties of hot and cold meats, and twenty-eight desserts. Alexis (center) was photographed before the banquet with his royal entourage, General Phil Sheridan (on Alexis's right), and General George Custer (in profile). (Denver Public Library Collection photo.)

disappeared in the rolling distance. Then he mounted his horse and returned with Beeson to Miguel Otero's camp, where he found a hilarious crowd of foot soldiers and Russian servants putting away the last of the grand duke's champagne and caviar.

Sheridan had to calm down and forgive in the end. As the special train pulled away from Kit Carson for Topeka and Kansas City, he mellowed himself with bourbon and conceded that the crazy hunt was a success after all. Alexis claimed a dozen kills out of the day's grand total of two hundred buffalo. Hundreds of pounds of hump meat were in the train's commissary, packed in ice for shipment to St. Petersburg. The grand duke was so ecstatic that he took Custer into his arms, hugged him and kissed him. Russo-American relations had never been (in James Russell Lowell's phrase) so "cordial and intimate."

THE ROYAL TOUR ENDED at St. Louis. The Pennsylvania Railroad recovered its olive-green Pullmans and Alexis went to Kentucky for a few weeks' vacation at Louisville with George and Elizabeth Custer. In mid-February, Custer escorted him to New Orleans and to Pensacola in Florida, where he boarded his flagship *Svetlana* and sailed for home by way of Cuba. Inspired by American ways, the grande duke's first act at St. Petersburg was to wed the commoner whom he had loved secretly for so long. The Czar annulled the marriage and Alexis accepted his father's ukase loyally.

His bachelor years passed pleasantly while the liberal Alexander II was Czar; less so after his death in 1881, when Alexander III, Alexis's nephew, took over and by his die-hard policies pointed his nation toward revolution. Alexis, the suave and gifted linguist, became front man for the Romanoffs, assigned to public funerals, weddings and dedications in London, Washington and Paris. The strong beauty of his face faded slowly from rich food, too much wine and lack of exercise. Fat replaced the muscle which had sustained him hunting in Nebraska with Buffalo Bill.

When Nicholas II became Czar in 1894, Alexis took an apartment in Paris on the Avenue Gabriel near the present U.S. Embassy and Place de la Concorde. He loved slumming in Montmartre. Nicholas made him nominal head of the Russian Navy though he was still as

Grand Duke Alexis never married after his first marriage was annulled, though he had quite a few mistresses. He spent his later years as diplomatic front man for the Romanoff rulers of Russia. Perhaps his buffalo hunt on the Great Plains was the most exciting time of his whole life. (Photo courtesy Library of Congress.)

bad a sailor as he had been on the *Svetlana*. He enjoyed strategy meetings with his admirals, over glasses of cognac in his Paris apartment. The impressive title amused him, but he was not amused in 1905 when the Japanese destroyed his Baltic fleet in the disaster at Tsushima. Alexis had had no part in causing the disaster but he resigned his command anyhow. Three years later, on November 14, 1908, he died in despair at the age of fifty-eight in the arms of his mistress, the French actress Madame Balleta. He was buried in the Romanoff mausoleum at St. Petersburg.

The man who gave Denver and the West some of their most entertaining memories deserved a happier fate.

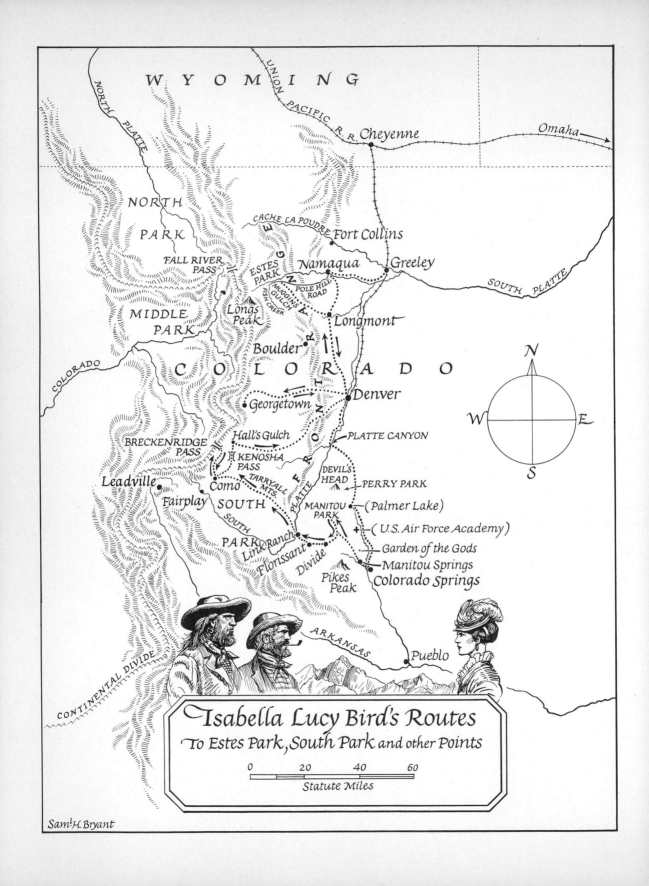

W Y O M I N G

UNION PACIFIC R.R. Cheyenne

Omaha →

NORTH PLATTE

NORTH PARK

CACHE LA POUDRE
Fort Collins

FALL RIVER PASS

ESTES PARK

Namaqua

Greeley

SOUTH PLATTE

MIDDLE PARK

Longs Peak

MUGGINS GULCH
FISH CREEK

POLE HILL ROAD

Longmont

COLORADO

Boulder

FRONTIER RANGE

C O L O R A D O

Denver

Georgetown

Hall's Gulch

PLATTE CANYON

BRECKENRIDGE PASS

KENOSHA PASS

DEVIL'S HEAD

PERRY PARK

Leadville

Como

TARRYALL MTS.

SOUTH

MANITOU PARK

(Palmer Lake)

Fairplay

SOUTH

PLATTE

(U.S. Air Force Academy)

PARK

Link Ranch

Garden of the Gods

Florissant

Divide

Manitou Springs

Pikes Peak

Colorado Springs

ARKANSAS

Pueblo

N

W   E

S

CONTINENTAL DIVIDE

Isabella Lucy Bird's Routes
To Estes Park, South Park and other Points

0   20   40   60
Statute Miles

Sam! H. Bryant

5

LOVE IN THE PARK

THE POOR INVALID, Isabella Lucy Bird, was down again in the spring of 1872, suffering from backache, headache, insomnia, bad teeth and nervous tension, to say nothing of the pain of having passed her fortieth virginal year. Her love of horses, which had meant so much since the death of her clergyman father, brought only more misery. Riding them sidesaddle, as became an English gentlewoman, was torture because of her ailing back.

Isabella was sick also of her own large sad eyes, her small white face, her squat figure four feet eleven inches tall which, she said, had "the padded look of a puffin." She was sick of the damp of Scotland's Isle of Mull where she was staying with her adored sister Henrietta. She was sick of nursing the poor, of teaching Sunday school, of lecturing on the evils of drink. In July when her doctor urged her to get out of bed and take a sea change by sailing to the Antipodes, she decided to do so. Being a person of means, she planned to spend a year in Auckland. She felt guilty about leaving Henrietta behind and meant to atone for it by sending her letters about her adventures.

She got to New Zealand safely but it supplied few adventures, so she left in January of '73 for the Hawaiian Archipelago, which gave her more exciting letter material. Hawaiian women, she found, rode horses astride on peaked Mexican saddles. Isabella bought "a dainty bloomer costume . . . full Turkish trousers gathered into frills which fall over the boots — a thoroughly serviceable and feminine costume."

*Nothing like Isabella Lucy Bird had ever happened to the Rockies before, or to Mountain Jim Nugent, either. She was smallish, fortyish, and usually wore a huge hat, bloomers, and full Turkish trousers with frills falling over her boots. She rode astride like a man on a frisky mare named Birdie.**

Riding astride seemed to cure the pain in her back. She roamed the islands for six months, reporting to Henrietta on Hilo, lepers and the liquor problem. She even climbed Mauna Loa, rising nearly fourteen thousand feet above the sea, and slept in a tent at the edge of its crater

*The sketches in this chapter were photographed by Clarence Coil from the seventh edition of Isabella Bird's *A Lady's Life in the Rocky Mountains* and are presented here with the kind permission of the original publisher, John Murray, 50 Albemarle Street, London.

with a kind and considerate Englishman named Mr. Wilson — so kind and considerate that she never slept better in her life.

She loved these Sandwich Islands. But she pushed on in August of '73 to San Francisco, to Cheyenne, Wyoming, and to Greeley, Colorado, an odd colony of socialists on the plains just east of the Rocky Mountains. This was not by accident. For one thing, Henrietta had threatened to join her in Hawaii, and that would not do. Furthermore, friends had told Isabella exciting things about the territory of Colorado. Rose Kingsley, Canon Charles Kingsley's daughter, had spent some months at Colorado Springs, which was full of Englishmen. Rose had described the pleasures of that "Little London" below Pikes Peak and had given Isabella letters to friends there.

Rose Kingsley's uncle, Dr. George Kingsley, had recommended to her quite a different kind of Colorado spot. Kingsley had gone West with the Earl of Dunraven in '71 and '72 to hunt and had heard of a secret valley of several thousand acres somewhere northwest of Denver. The valley was called Estes Park after its first settler, Joel Estes, who had moved away in the middle 1860's. A hard-drinking Welshman from Llanberis, Griffith Evans, had taken over the Estes ranch. Estes Park was drained by the Big Thompson River, the canyon of which was impassable. An obscure trail ran in from the Little Thompson up a gulch called Muggins. According to Kingsley, the Muggins Gulch entrance was guarded by an English desperado, Mountain Jim Nugent, a bachelor who had "black fits" and a tendency to commit mayhem during sprees in the grog-shops of Denver.

Isabella had mulled over these Estes Park matters and had concluded that she had to see the place. It would be interesting even to meet this English desperado, for she carried a Colt revolver somewhere about her padded puffin figure and had no fear of mere ruffians.

ON SEPTEMBER 9, 1873, a small prim lady in a gray and white dress over a crinoline stepped from the Denver Pacific train at Greeley, Colorado. Miss Isabella Bird was on her way to Estes Park. She was following directions in a letter received at Cheyenne from Colorado's ex-Governor A. H. Hunt, a friend of Rose Kingsley's and an associate of General Palmer in building the Denver and Rio Grande Railroad south from Denver to Colorado Springs.

The new Greeley before her was a ragged dream of Utopia. Westward were "the plains like the waves of a sea which had fallen asleep," merging into forested foothills, and then the great Front Range of the Rockies. She was able to observe and admire Greeley's morality (saloons were banned, as they are still). She disliked the rest of it — the heat, the black flies, the bugs that swarmed over her that night at Mrs. Graham's boardinghouse. But the morning brought the crisp clear air, the golden glow of cottonwoods, the cheerful gossip of magpies which make Colorado such a joy in early fall. She was thrilled by the view of Longs Peak, rising to more than fourteen thousand feet due west. "The Alps," she wrote Henrietta, "from the Lombard plains, are the finest mountain panorama I ever saw, but not equal to this; for not only do five high-peaked giants, each nearly the height of Mount Blanc, lift their dazzling summits above the lower ranges, but the expanse of mountains is so vast, and the whole lie in a transparent medium of the richest blue, not haze — something peculiar to the region."

Governor Hunt's letter was vague about the trail to Estes. He advised Isabella to go twenty-five miles further west to Fort Collins, south past the Namaqua trading post (near present Loveland), and on to another new town, Longmont, where Griffith Evans and Mountain Jim got their supplies. At Longmont she should be able to find someone to take her thirty-five miles west to Estes Park. Isabella donned her Turkish trousers and big hat but could not find a horse in Greeley which she could mount without a stepladder and so she rode a freight wagon to Fort Collins. That town pleased her no more than Greeley. "These new settlements," she informed Henrietta, "are altogether revolting, entirely utilitarian, given up to talk of dollars as well as making them, with coarse speech, coarse food, coarse everything." From Fort Collins, a "melancholy youth" who lost his way often, drove her in a buggy over the prairie to Namaqua and on to the impassable canyon of the Big Thompson where the Rockies began. Here he dumped her on Thomas Chalmers, a pioneer from Illinois, who possessed picturesqueness to Isabella mainly because his shoes did not match. Chalmers installed her in an open shed near his cabin. She did not find him lovable. She wrote, "he is slightly intelligent, very opinionated, and wishes to be thought well-informed, which he is not. He considers himself a profound theologian. . . . He hates England

Thomas Chalmers of Big Thompson Canyon thought he could take Isabella into Estes Park by a northern route. But all they found was "bad footing for horses."

with a bitter, personal hatred, and regards any allusions which I make to the progress of Victoria as a personal insult."

Chalmers claimed to know of a trail to Estes around the north side of Big Thompson Canyon. He and his fretful wife put Isabella on a skin-and-bones steed "like Don Quixote's charger" and bounced her about the wilds for three days. The hillsides blazed with groves of orange and yellow aspen. Gooseberry and scrub oak glowed crimson. Longs Peak was often in view — a tantalizing promise of Estes Park. But, scenery aside, the junket was a disaster. Chalmers did not find the Estes trail and the trio returned to the mouth of Big Thompson Canyon. Soon after, on September 25, Isabella escaped to Longmont in a passing wagon. The twenty-two-mile trip over the boiling prairie brought her to the end of her strength. Longmont's small St. Vrain Hotel was jammed and uncomfortable. All the ailments which had put her to bed on the Isle of Mull seemed to recur — "neuralgia, inflamed eyes, and a sense of extreme prostration."

At supper she described her fortnight of woe to the hotel's owner. She told him how her Estes Park plans had failed and how she must get to Denver somehow in the morning to take a train to New York because she was dying in this unendurable West. The owner was indignant. People get well in the Rockies, not sick. Besides, he said, Estes Park was a marvelous place and it would be a shame for her not to see it. He moved away, and returned in minutes to announce that her troubles were over. "You're in luck this time. Two young men have come in from Greeley and are going to take you with them to Estes tomorrow."

SHE WAS TERRIFIED. She lay sleepless through the hot Longmont night worrying about her neuralgia, about Muggins Gulch, about Mountain Jim Nugent's "black fits," about the accommodations she would — or wouldn't — find at the Evans ranch. The magic of the Colorado morning bucked her up a little, but the big horse she rented seemed skittish. She wondered about her young guides (the innkeeper called them "innocent," whatever that meant). Their names were S. S. Downer (a future Greeley judge) and Platt Rogers (a future mayor of Denver), and they were wondering in turn about Isabella. Platt Rogers, who had just graduated from Columbia Law School, recalled later: "The proprietor of the hotel asked that a lady might accompany us. We were not at all partial to such an arrangement as we were traveling light and free and the presence of a woman would naturally operate as a restraint upon our movements. However, we could not refuse and we consoled ourselves with the hope that she would prove young, beautiful and vivacious. Our hopes were dispelled when, in the morning, Miss Bird appeared, wearing bloomers, riding cowboy fashion, with a face and figure not corresponding to our ideals.''

Isabella revived rapidly once she got in her saddle, pack of ''indispensables'' behind and black umbrella hanging from the pommel. The air was ''keener and purer with every mile,'' the horse ''a blithe, joyous animal,'' the ride ''a recurrence of surprises.'' The travelers climbed from the hot prairie into the cool red canyon of North St. Vrain River, and on up through Little Elk Park to Little Thompson River — ''loveliness to bewilder and grandeur to awe.'' In late afternoon they ascended Muggins Gulch, riding in the bed of the crystal stream when the walls pressed in. Isabella watched for Mountain Jim, whom people called ''humbug,'' ''fourflusher,'' ''scoundrel,'' ''braggart.'' They approached a ''rude, black log cabin'' set in a scrub oak glade, and suddenly there he was at the door. The tiny spinster, fortyish, as Victorian as a gazebo, gazed at Jim Nugent curiously and described the moment later for Henrietta:

> Roused by the growling of the dog, his owner came out, a broad, thickset man, about the middle height, with an old cap on his head, and wearing a grey hunting-suit much the worse for wear (almost falling to pieces, in fact), a digger's scarf knotted round his waist, a knife in his belt, and ''a bosom friend,'' a revolver, sticking out of the breast-pocket of his coat; his feet, which were very small, were bare, except for some dilapidated moccasins made of horse hide. The marvel was how his clothes hung together, and on him. The scarf round his waist must have had something to do with it. His face was remarkable. He is a man about forty-five, and must have been strikingly handsome. He has large grey-blue eyes, deeply set, with well-marked eyebrows, a handsome aquiline nose, and a very handsome mouth. His face was smooth-shaven except for a dense moustache and imperial. Tawny hair, in thin uncared-for curls, fell from under his hunter's cap and over his collar. One eye was entirely gone, and the loss made one side of the face repulsive, while the other might have been modelled in marble. ''Desperado'' was written in large letters all over him. I almost repented of having sought his acquaintance. His first impulse was to swear at the dog, but on seeing a lady he contented himself with kick-

ing him, and coming up to me he raised his cap, showing as he did so a magnificently-formed brow and head, and in a cultured tone of voice asked if there were anything he could do for me?

As Isabella wrote these lines she may have smiled, thinking of the contrast between his polished manners and the rude behavior she had expected. She went on:

I asked for some water, and he brought some in a battered tin, gracefully apologizing for not having anything more presentable. We entered into conversation, and as he spoke I forgot both his reputation and appearance, for his manner was that of a chivalrous gentleman, his accent refined, and his language easy and elegant. I inquired about some beavers' paws which were drying, and in a moment they hung on the horn of my saddle. . . . As we rode away, for the sun was sinking, he said courteously, "You are not an American. I know from your voice that you are a countrywoman of mine. I hope you will allow me the pleasure of calling on you."

Soon after, Isabella and her guides reached Park Hill at the head of Muggins Gulch and she looked at last on the valley of her dreams lying below in the soft light of the setting sun — the view which has moved many millions of tourists on the highway from Lyons to Estes Park Village, on the route to Rocky Mountain National Park. Her description seems as fresh and true as when she wrote it nearly a century ago:

[It is] an irregular basin, lighted up by the bright waters of the rushing Thompson, guarded by sentinel mountains of fantastic shape and monstrous size, with Long's Peak rising above them all in unapproachable grandeur, while the Snowy Range, with its outlying spurs heavily timbered, come down upon the Park slashed by stupendous canyons lying deep in purple gloom. The rushing river was blood-red, Long's Peak was aflame, the glory of the glowing heaven was given back from earth. Never, nowhere, have I seen anything to equal the view into Estes Park. The mountains "of the land which is very far off" are very near now, but the near is more glorious than the far, and reality than dreamland. The mountain fever seized me, and giving my tireless horse an encouraging word, he dashed at full gallop over a mile of smooth sward at delirious speed.

The gallop brought her into Estes near the junction of Fish Creek and the Big Thompson, where the small Joel Estes memorial stone

Isabella suffered, but when she reached Griff Evans's dude ranch in Estes at last it was worth all the trouble. Her little cabin by the lake was drafty and had a skunk living beneath, but she woke each morning to find Longs Peak gloriously aflame and rising over all "in unapproachable grandeur."

stands now. The Griffith Evans establishment lay beside a small blue lake a short way up Fish Creek towards Longs Peak. The scope of the property surprised her — four comfortable-looking log cabins around a long central cabin, with two corrals of riding horses, a dairy house, milk cows strolling in to be milked, and hundreds of beef cattle in the distance. Actually, Griff Evans was running a dude ranch, thirty years before dude ranches were officially invented. He came running from the central cabin to welcome his new guests (he had nine men and women already), and he told Isabella that she could have the log cabin nearest the lake for herself. The charge would be eight dollars a week for cabin, board and riding horse.

She liked Griff on sight, though the smell of bourbon emanated from his bushy beard. She learned that he had bought the Estes buildings for a few dollars in '67, a year before Mountain Jim had taken his shack in Muggins Gulch. Both were squatters, holding land without titles to it, since the region would not be surveyed for homestead entry until 1874. Bad blood existed between them, partly because they competed in guiding parties up Longs Peak or westward over Fall River Pass to Grand Lake and Middle Park. Isabella got an impression from Griff that Jim in his cups made improper advances to Griff's seventeen-year-old daughter, Jinny. All of which made good material to send to Henrietta. Isabella wrote happily, "Jim's 'I'll shoot you' has more than once been heard in Griff's cabin."

Everything about Estes entranced Miss Bird — the great ranges enclosing it, the indescribable dawns and sunsets, the noisy skunk under her lake cabin, the bighorn sheep drinking there, the rides up Fish Creek toward Longs among the big yellow pines or over the Big Thompson to Black Canyon. She enjoyed being useful. She treated Griff's bad hangovers with bromide of potash, cooked and scrubbed in the main cabin, played the reed organ in the evenings for the dudes. She learned how to herd Griff's cattle with the tenderfeet cowboys, Rogers and Downer. She watched the progress of two dude love affairs but declined to see a parallel in Mountain Jim's daily calls on her as he went to check his traps in Black Canyon.

He called and called — always charming, respectful. He was a gay and witty man, obviously well educated, versed in the world's literature. He told her of his past, but warily, as though he were making it up and wanted the inventions to dovetail — his alleged birth in Montreal, his Irish father who had served as a high officer in the British army, his early affair with a seventeen-year-old girl which ended darkly and drove him to drink, his jobs in Canada teaching and trapping for the Hudson's Bay Company, his scouting in Sioux country for the U.S. Army, and his strange withdrawal at last to Muggins Gulch. He read to her poems of his own — not very good — mostly about the girl of his youth, or Jinny perhaps. He told of the grizzly bear attack in July of 1871 while he was in Middle Park ascending the Grand (Colorado) River toward Grand Lake and Fall River Pass. His collie Ring had scared up the bear and her cubs. The dog ran to Jim for protection, with the bear after him. Jim put four balls into the grizzly without stopping her. She jumped on him, chewed his left arm through at the elbow, bit off a thumb at the first joint, and slashed his neck and the whole right side of his face. He fainted. When he came to in a pool of blood, the bear and her cubs were gone. He managed to get to his white mule and rode eight miles to Grand Lake, where a passing doctor sewed up fifty wounds. The claws of the bear did not destroy his right eye, but tore the skin in such a way that a carbuncle formed over it.

Jim's talk of Longs Peak enthralled Isabella. He said that the ubiquitous Editor Byers of the *Rocky Mountain News* had made the first ascent in '68, with Major Powell. Just recently, Dr. Hayden and his government surveyors had reached the northeast foot of Longs by a trail coming up from the south — roughly that of today's highway from Boulder to Ward through Raymond and Allenspark. As the Hayden party ascended the blazed trail, Griff Evans had appeared from his ranch twelve miles away with eight guests. One of them was the famous Philadelphia lecturer, Anna E. Dickinson, who planned to be the first woman to climb the mountain. The two parties had camped together that night and had reached the top next morning, September 13, 1873, in three and a half hours.

Often Isabella gazed at Longs from her cabin and dreamed of climbing it herself, with Jim as her guide. The climbing idea was too absurd. She still thought of herself as a sort of invalid. On October 15, she would be forty-two years old. Though she had climbed Mauna Loa, Longs Peak was more difficult. And Jim Nugent was hardly comparable to her gentle and considerate tentmate on Mauna Loa, Mr. Wilson. She ignored the dreams, until Jim happened to tell her what the remarkable Miss Dickinson had done, at the age of thirty-one. His admiration for Miss Dickinson may have aroused her competitive spirit. She determined to try. She persuaded Platt Rogers and Downer to go along, and to hire Jim as the guide. And so on Monday, September 29, the four of them loaded their horses with food and blankets and set out up Fish Creek to the start of the Longs Peak trail near Lily Lake.

As a great landmark, Longs Peak has guided man since the beginning of his time on this continent. It forms one of the most beautiful masses in all the Rockies. It rises to 14,256 feet above the sea — more than a mile above Rocky Mountain National Park, in which it lies. Its timber stops at eleven thousand feet. The rest is bleak granite — precipices, chasms, ridges, shelves, notches. There are tiny blue lakes and bits of tundra and ptarmigan and snow ravines and baleful ravens and falling water. It is hard to breathe, which gives drama and urgency to everything. The view is overwhelming — the Continental Divide trundling westward and southward, the elephantine Mummy Range and the Never Summers northward beyond Estes, the Great Plains in blue-gray infinity to the east. Longs's east face, two thousand feet of sheer rock, is one of the few expert climbs in the United States. Tens of thousands have reached the summit by other faces, but it is never an easy walk for amateurs. At least twenty-one people have lost their lives on Longs, and there have been many injuries.

This blazed "trail" of 1873 was not a trail really, but just blazes on trees every so often. It remained the standard route to the top for half a century, until cables were installed on the north face in 1925 to shorten the distance. For the able-bodied, the blazes marked a good summer route. For a frail, middle-aged spinster weighing less than a hundred pounds it was madness to try it as late as September 29. Besides physical strain, she risked the peril of bad weather.

And still, Isabella and her three men rode blithely up Fish Creek. Jim looked like a pirate in his smashed wideawake and falling-apart clothes, with a knife in his belt and a pistol in his pocket. Isabella wore her Turkish trousers — getting pretty tattered — and her Hawaiian blouse, threadbare from washing. Her shoes were worn through. They passed Lily Lake, maneuvered their horses through the evergreens along Alpine Brook drainage, and reached timberline at twilight. They camped near a snow bank in a grove of limber pine which is called "Jim's Grove" still. After supper Jim installed Isabella in a bower of evergreens and instructed Ring to keep her warm.

A half-moon shone down on the peak but she slept badly most of the night. The wind set up a roar in "Jim's Grove" and animals howled below. Tuesday dawned at last and Jim called her to look at the sunrise. "From the chill grey Peak above," she wrote Henrietta, "we

Isabella's Grand Crater, which she saw approaching Longs Peak from Fish Creek headwaters, would be labeled Mill's Glacier today. Whatever its name, the awesome east face still rises sheer 1675 feet above it, forming one of the most difficult of American rock climbs.

looked to where the Plains lay cold, in blue grey, like a morning sea against a far horizon. Suddenly, as a dazzling streak at first, but enlarging rapidly into a sphere, the sun wheeled above the grey line. . . . The grey of the Plains changed to purple, the sky was all one rose-red flush, on which vermilion cloud-streaks rested; the ghastly peaks gleamed like rubies, the earth and heavens were new-created.''

Soon after breakfast the four reached today's Boulderfield at twelve thousand feet, on the north side of Longs. They left the horses and scrambled to that odd overhung rock formation called, in modern Longs Peak nomenclature, the Keyhole. The summit was still a thousand vertical feet above them. Here there was a crisis. At the Keyhole, a path edged its uneven way some hundreds of feet across a pitch of broken rock called the Ledge to the middle part of a great ravine, the Trough. At the top of the Trough another frightening shelf passage, the Narrows, led to the brief Homestretch grind to the top. As Jim pointed out these details of the last thousand feet, Isabella's courage failed her. She could not go on. ''You know,'' she wrote Henrietta, ''I have no head and no ankles, and never ought to dream of mountaineering; and had I known that the ascent was a real mountaineering feat I should not have felt the slightest ambition to perform it.''

She was distressed further by a bitter argument. Platt Rogers and Downer favored crossing the Ledge to the Trough. Jim said the Ledge was too icy. They must take a much longer route, descending a thousand feet vertically to pick up the Trough below. The men split on the issue. And Jim refused to let Isabella give up. He seemed obsessed with the idea that she could do whatever Anna E. Dickinson had done. He roped her to him, and dragged her along ''like a bale of goods, by sheer force of muscle,'' down to a lower part of the Trough and up again. ''That part,'' Isabella wrote, ''to me was two hours of painful and unwilling submission to the inevitable. . . . Slipping, faltering, gasping from the exhausting toil in the rarefied air, with throbbing hearts and panting lungs, we reached the top of the gorge [the Trough] and squeezed ourselves between two gigantic fragments of rock by a passage called the 'Dog's Lift,' when I climbed on the shoulders of one man and then was hauled up.''

Rogers and Downer had had to wait for them at that Dog's Lift start of the Narrows. The reunited four crossed the Narrows and

(Isabella wrote) "as we crept from the ledge round a horn of rock, I beheld what made me perfectly sick and dizzy to look at — the terminal Peak itself — a smooth, cracked face or wall of pink granite. . . . *Scaling,* not climbing, is the correct term for this last ascent. It took one hour to accomplish, pausing for breath every minute or two. The only foothold was in narrow cracks or minute projections on the granite . . . but at last the Peak was won. A grand, well-defined mountaintop it is, a nearly level acre of boulders, with precipitous sides all around, the one we came up being the only accessible one. It was not possible to remain long."

Isabella and Jim returned to the Keyhole by the long Trough route of their ascent. By her own account, it was a tender process, "Jim going before me so that I might steady my feet against his powerful shoulders. I had various falls and once hung by my frock, which caught on a rock, and Jim severed it with his hunting-knife, upon which I fell into a crevice full of soft snow. . . . Sometimes I drew myself up on hands and knees, sometimes crawled; sometimes Jim pulled me up by my arms or a lariat, and sometimes I stood on his shoulders, or he made steps for me of his feet and hands. But at six we stood on the Notch [the Keyhole] in the splendour of the sinking sun, all colour deepening, all peaks glorifying, all shadows purpling, all peril past." Jim carried her — a light burden — in his arms across part of the Boulderfield, lifted her onto her horse there, lifted her off at the "Jim's Grove" camp and rolled her in blankets near the campfire.

While Rogers and Downer slept, the older people talked awhile. Jim sang ballads in his soft Irish tenor. They discovered that both believed in spiritualism and each promised to appear to the other after death. Isabella confided to Henrietta: "Jim, or Mr. Nugent, as I always scrupulously called him, told stories of his early youth, and of a great sorrow which had led him to embark on a lawless and desperate life. His voice trembled, and tears rolled down his cheek."

And then it happened, though just what happened Isabella refused to reveal, even to her sister. Perhaps Jim kissed her, caressed her, made love. Whatever it was, she knew that the desperado had fallen in love with her, and she with him. "For five minutes," she wrote Henrietta, "at the camping ground his manner was such that I thought this possible. I put it away as egregious vanity, unpardonable in a woman of forty."

When Isabella had her romance with Mountain Jim while climbing Longs
Peak, people called this high stretch at twelve thousand feet the Lava
Beds — geologists claiming that the mountain was of volcanic origin.
Today they know better, Longs being the product of glacial action. So the
rocky stretch is called the Boulderfield.

But Isabella Lucy Bird did not really put it away. The thought of marrying this disreputable person colored everything she did for the remaining two months of her Colorado adventure. She planned a trip to Rose Kingsley's Colorado Springs but kept putting it off. She threw herself into the frantic activity of a woman troubled by love. She scrubbed her cabin, repaired her clothes, tried to get the roughness from her brown hands. She revealed her heart to Henrietta after a ride with Jim:

> I changed my horse for his beautiful mare, and we galloped and raced in the beautiful twilight, in the intoxicating frosty air. [I wish] you could have seen us as we galloped down the pass, the fearful looking ruffian on my heavy waggon-horse, and I on his bare wooden saddle, from which beaver, mink and marten tails and pieces of skin were hanging raggedly, with one spur, and feet not in the stirrups, the mare looking so aristocratic and I so beggarly! Mr. Nugent is what is called "splendid company." Ruffian as he looks, the first word he speaks — to a woman at least — places him on a level with educated gentlemen. . . . Yet, on the whole, he is a most painful spectacle. His magnificent head shows so plainly the better possibilities which might have been his. His life, in spite of a certain dazzle which belongs to it, is a ruined and wasted one, and one asks what good can the future have in store for one who has for so long chosen evil?

> Shall I ever get away?

She did get away on Monday, October 20, escorted by one of the dudes to Longmont and the St. Vrain Hotel. She rode "a bay Indian pony, Birdie, a little beauty, with legs of iron, fast, enduring, gentle and wise; and with luggage for some weeks, including a black silk dress, behind my saddle." She was no longer the frightened, ailing woman of the month before. Her small face must have had a new attractiveness. No man had made a play for her in a hotel lobby in years. But now here was this Colonel Heath — "an amateur sculptor and a colonel in the rebel Army, a dreadful man" — pestering her while she was trying to write Henrietta:

> If my sense of the ludicrous had not predominated, I should have thought of [using] the deadly weapon in my jacket. He was egregious. "Making love" was the only phrase that could be used — delicate flattery, all arts by which he supposed he could make himself agreeable. I might have said he proposed ten times. If I had any means of knowing when I

should get back I would get Mountain Jim to come for me, for there are things which become unendurable.

Isabella avoided the smitten colonel in the morning, and rode Birdie south over the prairie trail to Denver. In late afternoon she put a skirt over her Turkish trousers, mounted sidesaddle and moved on. "There the great braggart city lay spread out," she wrote, "brown and treeless, upon the brown and treeless plain. The shallow Platte, shrivelled in a narrow stream with a shingly bed six times too large for it, and fringed by shrivelled cottonwoods, wound along by Denver." She spent that night with members of Griff Evans's family on Seventeenth Street, west of the river. Birdie carried her across the Fifteenth Street bridge in the morning to breakfast at Charpiot's and to call on Governor Hunt and Editor Byers. She planned to take General Palmer's new train to Colorado Springs but Hunt urged her to ride Birdie instead. He gave her the names of ranching friends of his along the way, where she and Birdie would be welcome to spend the nights.

The Springs trip of eighty miles was not as easy as Hunt seemed to think. Isabella lost the trail twice and spent five days getting to Pikes Peak. She and Birdie stayed close to the Front Range, passing the mouth of South Platte Canyon, and then past Devil's Head in the serene, sheltered West Plum Creek valley. Today's tourists never see this lovely region; the four-lane highway passes east of it. Isabella spent one night of luxury near present Larkspur at the still-famous Perry Park Ranch (John D. Perry was a wealthy Union Pacific official). Thereafter Birdie trudged through deepening snow over the desolate, South Platte-Arkansas divide (present Palmer Lake) and on down and across the empty pine-land site of today's Air Force Academy. They went by General Palmer's Glen Eyrie mansion and through the Garden of the Gods, a multi-colored sandstone caricature of Gothic architecture "in which," Isabella remarked tartly, "were I a divinity, I certainly would not choose to dwell." On Monday afternoon, October 27, Birdie paused on the hill just west of Colorado Springs. Miss Bird was not pleased with Rose Kingsley's Little London:

I got off Birdie, put on a long skirt, and rode sidewise, though the settlement scarcely looked like a place where any deference to prejudices was necessary. A queer embryo-looking place it is, out on the bare Plains, yet it is rising and likely to rise, and has some big hotels much resorted to. It has a fine view of the mountains, specially of Pike's Peak, but the celebrated springs are at Manitou, three miles off, in really fine scenery. To me no place could be more unattractive than Colorado Springs, from its utter treelessness.

She had meant to spend weeks in Little London but she was restless from the start, wondering how the Estes Park dudes were doing without her, wondering if Jim was staying off whiskey and attending to his traps. She put up at a Kiowa Street boardinghouse for consumptives and called on Rose Kingsley's friends, the J. E. Lillers, who had come from England to edit the *Colorado Springs Gazette*. Liller was an intense young man, obsessed by fear that liquor was ruining the Springs' moral climate. Isabella thought him extreme, her own temperance stand having moderated lately. She gave him a big dose of bromide of potash to help him sleep, and did not explain that she gave the same dose to Griff Evans for his hangovers. The commons room of her consumptives' boardinghouse was crowded, noisy and gay on Tuesday night. The landlady and her guests laughed and sang for hours. Isabella was distracted by her view into the next room where,

I saw two large white feet sticking up at the end of the bed. I watched and watched, hoping these feet would move, but they did not, and, somehow, to my thinking, they grew stiffer and whiter, and then my horrible suspicion deepened, that while we were sitting there a human spirit, unattended and desolate, had passed forth into the night. . . . And still the landlady laughed and talked, and afterwards said to me, ''it turns the house upside down when they just come here and die; we shall be half the night laying him out.''

Early Wednesday morning, before anyone else died, Isabella and Birdie were on the road again. Governor Hunt had praised the beauties of South Park, and Isabella decided to return to Denver and Estes Park by that long wilderness route. She spent a night at a Manitou hotel and rode up the Ute Pass wagon road, which had just been blasted out of the canyon of Fountain Creek. At Rose Kingsley's insistence, she visited the Manitou Park ranch of the Englishman Dr. William A. Bell, north of Pikes Peak, thinking that ''it would put me out of conceit with Estes Park. Never! It is long and featureless, and its immediate surroundings are mean. It reminds me in itself of some dismal Highland strath — Glenshee, possibly.'' On Friday Birdie carried her across ''a hideous place,'' Hayden's Divide (the Divide of today's U.S. 24), and into the ''pine-sprinkled grassy hills'' of the Twin Rocks wagon road. To the south she could see the lacy spires of the Sangre de Cristo Mountains. Darkness caught her at a small Twin Rocks cabin where a man and his wife made her feel at home, though warning her that she risked her life traveling in November in the South Park country ''where if snow comes you will never be heard of again.'' She was warned again when she spent Saturday and Sunday at Colonel Kittridge's place on Oil Creek near Florissant, and again Monday night at the Link ranch (today's Lake George on the South Platte). She would not be deterred. Birdie, she said was a miracle horse, and those first November days were miracles too —

> As bright and warm as June, and the atmosphere has resumed its exquisite purity. . . . I have developed much sagacity in finding a trail, or I should not be able to make use of such directions as these: ''Keep along a gulch four or five miles till you get Pike's Peak on your left, then follow some wheel-marks till you get to some timber, and keep to the north till you come to a creek, where you'll find a great many elk tracks; then go to your right and cross the creek three times, then you'll see a red rock to your left,'' etc.

The Links directed her thirty miles northward to their daughter's place on Tarryall River above today's Tarryall Reservoir — northward through the flamboyant red-orange-purple Tarryall Mountains. Next day she ran into light snow as she entered the high north end of South Park, a vast grassy basin bounded by Mount Silverheels and other great round summits. But the summer weather returned, so she was bound to ride Birdie up the last bright trickle of the Tarryall, and a mile more above timberline to the bleak, tense spine of the continent at Breckenridge Pass, some 11,500 feet above sea level. Birdie brought her right back down and got her out of South Park that same day by the lower Kenosha Pass to Hall's Gulch, the miners of which had just hanged somebody. The rest of the trek was easy downhill to Denver, which she reached on Saturday, November 8.

She was quite worn out, and longing to see Estes, Mountain Jim and Griff's dudes. But she was an indefatigable tourist. After giving

The little mare Birdie carried Isabella above South Park to the top of the Continental Divide at Breckenridge Pass, which is called Boreas Pass now. The sketch shows a north-trending ridge near the top of Boreas Mountain, a thousand feet higher than the pass itself.

Birdie a few days of rest, she rode west to that gate of the mining country, Golden ("every other house a saloon") and by train and stage up Clear Creek Canyon to see the "fashionable resort" of Georgetown. She returned to Golden, and Birdie got her to Longmont on the fourteenth. The ardent Colonel Heath was not on hand to woo her, having left town because of wife trouble — too many wives. Early next morning, Birdie carried her up the Estes trail toward Muggins

Gulch, which, she declared, was "infinitely more beautiful than the much-vaunted parts I have seen elsewhere."

IT IS NOT POSSIBLE to comment quietly on Isabella's Pikes Peak circuit. It was incredible. Even today, her route makes a rugged motor trip of five hundred miles, some of it negotiable only by jeep. Isabella covered the terrain at that period of late fall when bad things can happen to the weather. She wore tropical clothes in shredded condition. Her health was poor and her horse was not much larger than herself. She had no money to speak of, because the Panic of '73 had reached Colorado and banks were not cashing checks. She picked her way through the empty land without compass or guide. When night came, she trusted to luck that someone would take her in.

From that day to this, no one, man or woman, has duplicated her feat. She herself seemed to think nothing of it; she was too busy observing Colorado — its ranching, mining, towns, people. She had published things before and she felt that her letters to Henrietta might contain material for travel books. She observed the scene, and also she considered her heart's yearning for Jim Nugent. "It takes peace away," she wrote Henrietta. She wondered if she could be a good wife to a man, after forty-two years of independence. When, in the soft twilight of November 15, she came to Jim's cabin in Muggins Gulch, no light shone through the chinks and all was silent. She was disappointed, and she was relieved also. Perhaps he had gone off and she would not have to make a decision. But:

> Soon I heard the welcome sound of a barking dog. . . . Calling "Ring" at a venture, the noble dog's large paws and grand head were in a moment on my saddle, and he greeted me with all those inarticulate but perfectly comprehensible noises with which dogs welcome their human friends. Of the two men on horses who accompanied him, one was his master, as I knew by the musical voice and grace of manner. . . . Jim leant on my horse and said, "I'm so happy to have met you, so very happy. God bless you." And his poor disfigured face literally beamed with nice kindly feelings . . . and sending the [other man] and fur-laden horse on to his cabin, he turned with me to Evans's.

The next eight days were days of anguish for both of them, the bitter-sweet anguish of middle-aged people perceiving what might have been and knowing nothing can be done about it. On Monday, Jim took her riding across the Big Thompson to see the Black Canyon beaver dams, "his mood as dark as the sky overhead." She wrote of the ride later, laying it on a bit thick perhaps, to thrill Henrietta:

> He was quite silent, struck his horse often, started off on a furious gallop, and then throwing his mare on her haunches close to me, said, "You're the first man or woman who's treated me like a human being for many years." . . . Then came a terrible revelation that as soon as I had gone away he had discovered he was attached to me and it was killing him. It began on Longs Peak, he said. I was terrified. It made me shake all over and even cry. He is a man whom any woman might love, but who no sane woman would marry. Nor did he ask me to marry him, he knew enough for that. . . . He has a squatter's claim, and forty head of cattle, and is a successful trapper besides, but envy and vindictiveness are raging within him. He gets money, goes to Denver, and spends large sums in the maddest dissipation, making himself a terror. . . . Of course I can't give details. A less ungovernable nature would never have said a word but his dark proud fierce soul all came out then. . . . He stopped his horse and said, "Now you see a man who has made a devil of himself! Lost! Lost! Lost! I believe in God. I've given Him no choice but to put me with the devil and his angels. I'm afraid to die. You've stirred the better nature in me too late. . . . Don't speak to me of repentance and reformation. I can't reform." . . . My heart dissolved for pity for him and his dark lost self-ruined life. He is so lovable and fascinating yet so terrible. I told him I could not speak to him, I was so nervous, and he said if I could not speak to him he would not see me again. He would go and camp out on the Snowy Range till I was gone.

On Tuesday, a tragi-comic war of love's frustration began. Jim, pale, haggard and more than a little drunk, called for her late in the afternoon, "but it was a dismal and depressing ride. Jim's manner was courteous but freezing." He coughed constantly, the implication being that it was all her fault. He repeated that he was off to the Snowy Range. That night Isabella dreamed "that as we were sitting by the fire Mr. Nugent came in with his revolver in his hand and shot me. But there is no such peril. I wonder if he really will stay up on the range?"

Jim kept her wondering all through Wednesday and Thursday. She busied herself with preparations to leave Estes for good. She washed her hair, made drawers out of a nightgown, and sat in the middle of her cabin "without nearly all my clothes," mending everything. But she had to unburden herself to Henrietta:

> If only it were not for Jim. It is so sad to think of him and no more to see his Arab mare tied in front of the house. It was very wrong of him to speak as he did, he should have let me go without the sorrow of knowing this. Thus again that hideous whiskey fiend crossed my path. You would like him so. He is so quick, like a needle, a thoroughly cultured Irishman . . . such an agreeable facility of speech. I cannot but think of poor Mr. Wilson on Hawaii and his quiet, undemonstrative, unannoying ways and compare him with this dark, tempestuous, terrible character, wondering how it is that the last is so fascinating.

On Friday, November 21, Griff Evans's last two lingering dudes told Isabella that they had seen Jim (still coughing and with "an awfully ugly fit on him") returning to his cabin by the lower ford of the Big Thompson. His use of the lower ford meant that he had avoided passing her cabin. This, she decided, was the end. She would deliver her last word to him herself. She wrote the icy phrases in her small spidery hand:

> Dear Sir:
> In consequence of the very blameworthy way in which you spoke to me on Monday, there can be nothing but constraint between us. Therefore it is my wish that our acquaintance shall at once terminate.
> Yours truly,
Isabella Lucy Bird

Late that afternoon, in a spirit of regained freedom, she saddled a big horse and went galloping down Muggins Gulch "in my ragged Hawaiian dress with two huge hounds with me — the very picture of outlawed free leggism." And there on the trail she met a changed Jim, his manner irresistibly appealing, as suited a man suffering from unrequited love. Her heart melted.

> I was terrified to encounter him but he was quiet and courteous. I had the note in my pocket and told him I was going to give it to him. He said I was very kind to write and put it in his pocket. He said that he was feeling so very ill that he was going home, that he had caught a very bad cold

on the Range, and that an old arrow wound in his lung had become very painful. He looked so ill and wretched going to his dark lonely lair, and I felt I had stabbed him and had not made sufficient allowance for him. He said if he was better he would like to call tomorrow evening. I said nothing, for well I knew he would never call after reading my note. I wished him good-bye, wishing I could bring him here and make him warm tea and be kind to him, rather than kill him as I had done.

But her note did not kill Jim. Instead it was like the last clap of thunder ending a storm. It brought them to an understanding, to acceptance of the inevitable, even to a sort of sad serenity. Jim's way of life, alcoholic and violent, stood between them, and he could not change. They would part, and still they would be friends. That was clear when she saw him Sunday and found him relaxed and charming again.

Thereafter, the days passed pleasantly. Isabella saw no reason now to be in a rush about leaving Estes. She made a splendid four-pound cake for Griff's dudes on Thanksgiving Day, and she wrote an article on her Longs Peak trip which Editor Liller would publish in Colorado Springs. Jim corrected the piece for her while she watched "the wind lifting his thin curls from as grand a head as was ever modelled . . . may our Father which is in Heaven yet show mercy to his Outcast child." The time of her departure for the railroad station at Greeley came on Tuesday morning, December 9, 1873. She had accepted Jim's offer to escort her as far as the Greeley stage on the Big Thompson near Namaqua. Griff Evans rode with her from the ranch as far as Jim's cabin. "At the top of the hill," she wrote, "I forgot to turn round and take a last look at my colossal, resplendent, lonely sunlit den, but it was needless for I carry it away with me." Jim loaned her his Arab mare for the Namaqua trip and gave her a farewell present — "a mouse-colored kitten beaver's skin."

He and his white mule brought her out of the wilds by a trail which became today's Pole Hill Road, partly along the North Fork of the Little Thompson. Their arrival Wednesday evening at the St. Louis stage station inn near Namaqua caused excitement. Isabella wrote:

The landlady asked, with great eagerness, who the gentleman was with me, and said that the men outside were saying that they were sure that it was "Rocky Mountain Jim," but she was sure it was not. When I told her that the men were right, she exclaimed, "Do tell! I want to know! that quiet, kind gentleman!" and she said she used to frighten her children when they were naughty by telling them that "he would get them, for he came down from the mountains every week, and took back a child with him to eat!"

It was bitter cold Thursday morning. Seventy-five days had passed since Isabella and Jim had met in the park, many of them tumultuous with the heartbreak of an impossible love. But their parting was casual. The Greeley stage arrived and Isabella found a friend on it, an Englishman whom she introduced to Jim as Mr. Fodder (his real name was Haig, a land agent for the Earl of Dunraven). She wrote:

> He [Mr. Fodder] was now dressed in the extreme of English dandyism, and when I introduced them, he put out a small hand cased in a perfectly-fitting lemon-colored kid glove. As the trapper stood there in his grotesque rags and odds and ends of apparel, his gentlemanliness of deportment brought into relief the innate vulgarity of the rich *parvenu*. Mr. Fodder rattled on so amusingly as we drove away that I never realized that my Rocky Mountain life was at an end, not even when I saw Mountain Jim, with his golden hair yellow in the sunshine, slowly leading the beautiful mare over the snowy Plains back to Estes Park. . . . A drive of several hours brought us to Greeley, and a few hours later, in the far blue distance, the Rocky Mountains, and all that they enclose, went down below the prairie seas.

JIM NUGENT is a Colorado legend now, a tragic figure of romance immortalized by the pen of Isabella Bird because of her love and pity for him. He did not live long after Isabella watched him and the rest of her Estes Park world go "down below the prairie seas." In June of '74, Griff Evans blasted him with a shotgun from his ranch-house porch in the presence of Isabella's English "parvenu" Mr. Haig. Griff pleaded self-defense, and was acquitted after Jim died from the wounds three months later in Fort Collins. Gossip had it, and still has it, that Griff shot Jim in a showdown involving Jim's attentions to Jinny Evans and Jim's fear that Griff was conniving with the Earl of Dunraven to take Estes Park from the squatters. On the day Jim died, Isabella was in Interlaken, Switzerland. She wrote later that he appeared in her hotel then to say good-bye to her, as he had promised to do that night on Longs Peak when love and marriage had seemed possible. He wore his tattered trapper's garb, bowed low with courtly grace and vanished.

And Isabella? That tiny, frail, tenderhearted, indomitable woman is an Estes legend too. The story of the park, as millions know it, is largely her creation. Her book, *A Lady's Life in the Rocky Mountains,* is as widely read today as it was when it appeared in 1879. Her fantastic activity increased as she grew older but her health got worse and worse — spots on her lungs, rheumatism, and a balky heart being added to her other ailments. She almost married Henrietta's doctor, John Bishop, in 1878, when she was forty-seven, but could not face "being an invalid wife" and fled to Japan to rest up among the Hairy Ainu of Hokkaido. Bishop, ten years her junior, contined to woo, and married her soon after Henrietta's death in 1880. Isabella buried Bishop five years later.

Her many travel books, immensely popular, told of her adventures in Hawaii, in the Malayas, in India, in Persia, in Turkestan, in China. How she survived these exhausting trips might be explained by her husband's remark that she had the appetite of a tiger and the digestion of an ostrich. Besides writing, she worked at photography, at chemistry, and at nursing. She used her fame as an author to establish mission hospitals in Kashmir, Seoul, and up the Yangtze. She died in Edinburgh on October 7, 1904, aged seventy-two, not long after crossing the Atlas Mountains of North Africa on an Arab mare loaned to her by the Sultan of Morocco, a mare as beautiful as the mare Mountain Jim had loaned her in Estes.

Lord Dunraven (standing) is passing his field glasses to Dr. George Kingsley somewhere in the Nebraska sandhills north of the Platte River. They are looking for elk or, perhaps, their guides Buffalo Bill Cody and Texas Jack. The year is 1871.*

*All the sketches of Lord Dunraven's hunting trips were made in England by Valentine W. Bromley and they are fine examples of how writers illustrated their books in the days before photographic reproduction. The earl gave Bromley general photographs of Western scenes for background and his own rough sketches of specific terrain, with details about how members of his party looked. In the preface to *The Great Divide*, Dunraven wrote: ''Of the illustrations in which Mr. Valentine Bromley has so graphically carried out my ideas, I will say nothing. The reader will agree with me that they speak for themselves.'' The original sketches are owned by Lord Dunraven's grandson, the Earl of Meath. The book versions of them are reproduced here with his kind consent.

6

THE DUDE FROM LIMERICK

ALL OUR DUDES had traveled widely before they went to the American West, and none more than Windham Thomas Wyndham-Quin, the fourth Earl of Dunraven and Mountearl in the Peerage of Ireland, second Baron Kenry of the United Kingdom, Knight of the Order of St. Patrick and Companion of the Order of St. Michael and St. George.

In his autobiography, Dunraven wrote that he was born in 1841 "at Adare, in the good little old County of Limerick." It was his fate to have a stern Roman Catholic for a father and a determined Low Church Protestant for a mother. The two could not agree on a religion for their only son so the father shipped him off to Rome for High Church instruction near the Vatican and forbade the mother to write to him. But she got her messages through somehow. She even managed to have him schooled briefly in Paris where he learned fluent and vernacular French along the Boul'-Mich, and picked up all manner of bad habits and an appreciation of fine wines and pretty girls. "It is most annoying," he complained later, "that everything that is pleasant is all wrong."

He was almost seventeen — very tall, very skinny, very positive — when he told his parents gently, for he was fond of them, to have their religious difference over somebody else. At the same time, he disobeyed them by going to Oxford instead of to some sort of church training place. Life, he had decided, was too short and too full of wonderful things to see and do to waste time on High or Low religion.

His three years at Oxford were fine. Study was not a required part of the curriculum. He raced his horses and played cricket and practiced on his violin to his heart's content, and cruised around the Isles on his yacht, the *Cripple*. Then he was a soldier more or less — cornet-of-horse in the First Life Guards — during which service he fought the Battle of Hyde Park when the Reform League mob stormed the area. In '67, he studied spiritualism under the renowned table-lifter, Daniel Dunglas Home. The medium's seances, with rappings and handless guitar-playing, convinced Dunraven that people could communicate after death, but he preferred the living for company. When Sir Robert Napier went to war in Abyssinia, Dunraven went along as a reporter for the *London Daily Telegraph*. A year later he married Florence Elizabeth Kerr, one of the highborn Lothian tribe, and took her to the United States for their honeymoon.

The honeymoon part was an excuse merely. Dunraven had been around, as we have said — to the Holy Land, Rhodes, Constantinople, Greece, Sicily, North Africa, and so on. But always he had dreamed of going West, particularly west of the Mississippi to hunt. In his autobiography he recalled his feelings on his way to New York in the summer of 1869: "I was young — not twenty-eight years of age; and my boyish brain-cells were stored to bursting with tales of Red Indians and grizzly b'ars; caballeros and haciendas, prairies and buffaloes, Texans and Mexicans, cowboys and voyageurs, and had not yet discharged or jettisoned their cargo. I was in search of such sport and adventure as, under the circumstances, were to be found."

Many people had posted him on Western affairs. An uncle from Sligo had known Sir St. George Gore and had told him of Gore's hunting years in Wyoming. Captain John Palliser, whose home was in Tipperary, had often visited Adare and had brought him more stories. Palliser had roamed the Upper Missouri country in 1847-1848 and had headed the government's Palliser Expedition to the Canadian Rockies in the late 1850's. Palliser was a child's ideal — the mighty hunter who enjoyed romping around Adare playing trappers and Indians with the future fourth Earl.

After landing in New York in '69, the impatient Dunraven first had to do the social rounds with his bride — the Brevoort House, Delmonico's, Newport, Lake George, Washington, D.C., Richmond — as a preamble to westering. And in Richmond he collapsed of sunstroke,

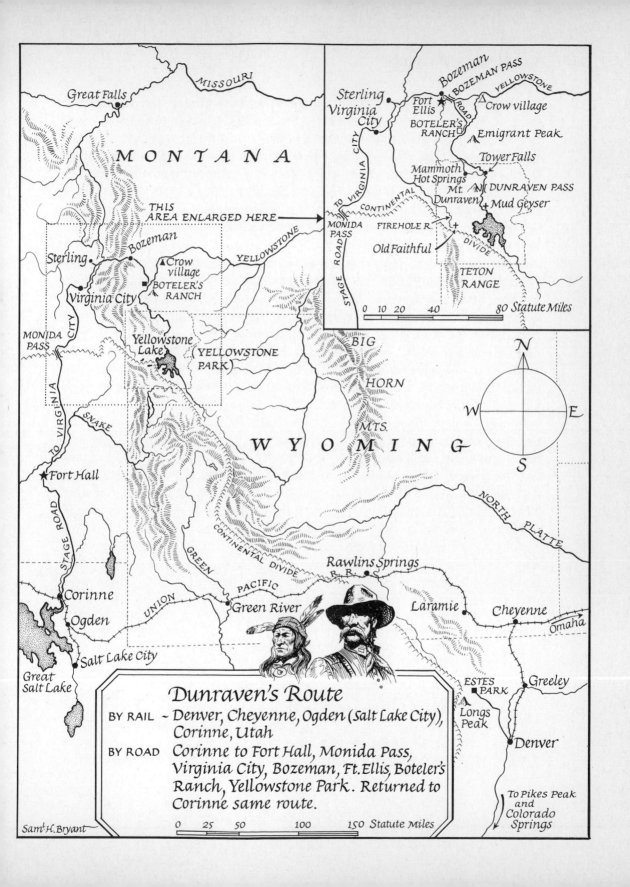

Great Falls

MISSOURI

MONTANA

Sterling
Bozeman
Virginia City

THIS
AREA ENLARGED HERE

Crow
village
BOTELER'S
RANCH

YELLOWSTONE

MONIDA
PASS

VIRGINIA CITY

SNAKE

Yellowstone
Lake

(YELLOWSTONE
PARK)

BIG

HORN

MTS.

W Y O M I N G

N
W   E
S

Fort Hall

CONTINENTAL DIVIDE

GREEN

RIVER

NORTH

PLATTE

STAGE ROAD

Rawlins Springs
R.R.

PACIFIC

UNION

Green River

Laramie

Cheyenne

Omaha

Corinne

Ogden

Salt Lake City

Great
Salt Lake

ESTES
PARK

Longs
Peak

Greeley

Denver

Dunraven's Route

BY RAIL — Denver, Cheyenne, Ogden (Salt Lake City),
            Corinne, Utah
BY ROAD   Corinne to Fort Hall, Monida Pass,
            Virginia City, Bozeman, Ft. Ellis, Boteler's
            Ranch, Yellowstone Park. Returned to
            Corinne same route.

To Pikes Peak
and
Colorado
Springs

Sam¹ H. Bryant

0   25   50   100   150 Statute Miles

Bozeman
BOZEMAN PASS
YELLOWSTONE

Sterling
Virginia
City

Fort
Ellis

ROAD

Crow village

BOTELER'S
RANCH

Emigrant Peak

Tower Falls

Mammoth
Hot Springs

DUNRAVEN PASS

Mt.
Dunraven

Mud Geyser

TO VIRGINIA CITY

CONTINENTAL

MONIDA
PASS

FIREHOLE R.

DIVIDE

STAGE ROAD

Old Faithful

TETON
RANGE

0 10 20   40   80 Statute Miles

forcing him to cut short the honeymoon and go home. He did not get back to the United States until the fall of 1871, after having covered the Franco-Prussian War for the *London Daily Telegraph*. His father had died recently and he was Lord Dunraven now, master of thirty thousand acres in Ireland and in Wales. He followed custom by taking along his own doctor, George Henry Kingsley, who was Isabella Bird's friend. George Kingsley was getting on in years — he was forty-five — but he had hunted far and wide as physician for various dukes and earls, and he was tough.

On this second American trip, Dunraven hurried with Kingsley straight to Chicago, having a letter of introduction to General Philip H. Sheridan, our hero of the overhung stomach. The earl found the general to be "a great soldier and a delightful man, with the one peculiarity of using the most astounding swear words quite calmly and dispassionately in ordinary conversation." Sheridan had an antlered trophy hanging in his Army headquarters office. Dunraven called it a wapiti, which amused Sheridan. It was, the general said, an elk. His Lordship retorted that, properly, an "elk" was a "moose," explaining further that Americans called an elk an "elk" for the same reason, or lack of reason, that they called thrushes "robins" and grouse "partridges."

Next day, the general wired Fort McPherson for hunting guides, and sent Dunraven and Kingsley along by train to that same town of North Platte, Nebraska, which we mentioned in the Grand Duke Alexis chapter. Two guides met them at the North Platte station. One, of course, was Buffalo Bill Cody; the other Texas Jack Omohundro, who was white mostly, for all his Indian name. Dunraven described the two in his autobiography:

Both were tall, well-built, active-looking men, with singularly handsome features. Bill was dressed in a pair of corduroys tucked into his high boots, and a blue flannel shirt. He wore a broad-brimmed hat, or sombrero, and had a white handkerchief folded like a little shawl loosely fastened around his neck to keep off the fierce rays of the afternoon sun. Jack's costume was similar, with the exception that he wore moccasins, and had his lower limbs encased in a pair of comfortable greasy deerskin trousers, ornamented with a fringe along the seams. Round his waist was a belt supporting a revolver, two butcher knives, and, in his hand he carried his trusty rifle, the "Widow" — now in my possession. Jack, tall and lithe,

Texas Jack Omohundro was a professional hunters' guide known through-out the West both for skill and personal charm. He was with Dunraven in Nebraska, Yellowstone Park and many other places.

with light brown close-cropped hair, clear laughing honest blue eyes, and a soft and winning smile, might have sat as a model for a typical modern Anglo-Saxon — if ethnologists will excuse the term. Bill was dark, with quick searching eyes, aquiline nose, and delicately cut features, and he wore his hair falling in long ringlets over his shoulders, in true Western style. As he cantered up, with his flowing locks and broad-brimmed hat, he looked like a picture of a cavalier of olden times.

The earl did his best to record the dialogue of his guides as they discussed the North Platte game outlook:

"Never you mind about deer and elk," cried Jack. "You have no call to worry about that. We will find game enough if you can hit them. You think the prairie don't look cheerful, eh! Well, it does seem kind of dismal, don't it, this time of year. Ah, but you should see it in the summer when the grass is all green, and the flowers is all a-blowing, and the little birdies is a-building of their nesties and boo-hooing around, and the deer are that fat they will scarcely trouble to get out of the way; and as to eating, they are just splendid, immense! I tell you — ain't they, Bill?"

"Yes, sir — ee, you bet your boots they are! But come on, Jack, let's fork our ponies and skin out for the fort. . . . We will see you in the morning and fix that hunt all right, I guess."

They passed the night in North Platte's small hotel. In the morning, Dunraven had the commonest of reactions to the Great Plains:

I was oppressed with the vastness of the country; the stillness and the boundlessness of the plains seemed to press like a weight upon my spirits and I was not sorry to get back into the bustle and busy life of Fort McPherson. After a while, I became accustomed to the plains. The feeling of depression of spirits which was at first occasioned by the monotony and quiet coloring of everything faded away and the limitlessness of the prairie only impressed me with a feeling of freedom, and created rather an exhilaration of spirits than otherwise.

Dunraven and Kingsley spent a happy month with Buffalo Bill and Texas Jack hunting elk north of the North Platte River. The earl berated the cowardly elk "stags" (bulls) for trying to save their skins by hiding among the "hinds" (cows), but he was very pleased to get a handsome trophy for the fireplace at Adare. His account of how his party looked arriving back at Fort McPherson seems to paraphrase Matt Field's account (page 29) of the return of Sir William Drummond Stewart's men from the Yellowstone in 1843. Dunraven wrote, "We were about the dirtiest, most blood-stained, hungriest, happiest, most contented, and most disreputable crowd to be found anywhere in the great territories of the West."

A YEAR LATER, in early November, 1872, the two dudes returned from Britain to Fort McPherson. This time Buffalo Bill and Texas Jack led them south of the Platte to Medicine Creek and Camp Alexis, but they did not find the buffalo herd which the grand duke had seen ten months before. Then they continued west along the Union Pacific, getting badly swindled at Sydney, Nebraska. "It would take too long," Kingsley commented, "to describe the unutterable villainy and ruffianism of that most infernal hole." They hunted bighorn sheep around Scottsbluff and went on to Cheyenne — "a funny town of the packing-case and kerosene-tin order," Kingsley wrote his wife. From Cheyenne they rode the new rails south through Denver to Pikes Peak, for a few days' hunting in South Park.

They holed up in Denver for the Christmas holidays at, Kingsley wrote, "a capital hotel — kept by one Charpool, a Swiss, having one of the best cooks and the best wine cellars in America. Lord! we hungered for its fleshpots when we were up in the mountains!" Charpool was Kingsley's name for Charpiot's, whose Hotel and Restaurant was "the Delmonico of the West." They spent a convivial evening at the Corkscrew Club, near Broadway, a hangout for prominent foreigners where women, nice women anyhow, were not permitted. And that was where they heard first of the charms of Estes Park, of Longs Peak, of Griff Evans's dude ranch, of the mysterious Mountain Jim Nugent.

One of their informants was a lively young mining man named Theodore Whyte, aged twenty-six, whose father was said to be some kind of Irish hussar and whose mother was a French-Canadian heiress. Whyte had grown up in Devonshire, had trapped three years for Hudson's Bay Company and had come to Colorado in the late 1860's to make a fortune. His talk about Estes, up the multicolored St. Vrain canyon and Muggins Gulch, inspired Lord Dunraven with a wild wish to see that hunter's paradise, even in the dead of winter. But Kingsley had commitments in Salt Lake City and San Francisco and didn't feel

On his first Estes Park visit in December, 1872, Dunraven (right) hunted bighorn sheep around Longs Peak with a "Scotch gillie named Sandie," whom he had met at Denver's Corkscrew Club.

up to Estes just then. They decided to separate temporarily. On the day after Christmas, 1872, the earl took the train for Longmont with a couple of Corkscrewers for company — "a Scotch gillie" and "a friend from Sligo." During the short trip, a magnificent parhelion or "sun dog" entertained them — a lighting up of the sky by brilliant mock suns, in rainbow hues.

In Longmont, Dunraven rented mules and a wagon and spent a day with his friends riding up the Muggins Gulch trail past Mount Olympus to Estes — "undulating," the earl would write, "grass-covered, dotted with trees, peaceful and quiet, with a silver thread of water curving and twining through its midst." The weather was mild. There was little snow, though the temperature was well below zero in the shade. Sap oozed from the pines in the blazing sun and the travelers heard insects buzzing. Longs Peak soared to blue heaven — serene king of its court of Continental Divide mountains, magnified by their mantles of glittering snow. It was a marvelous sight. The dude ranch at the mouth of Fish Creek was still open. Griff Evans assigned the Dunraven party to the two-room cabin near the little lake.

The earl could not tarry long, but he stayed long enough to hunt "wapiti" up Black Canyon toward the Mummy Range, up Fall River toward Middle Thompson, up the Big Thompson to Bear Lake, up Fish Creek to the Twin Sisters, down Muggins Gulch as far as Mountain Jim's. Perhaps he explored north a few miles, to the head of Devil's Gulch (near Tallant's today, named for the landscape artist) and down the gulch to the north fork of the Big Thompson and on to present Dunraven Glade and Dunraven Park under Mount Dunraven. He saw a lot of Estes, and succumbed to its blandishments. "The climate of Colorado," he would write, "is health-giving — unsurpassed, as I believe, anywhere — giving to the jaded spirit, the unstrung nerves, and weakened body, a stimulant, a tone and vigor that can only be appreciated by those who have had the good fortune to travel or reside in that region."

He saw a lot of Estes — and he talked to Griff Evans and Theodore Whyte about it. On his voyage back to Ireland he could not get what he had seen off his mind. During that winter of 1873 he began to dream of acquiring the park's ten or fifteen thousand acres all for himself, with the Evans ranch as a nucleus. Lord Dunraven was a very rich man now. He could afford to maintain a private hunting preserve in America, a safe retreat from civilization. Griff's talk had made him realize that there was no time to lose. He must find a real estate agent to start buying land soon. Evans and Mountain Jim now had Estes Park to themselves, but Dr. Hayden's surveyors were about to map the

Longs Peak region, and homesteaders always flocked in after an area had been surveyed.

The earl's choice for his purchasing agent was the Englishman, Isabella Bird's "Mr. Fodder" whose real name was Haig. And so our chronology brings us to that farewell in December of 1873, when Isabella put love and Estes Park behind her, and Mountain Jim helped her and her Turkish trousers on the Greeley-bound stage. You will recall that she introduced Jim to the dudish Mr. Haig, while comparing Jim's picturesque tatters to Haig's lemon-colored kid gloves and finding Jim ever so much more attractive.

Mr. Haig seems to have spent the winter of 1873-1874 in Denver studying U.S. laws for distributing the public domain. He found that Dunraven, being a foreigner, could not apply for a free 160-acre homestead in Estes, or for a small preemption holding at one dollar and a quarter an acre. Even Americans were limited to one homestead and one preemption per person. But speculators everywhere were getting around the laws. In Colorado, cowboys, prospectors and such were paid by these speculators to file for homesteads after agreeing to sign the land over to the real purchaser as soon as patents were issued by the Land Office. The requirements for improvement of the land were met by laying logs on the ground in squares, representing houses.

By the time of Dunraven's return West, Haig had bought Griff Evans' squatter's rights and his Fish Creek ranch buildings, retaining Griff as caretaker. But Mountain Jim had refused to sell, and had frightened the Englishman almost out of his lemon-colored gloves just by waving his gun. Meanwhile, Haig had put Theodore Whyte to finding dummy filers in Denver. Whyte had rummaged around Larimer Street during May and early June of '74, and had induced thirteen men to apply for Estes Park homesteads and preemptions. The applications involved nearly four thousand acres of land, counting the Evans ranch — a fair beginning for the private hunting preserve.

WHYTE REPORTED THESE MATTERS to Dunraven when the earl and George Kingsley turned up at the Evans Ranch for a bit of late spring hunting. Dunraven was pleased, but soon began to have doubts about his preserve. Estes Park was very beautiful, and that was the trouble. Besides, it looked like gold country. With warm weather people from everywhere piled in by the hundreds to picnic and camp and prospect.

More came to climb Longs Peak. One climber found the coat Anna E. Dickinson had left on top in '73. The newspapers wrote it up and that brought more climbers. On Sundays ministers held Low Church services in plain view of the ranch. The earl hired Theodore Whyte to fence people out and to heckle trespassers but Whyte could not supply proof that Dunraven owned anything. When Whyte told the picnickers and campers and prospectors and Low Church ministers to get their tents off the earl's property they wanted to know how the dude furriner got aholt of it.

Years later Dunraven remembered that it was in mid-June that he started to think about modifying the whole hunting preserve idea. He was enjoying a nap in his cabin at Griff's when somebody knocked on his door. He woke, opened the door grumpily, and found a ragged little old man standing there with a donkey beside him. The earl recorded the conversation:

> *Little old man:* Say, is this a pretty good place to drink whiskey in?
> *Lord Dunraven:* Yes. What place isn't?
> *Little old man:* Well, have you any to sell?
> *Dunraven:* Got none. Good day, sir!

Civilization! All the earl's fences couldn't keep a little old man and his donkey from disturbing his nap! And the last straw was the shooting of Mountain Jim during that same June of '74. Dunraven gave his view of what happened, half a century later when he was nearly eighty years old:

> Estes Park was inhabited by a little Welshman, Evans, who made a living I don't know how; and by Mountain Jim, who trapped — an extraordinary character, civil enough when sober, but when drunk, which was as often as he could manage, violent and abusive, and given to declamation in Greek and Latin. Evans lived in quite a decent, comfortable log-house, and Jim in a shanty some fifteen miles away. Evans and Jim had a feud, as per usual about a woman — Evans' daughter.
>
> One fine day I was setting by the fire, and Evans asleep on a sort of sofa, when some one rushed in shouting, "Get up; here's Mountain Jim in the corral. He is looking very ugly." Up jumped Evans, grabbed a shotgun, and went out. A sort of duel eventuated, which ended in Jim getting all shot up with slugs. Jim was not dead, but refused to be carried into Evans' house. We carried him down to the creek, and fixed him up as

well as we could, and he made a solemn declaration, as a man who would presently be before his Maker, that he had not begun the scrap, and that it was sheer murder.

However, he did not go before his Maker, and after a while we got him back to his shanty. Dr. Kingsley went with him and reported that he could not possibly live, for he had one bullet in his skull and his brains were oozing out, and he did not know how many more slugs were embedded in various parts of his person. But it is hard to die in the wonderful air of that great altitude. Before many weeks had passed he was packed down to the settlements, where some months later he did die.

The shooting lured to Estes the morbidly curious as well as the tourists. Within a month Dunraven had made up his mind. He would set up his hunting lodge and game preserve far from this madding crowd, in the glade north and west of Devil's Gulch. Estes Park itself would be developed by a stock company as a summer resort and cattle ranch. The earl would be the major stockholder, Theodore Whyte the general manager, and Griff Evans would continue to run the ranch. Dunraven's scheme was announced in Denver papers on July 29, 1874. Thereafter Whyte went to work, modernizing Griff's ranch buildings with clapboard, bringing in machinery for a sawmill and enlarging the ranch herd with mouse-colored Swiss cattle to twelve hundred head. Whyte hired carpenters to begin building a gabled cottage for Dunraven's use, half a mile up Fish Creek from the ranch, and a hunting lodge in Dunraven Glade on the secluded north fork of the Big Thompson. Also he made plans for roads and trails radiating from a proposed big hotel to be built on a small lake in the vicinity of the Dunraven cottage site.

By the middle of August Dunraven had had his fill of the Estes hustle and bustle and was ready to forget his real estate troubles and head north for some hunting out of Fort Ellis (Bozeman) in Montana Territory. And he longed to see Yellowstone Park, having heard the same kind of incredible reports which had thrilled Sir William Drummond Stewart in the 1830's. Perhaps John Palliser had told the young Dunraven things about "Geyserland," as Yellowstone Park was called in the '60's. Certainly the earl had read of the Yellowstone expedition of 1870 under Henry D. Washburn and N. P. Langford, and in Washington he may have seen Thomas Moran's celebrated painting of the

Grand Canyon of the Yellowstone — the painting which had helped to influence Congress to create the Park in 1872.

Texas Jack Omohundro had agreed to lead the earl's party. Dunraven and Kingsley met Jack in Denver and they bought their outfit in Salt Lake City — "a peculiar place," the earl would recall, "like a jar of mixed human pickles, saints and gentiles, elders and sinners, Mormons and Christians." They had planned to reach Fort Ellis from Rawlins, Wyoming, and the east side of the Continental Divide, using Jim Bridger's old route to Virginia City west of the Big Horns, to Yellowstone River and over Bozeman Pass. But Sioux Indians were restive in the Big Horns. So Dunraven, Kingsley and Texas Jack, plus the earl's Scotch servant, Campbell, and his colored valet, Maxwell, took the stage coach from the Union Pacific station at Corinne, Utah. The stage ran north to Fort Hall in Idaho and over Monida Pass into Montana — three hundred miles and more. Idaho's strange beauty lifted Dunraven's spirits and as they neared Fort Hall, the sunrise inspired him to wax poetic:

> The dawn approaches, flinging over all the eastern sky a veil of the most delicate primrose that warms into the rich lustre of the topaz, hiding the sad eyes of the fading stars. The yellow light sweeping across the sky is followed by a lovely rosy tint which, slowly creeping over the arch of heaven, dyes the earth and firmament with its soft colouring and throws back the mountains and valleys into deepest gloom. Stronger and stronger grows the morn. Higher and warmer spreads the now crimson flood. The mountains all flush up; then blaze into sudden life. A great ball of fire clears the horizon, and strikes broad avenues of white light across the plain. The sun is up! and it is day.

They spent a night or two at the gold camp of Virginia City, which was in decline but still specializing in such interesting ladies as to cause Dunraven to exclaim, "Virginia City! Good Lord! What a name for the place!" Short of Bozeman, they stopped off at the little ghost camp of Sterling to look at a mine. They would never forget the spot because a small Irishman there, who said his name was Mahogany Bogstick, harangued the earl for hours on England's perfidy and the virtues of a milk diet. They continued to Fort Ellis, admiring the serene beauty of Montana's Madison and Gallatin and Tobacco Root

Ranges, and they dined lavishly in the "clean all-alive and wide-awake town of Bozeman."

General Sweitzer put them up at Fort Ellis and some of the soldiers instructed them with stories about how mean Indians were and how they cut up people and broiled the pieces, still wriggling. The earl discounted these stories of Indian misbehavior, having heard Buffalo Bill on the subject of government mistreatment of Indians — the story of a century of injustice, of rights withheld, of treaties broken, of promises unfulfilled. General Sweitzer said that there was a Crow Indian camp beyond Bozeman Pass, near the big bend of the Yellowstone. The camp was on the road upstream, leading to Yellowstone Park and to Fred Boteler's ranch, which Texas Jack had chosen as headquarters for the hunt.

Dunraven and Kingsley made it a point to visit the Crow camp, sending the others on ahead to Boteler's in the handsome shadow of Emigrant Peak. The Crow chiefs felt themselves honored by the two Europeans and the whole village turned out to entertain them. Dunraven admired what he saw that day and praised the way of life of the Crows later in his superb book about Yellowstone, *The Great Divide*. The average male Crow seemed to him a lot like anybody else in his desire "to appear formidable to his enemies and attractive to the women. . . . In short, he is the greatest coxcomb on the face of the earth, not to be surpassed even in London for inordinate vanity, stupendous egotism, and love of self."

A ceremonial was arranged, with a *coup* dance by a young brave as the high point. Dunraven wrote in *The Great Divide*:

> I cannot describe an Indian dance. The only way to convey an idea of it would be for me to put on a blanket and jump around loose, and for some one else to take shorthand notes of my appearance and antics. I tried it the other day in my English home; but the shorthand writer had a fit; my elder children howled in terror; the baby went into convulsions, and had oil poured on its head; the wife of my bosom fled shrieking from the room, and my dearest male relative threatened to apply for a writ *de lunatico;* so I abandoned the attempt.

An alarming spectacle, the *coup* dance, and accompanied by a frightful tale of savage conquest. But the earl did not find it strange at all. It reminded him of his own *coup* dancing days at Oxford:

At the Crow village near present Livingston, Montana, Dunraven (right) and George Kingsley heard a young brave tell a "bloodthirsty" tale of "savage" warfare. It reminded the earl of his own battles as an undergraduate after the Oxford-Cambridge boat race.

Well, this young Crow brave postured so cleverly, and signified so plainly by his signs what he was doing, how long he was out, when he met his enemy, &c. &c.; that I could pretty well make out his meaning. . . . It was last spring, soon after the snows had melted from the hills, about the time when those infernal east winds do blow, raising clouds of dust in King's Road, Chelsea, that I and five others (Charley Smashington led the party) who had come up to town to see the Oxford and Cambridge boat race, drove up to Cremorne in two hansoms. We were in our war-paint, white ties encircled our necks, our feet were shod in patent leather; our hearts were good, our backs strong, our bellies full of inferior dinner and bad wine. We were all partially disguised in liquor, and our hearts and faces were Light Blue. Elated with our late triumph, we danced the valse-dance far into the night, and loudly proclaimed the great deeds of our tribe and jeered at the insignificant Dark Blue. I was standing on a chair waving a champagne bottle around my head, when without a moment's warning the war-cry of the Dark Blues rang through the air. I received the contents of a tumbler of B. and S. full in the face, and, stunned and dripping with drink, was pulled out of the conflict by my friends and my heels.

What a row there was! — bottles flying, glasses smashing, tables falling, fists smacking, yells, howls, screams, oaths and every other kind of missile hurled through the air. I espied a timid youth in spectacles crawling terror-stricken beneath a table. Yelling "I'll have those gig-lamps," I sprang upon him; with one blow I knocked his hat off; another, and the crimson flood flowed out upon his vest; I dashed the glasses from his face, I ground him in the dust, I tore the reeking necktie from his dishonored head, and with a howl of triumph fled from the scene, followed by my friends. They are here, and know that my tongue is not forked, and that I speak straight, and here is the tie.

Next morning, Dunraven and Kingsley said good-bye to their Crow hosts and rode up the lovely Yellowstone Valley. As they neared Boteler's Ranch they fell to discussing the drinking problem, and Texas Jack's habit of having a "tot or two" of whiskey before breakfast, and whether they themselves ought to drink more milk as Mahogany Bogstick had urged. It was time for a "wee droppie" anyhow. Kingsley reached in his pocket for their common whiskey flask and discovered nothing but a big hole where the flask should have been. The loss was a serious matter, of course. They turned back and came upon the flask an hour later, just as night came. And not the flask only —

beside it was Kingsley's wallet stuffed with everybody's money, letters
of credit and passports. Plainly their yearning for a drink had saved
them all from financial loss and much trouble. And so a resolution of
penitence was in order. Dunraven drew it up:

> Resolved: Never to join any temperance society except one recently
> started in San Francisco where it is ruled that "nothing stronger than
> wine, beer, or cider shall be drunk on the premises, unless any member be
> suffering under a sense of discouragement, in which case whiskey is al-
> lowed."

The hunting out from Boteler's Ranch with Fred Boteler as guide
was only fair, though the party had adventures enough chasing elk
and bear and antelope. The terrain was in those rugged foothills of
the Gallatin and Absaroka Mountains which border the Yellowstone
between present Livingston, Montana, and the Gardiner entrance to
Yellowstone Park. There was much too much rain, but the worst trial
was the journeying with pack mules. Getting the packs tied down on
the mules at the start of day was misery enough. The earl described
what usually happened thereafter:

> At last things are all fixed. Boteler leads off on his riding horse, old
> Billy, for the mules know him and will follow him anywhere; and the
> pack animals straggle after. We take a careful look over the place lately
> occupied by our camp, to see that nothing is left behind; coil up our lariats,
> tie them behind the cantle, take our rifles, swing into the saddle, and spread
> out in open files, some behind, some on the flanks, to keep the cavalcade in
> order. All goes very nicely for awhile; the beasts are plodding along, very
> slowly it is true, for some will wander, while others will stop to graze;
> when suddenly Satan enters into the heart of the hindermost animal. A
> wild ambition fires his soul; he breaks into a trot, and tries to pass to the
> front. A tin bucket begins jangling on his back; he gets frightened at the
> noise, and breaks into a canter. The bucket bangs from side to side; all
> the small articles in the pack rattle and shake; an ax gets loose, and
> the handle drops and strikes against his ribs; he fancies that there must
> be something alive upon his back hurting and belaboring him — something
> that must at any price be got rid of. A panic seizes him, and wild with
> fright, he breaks into a mad gallop. Yells of entreaty, volleys of oaths
> are hurled at him; two of us try to cut him off, and only add to his terror

The Dunraven party met Indians now and then along the Yellowstone
south of Boteler's Ranch. They proved to be friendly, but it was best to
be on guard. Party members, left to right, are Texas Jack, Maxwell (the
earl's servant), Dunraven, Kingsley and Fred Boteler, of Boteler's Ranch.
The trees are lodgepole pines which are predominant in the area.

and make matters worse. The pack begins to slip over his tail; mad with ungovernable fear, blind with terror, he kicks, squeals, and plunges. A saucepan flies out here, a lot of meatcans there; a sack of flour bursts open and spills its precious contents over the ground; the hatchet, innocent cause of all the row, is dangling round his neck; a frying-pan is wildly banging about his quarters; until at last he bucks himself clean out of the whole affair and, trembling and sweating with fear, he stands looking on the havoc he has wrought, and wondering what on earth the noise was all about.

For a solid fortnight, the wet hunters endured stiff joints, bleary eyes and rheumatism. But the autumn weather cleared when they reached Mammoth Hot Springs, just inside Yellowstone Park, for the tourist part of their Montana journey. Captain C. Wynne, the earl's cousin, joined the party there on September 20. Soon after, Fred Boteler led the way east from Mammoth to Tower Fall, which they watched splashing down out of its Devil's Den cradle of rock. Before them was the foot of the Grand Canyon of the Yellowstone, running south for twenty miles in a westerly curve of dark spruce and gold aspen. Mount Washburn blocked their view of the to-be-famous falls above Inspiration Point.

Boteler took them on south next day by a trail known now as the Canyon-Dunraven-Tower Fall Road. They camped at nightfall near the present Dunraven Pass Ranger Station. Just above them westward was a peak 9700 feet high — today's Mount Dunraven. He was thrilled by the landscape and so were the rest. It had a remarkable effect on their appetites, Dunraven's in particular. His words on the subject recall those of Dr. Cheadle (page 90) about dining in Kamloops. Dunraven wrote:

And what a supper I did eat! It may seem strange, and it may be very shocking to think and talk about one's material comforts and gross appetites: but the recollection of antelope steak is still fresh and distinct, savouring in my nostrils and bringing moisture to my lips and overpowering all other thought. . . . If people deny that one of the greatest enjoyments of life is eating when you are famishing, then those people either are devoid of the first principles of morality or have never been hungry; and they had better learn to speak the truth, or live on spare diet for a week, then get into vigorous health, and so know what a good appetite really means.

Valentine Bromley's sketch of Mammoth Hot Springs in Yellowstone Park was based on a photograph made by W. H. Jackson during Dr. Hayden's expedition in 1871. Jackson labeled it Gardiner's River Hot Springs. Dunraven got his Jackson photos from his English friend William Blackmore, whose brother had just become famous as the author of the novel Lorna Doone. William Blackmore financed Hayden's Yellowstone trip and was a main backer also of the Denver and Rio Grande Railroad and the town of Colorado Springs.

Bromley's sketch of a W. H. Jackson photo shows the Upper Geyser Basin of Yellowstone Park looking northwest from Grand Geyser, not far from Old Faithful. Dunraven wrote, "The whole face of the country is honey-combed and pitted with springs . . . boiling streams . . . fissures . . . chasms from which issue hollow rumblings . . . angry snarls and roars."

The earl ate that antelope supper on a Tuesday evening. Seven days of heaven followed. "I never enjoyed a ride more in my life," Dunraven would remember, "and never expect to have so pleasant a one again." On Wednesday morning, they stood on Inspiration Point to gawk at the water tearing and tossing over the upper and lower falls of the Yellowstone and boiling on down the yellow and purple gorge. They rode upstream a few miles in the afternoon to watch the comical pots of bubbling mud at Mud Geyser, and camped a bit to the west on the prairie flats of Trout Creek. They rested Thursday and Friday, living on the six-inch trout which the earl caught by the score.

On Saturday they continued west on the divide, past Mary Lake and across the marshy old lake bed of Nez Percé Creek to Lower Geyser Basin and Firehole River, blue-smoking and gay with migrating ducks and Canada geese enjoying the warm spots. They took in the minor paint pots and pellucid pools of the Lower Basin and rode on south through the rich grass along the Firehole to the real show, the Upper Geyser Basin. It brought them soon to Old Faithful, belching to the skies on the hour, and Castle Geyser, which thrilled them even more. The Upper Basin was not large — only a few thousand acres of clay plain holding up some dispirited lodgepoles here and there — but it was a sort of huge soapbox where nature could rant away without fear of police action. The earl put his Irish whimsy to work when he wrote:

> The whole face of the country is honeycombed and pitted with springs, ponds and mud-pots, furrowed with boiling streams, gashed with fissures, and gaping with chasms from which issue hollow rumblings, as if great stones were rolling round and round, or fierce, angry snarls and roars. The ground sounds hollow under foot. The trail winds in and out among holes that puff sulphur fumes or squirt water at you; by great caverns that reverberate hideously, and yawn to swallow you up, horse and all; crosses boiling streams which flow over beds composed of a hard crust, colored yellow, green, and red, and skirted by great cisterns of boiling, bubbling, seething water. The crust feels as if it might break through at any moment and drop you into fire and flames beneath, and the animals tread gingerly upon it. . . .
>
> The air is full of subdued, strange noises; distant grumblings as of dissatisfied ghosts, faint shrieks, satirical groans, and subterranean laughter; as if the imprisoned devils, though exceedingly uncomfortable, were not beyond being amused at seeing a fresh victim approach. You fancy

The earl loved wilderness travel but did not understate its miseries, such as packing uncooperative mules each morning. Party members left to right are: Dunraven, Captain Wynne (the earl's cousin), Maxwell (the earl's servant), Texas Jack (cinching up) and George Kingsley (valiantly hanging on to a bucker).

you can hear the rattle of the loom, the whir of wheels, the clang and clatter of machinery; and the impression is borne upon the mind that you are in the manufacturing department of Inferno, where the skilled hands and artisans doomed to hard labor are employed. I can compare it only to one's feelings in an iron foundry, where one expects every moment to step on a piece of hot iron, to be run through the stomach by a bar of white flowing metal, to be mistaken for a pig and cast headlong into a furnace, or to be in some other way burned, scalded and damaged.

They ran short of food and on Monday had to leave Geyserland for Mammoth Hot Springs, with a pause at Dunraven Pass to climb Mount Washburn. After Mammoth, they hunted as they rode down the Yellowstone, but Montana's game had mysteriously vanished. Even good grass was scarce and the horses were falling down from weakness before they found food back at Boteler's Ranch.

But somehow the gloomy end of the expedition didn't matter. Dunraven and his friends had had enough excitement. They were glad to pay Fred Boteler his due and quit the country, by way of Fort Ellis and Virginia City again. The stage ride thereafter to Corinne, Utah, was a horror of discomfort and delay. The party — Dunraven, Kingsley, Captain Wynne, Texas Jack and the two servants — arrived at Corinne's Union Pacific station eighteen hours late. They were worn out and sulky, but luck was with them. The eastbound express came in just as they did.

They recovered their good spirits quickly on the train. Dunraven closed *The Great Divide* with these lines:

How luxurious appeared the Pullman car, how smooth the motion, how soft the cushions, how snug the beds! With what awe did our unaccustomed eyes regard the ladies! How gorgeous they appeared, how graceful they were, how marvelous their costumes and how stupendous their back hair! How extraordinary seemed the harmonium, and the singing thereto! How full of pictures were the periodicals, how full of lies the newspapers! How clean one felt in a "boiled rag" and fresh suit of clothes, and how sound we all slept that night!

THEODORE WHYTE CARRIED ON ALONE with the Estes Park project during 1875. Lord Dunraven was out of touch most of the time. He was busy hunting moose and caribou in Nova Scotia and Newfoundland. He stopped in New York at the Brevoort now and then, and when he

*Rockies camping was no fun for Dunraven's men when it rained all
through a cold September night.*

yearned to see mountains he visited the Fifth Avenue galleries where
Albert Bierstadt's stunning Rockies landscapes were displayed. Often
the artist himself was around — a handsome, courtly man in his mid-
forties. Bierstadt had been born in Düsseldorf, Germany, but he had
grown up in Massachusetts. He had gone to Düsseldorf as a youth to
study landscape, and went West in the late '50's with Frederick W.

The German-American artist Albert Bierstadt was paid very high prices for his Rockies landscapes at age forty-seven when Dunraven brought him to Estes Park from New York to paint Longs Peak.

Miss Dorothy Dengler has disclosed in her article "The Earl, the Artist, and Estes Park" (Denver Brand Book, 1956), how Albert Bierstadt painted this view of Longs Peak as he saw it from Dunraven's Fish Creek cottage. The actual painting was done at Bierstadt's studio in New York, based on sketches which the artist made at Estes in December, 1876–January, 1877, and during the summer of 1877. Dunraven paid Bierstadt fifteen thousand dollars for the huge landscape which hangs now in the beautiful reading room of the Western Department, Denver Public Library.

After Dunraven's death, Miss Dengler has written, the painting was inherited by his daughter, the Countess of Meath, who gave it to a nephew, Desmond Fitzgerald. The late Dr. Malcolm G. Wyer, head of the Denver Public Library, located it through the art dealer Cyrus Boutwell, and it was purchased in 1955 for five thousand dollars (a real bargain!) and given to the Denver Public Library by Roger B. Mead.

Bierstadt's Longs Peak shows the Twin Sisters at left and Longs Peak (with Mount Meeker) at right. The painting has been criticized for being too dramatic and more like the Swiss Alps than the Rockies. The criticism is not valid. At any time of year, heavy clouds can come to Longs and produce this magnified effect of brooding tumult. (Denver Public Library Western Collection photo.)

Lander, the Washington engineer who was building the Central Over-
land Route to California. The Lander Cut-Off part of the route had
taken Bierstadt past various Rockies — Laramie Peak near Fort Laramie, for example, and the Wind Rivers at South Pass and Lander Peak
in western Wyoming.

He had sketched them all. Back in New York, he had used the
sketches in developing a lush and sensational way of painting mountains on a grand scale. By 1865, he was the nation's best-paid landscape painter, which was not surprising since only millionaires had
enough room in their homes for his huge canvases. From his Rockies
specialty he had branched out to make showpieces of other piles of
stone out West, including Mount Whitney, Mount Hood, and Mount
Sir Donald in the Selkirks of Canada.

When Lord Dunraven returned to Estes Park in the late fall of
1876 he brought Albert Bierstadt out with him. The earl wanted one
of those spectacular landscapes to hang with his game trophies at
Adare, and Longs Peak seemed a perfect subject. Also the artist could
advise him on the placing of the proposed English Hotel, the lumber
for which had been cut by Theodore Whyte and piled along Fish
Creek. Bierstadt went happily to work sketching Longs Peak from
every angle and in all lights and weathers, while Dunraven tried out
his Fish Creek cottage and his hunting lodge in Dunraven Glade. The
lodge was well equipped. It even had a whiskey cave so that Dunraven
could always count on a "wee droppie."

By mid-January of '77, Bierstadt was through sketching, Dunraven had another elk trophy, and it was time to head East. The earl
was not sorry to go. He had enjoyed the hunting, but everything else
at Estes depressed him now. He could not understand how things had
come to such a pass. His original plan for the park had been merely
the whim of a sportsman and nature-lover seeking variety. He had
never intended to make a career of the place.

Estes these days was bringing him nothing but pain. Many of the
homestead filings which Haig and Whyte had arranged were being
challenged in the Colorado courts. Men were squatting on choice Estes
tracts near Black Canyon and in Moraine Park — tracts which had
cost Dunraven thousands of dollars. The squatters charged that he
held them illegally. The Denver newspapers treated him like a crimi-
nal for doing what native land-grabbers were admired for doing. Wild

Dunraven's English Hotel was opened by Theodore Whyte a mile up Fish Creek in the summer of 1877 on a lake site chosen by Albert Bierstadt. It was renamed the Estes Park Hotel in '93 and it burned down in 1911. Whyte's little manufactured lake is gone too. (William H. Jackson photo, State Historical Society of Colorado.)

yarns were appearing in print about a rascal in dude clothes who claimed to be Dunraven. The imposter ran up bills and behaved scandalously in Blake Street's bawdy houses. The earl knew that it was useless to protest.

It was all most upsetting, worse than his parents' High-Low Church dispute in his childhood. It robbed him of happiness and he could not allow that, and so he began a policy of visiting Estes infrequently, briefly and incognito. He was present with Albert Bierstadt when Theodore Whyte opened the English Hotel in the summer of '77 — and wished he hadn't been. Soon after, the tale spread that a righteous room clerk kicked the earl out of his own hotel when he demanded (allegedly) lodging for himself and a young lady. The tale was pattern folklore. It would be applied later to Winfield Scott Stratton, the Cripple Creek gold king, who was mortgage-owner of the Brown Palace Hotel in Denver, and to Spencer Penrose, owner of the Broadmoor Hotel in Colorado Springs.

The earl had one last hunt up Dunraven Glade in 1880, and a farewell "wee droppie" from his whiskey cave. Then he left Estes Park for good and all — left the noble Longs Peak, and his gabled cottage and English Hotel and the Evans ranch on Fish Creek, his Swiss cattle herd, and 6600 acres of beautiful land which remained his after the lawsuits. In '83, he leased everything to Theodore Whyte, and in 1907 he sold out completely. One of the purchasers of the Dunraven property was Freelan O. Stanley, who had invented the Stanley Steamer auto with his twin brother.

And so the Dunraven era of Estes Park ended and the modern era began.

THE EARL LIVED ON AND ON, honorably, usefully, fully — and joyously, as he had planned to do as a child. He opposed sweatshop labor in the House of Lords and worked for Irish land reform against his own interests. He served Queen Victoria as her Undersecretary for the Colonies from 1885 to 1887 in Lord Salisbury's administration. At the century's turn he joined the cavalry in the Boer War. He operated his yacht *Grianaig* as a hospital ship through World War One. Sailing was his greatest pleasure next to roaming the deep woods. He raced his yachts *Valkyrie II* and *Valkyrie III* for the America's Cup off New York in 1893 and 1895, losing both races. He protested the second race on the grounds that commercial spectator boats were permitted to run on the course, and he was struck off the membership of the New York Yacht Club. Basically his protest opposed the trend from amateur sport to professionalism. It nearly caused a break of diplomatic relations between Britain and the United States.

To the end he was a gay blade, tall, lean, handsome, trim and debonair. He had a gusto which can only be described as derived from the pride of being British. He loved horses, the sea, pipe smoking, smart clothes, euchre, whiskey and good food — especially canvasback ducks, soft-shelled crabs and corn on the cob. He loved intelligent conversation, and lovely women to look at. He loved his London clubs

Lord Dunraven had lost all interest in Estes Park by the late 1880's when John Singer Sargent, the American portrait painter, sketched him. (Sargent sketch reproduced through the kindness of its owner, the Earl of Meath.)

To the end, Dunraven remained tall, lean, handsome and debonair. He had a gusto which may be described as deriving from the pride of being British. (Sir Arthur S. Cope's painting reproduced from Past Times and Pastimes, *kindness of the Earl of Meath.)*

and restaurants — the Beefsteak, the Garrick, the Savage, the Blue Post in Cork Street, Long's Hotel in Bond Street, the Pall Mall. He knew celebrities on both sides of the ocean — Oscar Wilde, Texas Jack, Lord Strathcona, Buffalo Bill, Lord Kitchener, James McNeill Whistler, General Sherman, Sir John McDonald, Jay Gould, John Singer Sargent, Sam Ward, the famed Washington lobbyist. Ward's wife, Medora Grymes, was an aunt of Medora de Mores whom we will meet in the next chapter. The novelist Elinor Glyn, creator of those shocking love stories *Three Weeks, His Hour,* and *Six Days,* was a favorite of Dunraven's — "gifted in many respects," he wrote of her, "and in literature a genius."

He died at eighty-five in London on June 14, 1926 — a time when the elk were leaving Estes for summer pasture in higher country, and people with shovels were arriving in Dunraven Glade to look for the cave where his whiskey was supposed to be buried.

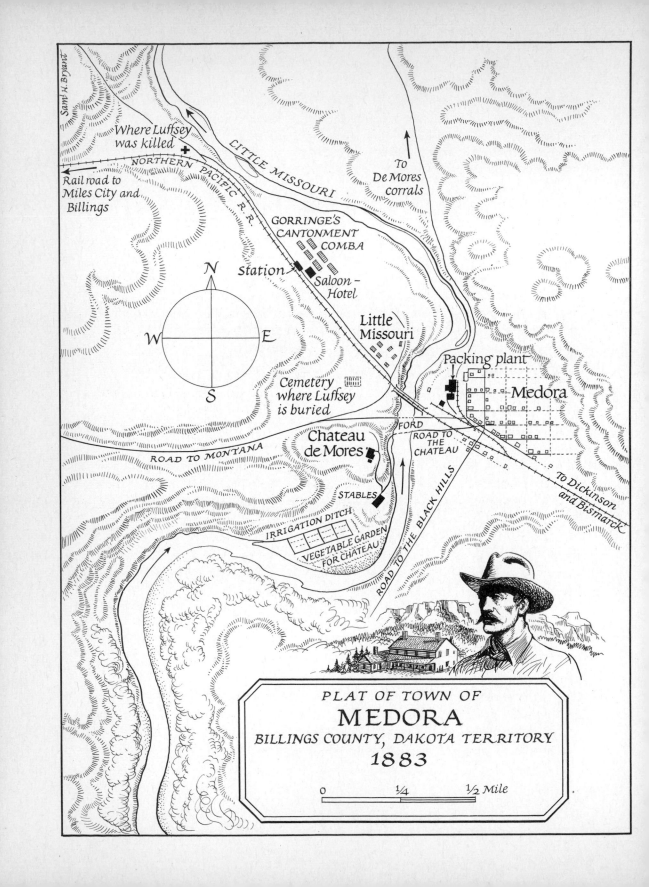

Sam. H. Bryant

Where Luffsey
was killed

Rail road to
Miles City and
Billings

LITTLE MISSOURI

NORTHERN PACIFIC R.R.

To
De Mores
corrals

GORRINGE'S
CANTONMENT
COMBA

Station

Saloon-
Hotel

N

W   E

S

Little
Missouri

Packing plant

Medora

Cemetery
where Luffsey
is buried

FORD

ROAD TO MONTANA

Chateau
de Mores

ROAD TO
THE
CHATEAU

To Dickinson
and Bismarck

Stables

IRRIGATION DITCH

VEGETABLE GARDEN
FOR CHATEAU

ROAD TO THE BLACK HILLS

PLAT OF TOWN OF
MEDORA
BILLINGS COUNTY, DAKOTA TERRITORY
1883

0   1/4   1/2 Mile

7

O TEMPORA! O MORES!

WE MUST REMEMBER that the Marquis de Mores of Paris, France, was very young when he went to the North Dakota Bad Lands in 1883 to work out a dream. He was only twenty-four, and had no use at all for any plodding, practical approach to life. His rashness and impatience derived from the way he had been put together. His Latin mind worked rapidly. He was horribly precocious. He had health, energy, instant reflexes and a melancholy beauty of form and face. His eyes were dark and heavy-lidded, his skin golden, his black hair thick and curly. He was just over six feet tall, and thin as a rapier. He moved with the ominous grace of a leopard.

He was very young, but part of him was very old, for his family traced back to the golden age of Spanish feudalism — Crusades, Jewish massacres, Mohammedan slaves and all the rest. His full name was Antoine-Amédée-Marie-Vincent Manca, and his line began in 1322 when Pedro Emmanuel Manca helped take Sardinia from the Pisans for the King of Aragon. This Manca got three Sardinian villages for his pains. The three formed a fief, the marquisata de Mores, under Spain's Philip V, who had founded the Spanish branch of the house of Bourbon. Sardinia went back to the Italians in 1720. In the process the Manca clan picked up a couple of Italian duchies — de Asinara, and de Vallombrosa, near Florence.

In the meantime, Vincent Manca married a French girl who was related to, or at least warmly connected with, King Henry of Navarre.

The American West, where freedom was freest and class distinctions were a joke, drew the oddest people — even the Marquis de Mores of Paris, France, who believed in the divine right of kings. Young De Mores with his waxed moustache looked like "a fop, or exquisite," but it was wiser not to challenge him to a duel. He was credited with shooting two men for sure who failed to beat him to the draw, and he poked his sword through several others. (State Historical Society of North Dakota photo of E. Chinot etching.)

Vincent was then the Marquis de Mores, as well as Marquis de Monte-Maggiore, Duke de Vallombrosa, Duke de Asinara, Count de San-Giorgio, and Baron de Tiese, Tissi, Ossi and Usini. In the 1850's, his son Richard settled on the fashionable Left Bank of Paris. Richard married a sister of the Duke des Cars, a partisan of King Louis-Philippe and the Orleanist branch of the Bourbon monarchy. Antoine, our Marquis de Mores, was born to the Duke and Duchess de Vallombrosa in Paris on June 14, 1858. North Dakota was not even a territory of the United States then, but just an unorganized remnant of the Louisiana Purchase which few people knew existed.

Young Antoine grew up a devout Catholic, and also an Orleanist, which meant that he was anti-republican and anti-Semitic by tradition. And still he was tinged with liberalism because he felt that royalism could regain power by popular demand. He had a Catholic priest as tutor to his fifteenth year, and an excellent English valet not much older than he was, William Van Driesche, to see that he dressed properly. Van Driesche's father was the Duke de Vallombrosa's valet. Van Driesche's grandfather had dressed the Duke's father, Vincent Manca. Antoine's parents shuttled him about with the weather from Paris to the Vallombrosa chateau at Cannes, or to the chateau at Dreux, where Louis-Philippe had built a tomb to hold Orleanist bones. By the time the marquis was thirteen, he could speak fluent English, German and Italian. He was quite mature politically and burned with anger and shame when the Germans seized Paris in 1870 and France was taken over by the Third Republic instead of by the Count de Paris, grandson of Louis-Philippe.

The Marquis de Mores entered the French cavalry and infantry school, St. Cyr, in 1877, and won a reputation as horseman, side-arms expert and duelist before he resigned unexpectedly from the service in 1881. The resignation was a turning point. The French Army, the marquis felt, was a disgrace. Its leaders were not seeking revenge on Germany. Antoine's fellow cadets were just as spineless. When he taunted them into duels — proper conduct for a royalist — they showed their fear by dueling badly. Antoine dueled, sword or pistol, without fear. He observed that his own father was as weak as the Army crowd. Even though France had accepted the Third Republic, the Duke de Vallombrosa did nothing for the cause of the Count de Paris, caring only to be seen at the opera or at the Cannes Yacht Club or the Cercle de l'Epatant. Like other aristocrats of the day, the duke was getting poor and watching out for an American heiress who could bring a large dowry to Antoine in exchange for the title of the Marquise de Mores.

But it was Antoine himself who found the heiress — at a party in Paris just before he left the Army. She was Miss Medora von Hoffmann, a shy, stately, intense, dark-eyed girl with glossy hair of a deep-red color. Medora was named for an aunt, a famous New Orleans beauty — wife of Dunraven's friend, Sam Ward. Her grandmother became immortal by interceding for the pirate Jean Lafitte while she was the wife of Louisiana's Governor Claiborne. When the governor died, she had married a Federal judge, John R. Grymes, who had settled her on Grymes Hill, Staten Island, New York. The Grymes daughter, Athenais, had married another Staten Islander, a German baron, Louis von Hoffmann, whose Wall Street firm was worth thirty millions and was only a little less rich and powerful than the firm of Drexel, Morgan & Co. Baron von Hoffmann was socially important, too, being a founder of New York's oh-so-British Knickerbocker Club in 1871.

Antoine took in the style and looks of twenty-year-old Medora and found that she was a Catholic, that she knew a lot about hunting and guns, and that her doting father gave her ninety thousand dollars a year for spending money. Then he fell in love with her. He proposed to her in the rose garden of the Hoffmann villa in Cannes and they were married on February 15, 1882, by the Bishop of Fréjus in the church of La Verrière, with the blue Mediterranean shining below.

That August, the Marquis and Marquise de Mores and the excellent valet William Van Driesche landed in New York. Hoffmann liked and admired his son-in-law from the start. He was proud of Medora for capturing a real marquis who would become a duke, only one rank below prince in the order of nobility. Hoffmann's younger daughter had done no better than marry a German baron like himself (barons were six ranks down). Hoffman gave Antoine half a million dollars for a dowry and put him to work in Wall Street learning foreign exchange.

The baron's idea of Antoine was not complex. He imagined him to be just another bright ambitious youngster whose confidence in himself was commendable. Hoffmann had no inkling of what made Antoine's wheels go around — his obsession with lineage and with the

Medora von Hoffmann was born on Staten Island, New York, of all places, but she was a princess in her secret heart and lived a royal role after she married the Marquis de Mores and moved with him to his own town of Medora, North Dakota. To this day, people in Medora town talk of her regal beauty and of her twenty servants, and of her hunting palace on wheels, with a bathroom and all. (Charles Jalabert portrait, State Historical Society of North Dakota photo.)

kind of heroism men had lived for when knighthood was in flower. Antoine believed that aristocrats alone were fit to rule the earth. While he wandered around Wall Street seeming to study foreign exchange, he was actually studying ways to make money in this booming America — pots of money far beyond the baron's thirty millions. Money was power. With plenty in hand, Antoine and Medora could go back to Paris, restore grandeur to the House of Vallombrosa and put new life into the cause of royalism.

It happened that before Antoine left Paris a cousin of his had told him of his trip West to the end of the Northern Pacific Railroad in Dakota Territory, and of the hunting in the Little Missouri Bad Lands. In New York, the marquis heard much more about these Bad Lands from a Greenwich Village naval celebrity, Commander Henry Honeychurch Gorringe, who had lately brought from Egypt and raised in Central Park the sixty-nine-foot obelisk called Cleopatra's Needle. Gorringe was a member of New York's horsey set, which centered around the Hotel Brunswick on Fifth Avenue at Twenty-sixth Street. Antoine and Medora were staying at the Brunswick during that winter of 1882-1883. The commander confided to Antoine that he had invested part of his obelisk fee in a Bad Lands property called the Little Missouri Land and Stock Company because the free-range cattle business was making millionaires out of so many people.

Gorringe explained further that his cattle syndicate had bought for ranch headquarters the U.S. Army's cantonment Comba, which had protected Northern Pacific construction crews from the Indians on the Little Missouri's west bank until '82, when the railroad pushed further toward the Montana Rockies. The commander stressed that he hated to part with such a bonanza property but his group had too many irons in the fire. The marquis could have the Little Missouri Land and Stock Company for twenty-five thousand dollars.

Antoine decided to investigate. Baron von Hoffmann agreed to share the financing as long as he was treasurer of the project and it involved buying land. And so, in March of '83, De Mores and his excellent valet, William Van Driesche, went West, stopping in Chicago to see how its stockyards and slaughterhouses compared with the famous La Villette abattoirs which the marquis had seen in Paris. At St. Paul, Minnesota, late that month they boarded a Northern Pacific train headed for Gorringe's Bad Lands.

TODAY, NORTH DAKOTA, nourished by the broad, languid Missouri, is one of the loveliest and most interesting of states. The flavor is north European — torrid summers mostly daylight, bitter cold winters with long nights. The Spartan climate makes the fine days seem that much finer. The faces of its people have the rugged cast of Norwegians, Baltic Germans, Russians. Everywhere the burnished prairie and the clusters of fat barns in cottonwood groves speak of hard work and the fruits thereof. The lake-flecked prairie is a sportsman's paradise for game birds — bobwhite, pheasant, geese, ducks. The windy capital, Bismarck, is the tidiest of cities. It has no poverty.

But the Bismarck in Dakota Territory which the marquis and Van Driesche visited in the spring of '83 was far from tidy. It was a rough, tough, Northern Pacific division point, mining supply center, outpost for outcasts and head of Missouri River navigation. Beyond Bismarck, the train passed, after a hundred miles, the gale-battered hamlet of Dickinson, an outpost of an outpost. An hour later, without warning, the travelers watched the drab Dakota prairie disappear as the train ran slowly out of the storm area and down into the Little Missouri Bad Lands below the prairie level. Around them was a stunning succession of multicolored draws and coulees, fluted puddings of striped hills with red gargoyles on top, purple pillars of clay, gothic arches of baked orange sandstone. Creeks trickled through the mud-pie world past cottonwood groves and flowering patches of pasture as green in late March as Ireland. They drained into the Little Missouri, which turned out to be a sickly thin sheet of muddy water some fifty yards wide.

If De Mores was uninspired by the stream as he stepped from the Northern Pacific train, the village of Little Missouri disappointed him still more. Dilapidation was everywhere. There was no station platform, and only a shed for a station. A dingy hotel, labeled Pyramid Park, stood north of the track. There was a long saloon, a boarding house and a general store. Not far off on the sage flat, and framed against the striped hills, were the gray buildings of cantonment Comba, looking as though nobody had tended them in years. Van Driesche rented two beds in the Pyramid Park's loft, and the two tenderfeet dined on cheese that night in a saloon full of dispirited men who seemed to be out-of-work cowboys, hunters, miners and plain bums.

Most of them were young men, but one was middle-aged, broad-shouldered with shifty eyes, a goatee, a handlebar moustache of excessive length, and a sharp ugly face. He presented himself to the marquis as Little Missouri's first settler and official greeter. He called himself Elbridge G. Paddock — Jerry to his friends. He offered his services to De Mores, and much talk ensued, continuing next day. In the end, Antoine hired Paddock as guide, though Van Driesche warned that Paddock must be some sort of desperado who would bear watching. But obviously he knew the region like the back of his hand, and he had interesting things to say about Gorringe's twenty-five-thousand-dollar ranch and the Bad Lands in general.

The "ranch," Paddock explained, was mostly a myth. Gorringe and his New York associates wanted to sell because they had been taken in. The decaying cantonment was its only real asset. The land around its decayed buildings was public domain, or maybe the Northern Pacific's. Gorringe's cattle, if any, were scattered among the hills and secret pastures of the Bad Lands. Their number would not be known until somebody rounded them up, assuming they had been branded properly and had not been sold in Canada by cattle thieves. The Bad Lands were long on these thieves, Paddock pointed out. Every other man in the region was handy at rustling. He added that ranching on the Little Missouri was only two years old. Howard Eaton had come out from Pittsburgh in '81 to start the Custer Trail Ranch five miles upstream (Custer's men had passed the site in '76 on their way to their deaths on the Little Big Horn). Bill Merrifield and Sylvane Ferris had their Chimney Butte-Maltese Cross spread two miles beyond it. These ranchers and a few more were squatters, awaiting the day when the public domain and the Northern Pacific land-grant holdings would be surveyed so they could know which belonged to which. Then they could apply for free homesteads from the government or buy land from the railroad.

The marquis, raised on Europe's tight civilization and ancient land tenure, listened with wonder to Paddock's talk. The Little Missouri Bad Lands, Jerry said, were in a Dakota county called Billings, but Billings County was as mythical as Gorringe's ranch. It had no organization, no county commissioners, no sheriff, no judge. The nearest official was the justice of the peace in Dickinson, and he didn't do much more than marry people. The nearest sheriff was a hundred and fifty miles away, at Mandan in Morton County, near Bismarck. Billings

County, Paddock declared, was a state in anarchy, governed by public opinion, and not much of that. The Little Missouri ranches had no legal boundaries, though they were part of a region, roughly one hundred miles long and fifty miles wide, called a round-up district. The ranches of the squatters were more like spheres of influence within the district. The size of each sphere depended on how many cattle the rancher owned. If he had five hundred cattle on a thousand acres of land and brought in another five hundred head from Texas or Iowa, he could claim influence over a thousand acres more. He couldn't fence the land because everybody's cattle ran together and grazed together wherever the grass was good in the round-up district. The system, therefore, was an extra-legal way of dividing up a free range of three million acres so that each rancher's cattle had enough to eat.

De Mores made haste to write Henry Gorringe declining his kind offer to sell him his troubles for twenty-five thousand dollars. But as Antoine horsebacked up and down the Little Missouri with Paddock, the belief seized him that the Bad Lands had a spectacular feature. Their strange situation — below the prairie level — protected them from the worst weather and assured them of water from springs and slow beaver-dam run-off to make shining pastures, winter and summer. The marquis knew that the Northern Pacific was due to reach Oregon and the Pacific in September. Soon trains of cattle would rattle east through Little Missouri, bound for Illinois feed-lots and Chicago's great packing houses. Finished beef from the packing houses would be carted west to supply the butcher shops of Bozeman and Helena and Spokane.

And then an old idea struck the marquis, but he thought it was new, for he was very young, as we have said. Why, he asked Paddock, was all this expensive hauling necessary — hauling live animals thousands of miles from the Great Plains to the East, and hauling them again as meat in the newly invented refrigerator cars back to the Far West? Why not fatten them on the year-round grass of the Bad Lands and butcher them in the area, just as cattle were fattened near Paris and delivered on the hoof to La Villette? Wouldn't that revolutionize the beef industry in the United States? Wouldn't cheaper beef increase the demand enormously, as the big fees of the middlemen in Chicago were eliminated? Wouldn't the Marquis de Mores become a multi-millionaire before he was thirty from cattle sales and abattoir profits, to say nothing of real-estate profits from the town he would plat for his hundreds of plant workers and cowboys?

Jerry Paddock, the shifty-eyed opportunist, expressed agreement. Also, he accepted De Mores's offer to be his agent in the land and cattle end of the revolution. What did Paddock have to lose?

OVERNIGHT THE LITTLE MISSOURI BAD LANDS exchanged their doldrums for activity. The saloon bums found themselves employed, as the marquis, wildly impatient to get going, passed out checks against Medora's dowry and Hoffmann's bank account. Antoine did not forget his beautiful wife, who had just produced a daughter, Athenais, back on Staten Island. He named his town in her honor, Medora, and planned it on both sides of the track, on the east bank of the river short of the railroad trestle. On April 1, 1883, he and Van Driesche evacuated their loft in the Pyramid Park and moved into a tent on the town site, which they toasted with champagne. The railroad laid a spur track northward some hundreds of yards to the spot where the abattoir would be. Soon after, the luxurious private car *Montana* was hauled to the spur for the marquis to live in, at a rental of fifteen dollars a day, while his chateau was being built on the high bluff across the river.

In May, Baron von Hoffmann pulled strings in Wall Street and the Northern Pacific sold Antoine some nine thousand acres of still unsurveyed land for thirty-two thousand dollars. The tract ran up and down the Little Missouri for twenty-five miles, in a strip twenty acres wide on each side. Hoffmann got more unpatented but guaranteed land from the government in June by buying Valentine scrip, which was a Dakota Territory adaptation of a California scheme for rewarding Civil War veterans. Carpenters and painters began arriving in Medora from Bismarck and St. Paul, and engineers and butchers came from the Chicago packing plants to see what went on. The marquis ordered corrals to be built, and a brick kiln. Freight cars appeared, loaded with boilers and pumps and vats and lumber. One car held Medora's square Kurtzmann piano and five tin bathtubs shaped like seashells.

It is often noted that residents of a community dislike the promoting newcomer. The more he helps them to prosper, the more they dislike him. Bob Roberts's saloon in Little Missouri became the place where people gathered to tear the marquis apart, to castigate the

*The Chateau de Mores, completed by the marquis in 1883 on its bluff
above the Little Missouri, looked like an overgrown American farmhouse.
But all was European within, including an indoor privy.*

tenderfoot for his dude ways, his bean-pole build, his aloof cordiality,
his seashell bathtubs, his purchase of water rights on the river. They
resented the publicity he was receiving in Eastern newspapers, such as
the *Detroit Free Press,* which reported in part:

> At the Little Missouri Station, on our return, a few of the party were
> introduced to the Marquis de Mores, who has lately established stock ranges
> in the Bad Lands. He made a picturesque figure in the costume of à
> plainsman. To begin with, De Mores is tall, well built and graceful. His
> face is ruddy brown with exposure, with an amiable expression, and certain
> French characteristics, made more conspicuous by a black moustache and

gleaming black eyes. His figure was set off to advantage by a leather hunt-
ing-coat with fringed seams and skirt. It had I know not how many pockets,
but each contained some essential — matches, cigars, tobacco, pistol car-
tridges, a flask, a solar compass of considerable size, a field glass, a ''Multum
parvo'' knife, very large with blades for every purpose, saws, corkscrews,
gimlet, etc. A great white hat with a leather band and an immense brim
made a contrast with his black hair. A blue flannel yachting shirt laced at
the bosom with yellow silk cord, corduroy trousers, leggings of the same material as the coat, and stout shoes and California spurs completed De
Mores' costume. Around his waist was a leather belt filled with gun car-
tridges; it also held two long-barrelled Colt's revolvers of heavy calibre
and a bowie knife which would bear inspection even in Arkansas. His gun
was double-barrelled, made in Paris, a breech loader of plain but accurate
finish, having a rubber shoulder piece at the butt to take up the shock
of the recoil. The arrangement of the locks permitted instant firing.

His own riding pony was short and mettlesome, of a deep cream color.
The equipments were a Mexican saddle of uncolored leather, ornamentally
stamped; heavy stirrups of a Mexican pattern, a bridle plainly ornamented
and Spanish bit, with bridle reins of braided horse hair, knotted and tas-
seled at short spaces. Attached to the saddle were rubber and Navajo
woolen blankets, a rope lariat, a feed bag for the pony, a bag of provisions,
and some articles of apparel.

The *Springfield* (Mass.) *Republican* reported that same summer:

It is quite the fashion to dwell upon the humorous sides of ranching as
practiced by the Duke of Vallombrosa's son, the Count de Mores, out in
Dakota, but if appearances were anything, the young Frenchman can well
afford to bide his time. With the completion of the Northern Pacific comes a
tide of immigration into Dakota, and the Count, having secured an indefi-
nite leave of absence and something like half a million of money, concluded
to speculate on the growth of the Northwest just as many Englishmen are
doing at the present time. The Marquis is said to have spent his half million
all on his ranch, and business men say he will succeed in his undertaking.

The handful of men in Little Missouri who took dudes out hunting
were especially rabid about the marquis, since his proposed cattle
kingdom would drive out their game. One of them was a blow-hard
Texan named Frank O'Donald who claimed he had buried a number
of men after beating them to the draw in Texas cow towns. In June
of '83, the marquis happened to install a drift fence across a hunting

trail on his tract, ten miles downstream from Medora, to hold some of his stock. O'Donald and his partner, a youngster named Riley Luffsey, rode up to the fence, cut it in two places and passed through without putting it together. When De Mores's men repaired it, they cut it again.

In Roberts's saloon on Saturday night late in June, O'Donald, very drunk, announced to the customers that he was going to shoot the marquis next day for putting up what he considered to be an illegal fence. There were cheers of approval. Then Riley Luffsey, also aglow, stood and demanded his chance to pump the Frenchman full of lead and share the glory. His statement brought down the house since the crowd knew that this nineteen-year-old Irish boy was so softhearted he could hardly stand to kill a rabbit. Moments later a third inebriate, a newcomer from Germany named "Dutch" Wannigan, joined the proposed shooting party. Wannigan explained that he had fought in the Franco-Prussian War of 1870 and was always ready to go after any Frenchman. Later that night somebody from the saloon went to De Mores's temporary abode and slipped a note under the door ordering the marquis to leave the Bad Lands at once.

Such was the background of the tragedy of errors that followed. Frank O'Donald probably had no idea of going through with his threats. He was just baiting a greenhorn who riled him, as was the custom out West. Luffsey and Wannigan had joined in to please the saloon crowd. The greenhorn De Mores was supposed to knuckle under because he didn't know any better. But the marquis was not that kind of greenhorn at all. He thought of himself as the representative of a thousand years of nobility. One of his reasons for coming to the Bad Lands had to do with restoring the honor of aristocrats, the honor he had trained himself to defend with great skill. When he found the note under his door and learned from Paddock that the three men spoke of gunning for him, he took them seriously. He cleaned his revolvers and his breech-loading rifle and wired the sheriff in Mandan to come to Little Missouri and arrest them.

The sheriff's deputy did come to Roberts's saloon but he never served his warrants because the contemptuous O'Donald told him to go back to Mandan before he got hurt. The marquis realized that he would have to arrest the three himself. With one of his cowboys, he took a stand late that same day on the main trail along the railroad tracks, a mile west of Medora. Jerry Paddock and three others were in the vicinity also. It was getting dark as O'Donald, Wannigan and Luffsey rode along, laughing about O'Donald's handling of the deputy sheriff. Suddenly they were astounded to find the greenhorn De Mores blocking their way and demanding their surrender. They spurred their horses toward him and began shooting, but not fast enough. When the firing ceased, O'Donald and Wannigan were in a heap on the ground by their dead horses, begging De Mores not to kill them. O'Donald had been shot in the thigh. The boy Luffsey was dead with a bullet hole in the neck. Next day Paddock took O'Donald and Wannigan on the train to the Mandan jail, where they were held for a time and released on bail, pending trial for assault.

Nobody threatened to shoot the marquis after that. His critics discussed him now with grudging respect and even exaggerated his exploits, as in the tale of how he killed a bear armed only with his "Multum parvo" knife, having decided that guns didn't give bears a fair shake. But feeling against him was very bitter when poor Luffsey was laid to rest in the cemetery near the chateau. Some ranchers tried to bring him to trial for the boy's death, but Judge Bateman in Mandan ruled that he had acted in self-defense. In the meantime the community was distracted from the tragedy by De Mores's ever-expanding plans for raising stock in the Bad Lands and packing meat and shipping it all over. They were distracted more when the chateau on the hill above Medora was completed and the marquise arrived from Staten Island to take over on August 5, 1883.

Architecturally the chateau had nothing "chateau" or French about it. Bismarck carpenters had designed it and it came out just an overgrown, comfortable American farmhouse two stories high, with fireplaces in every room, a long verandah, a red roof, shutters and clapboard sides painted gray. It was to be enclosed in time by a fence of elk horns which De Mores was gathering on his hunting trips. From Medora it was reached by a ford just upstream from the railroad trestle, and then by driveway across the cottonwooded bottomland near an irrigated plot of thirty acres for the vegetable-garden hill. The chateau had twenty-eight rooms altogether, including a modern marvel few Dakotans had heard about, an indoor privy.

The beautiful Marquise de Mores — everyone called her "Madame" — did not arrive alone. She brought some twenty servants

The Marquis de Mores went around Medora "armed like a battleship," as Hermann Hagedorn put it, after he accepted responsibility for the killing of Riley Luffsey in June of '83. (State Historical Society of North Dakota photo.)

with her — a French chef, a wine steward, six Italian upstairs and downstairs maids, an English butler, a seamstress, a laundress, a dishwasher, four German gardeners, and four men from Staten Island to handle the horses, carriages and pack of hunting dogs. If the community had grave doubts about the marquis, it fell in love with Madame. She was hardly more than a child, and there was something wonderfully romantic and appealing about her. She was gently regal. She was kindly strict. Her Catholic piety was picturesque and convincing. She brooked no criticism of her prince, making it plain that the marquis was divine and could do no wrong.

However, there was gossip that she did oppose him in the matter of William Van Driesche. It appeared that the excellent valet had slept in Antoine's room from his early childhood to serve him on call. The habit was continued at the chateau in the marquis's bedroom adjoining Medora's. Madame was said to have complained that the arrangement embarrassed her. The marquis did not need valet service as a prelude to joining Madame in the night when the spirit moved him. Antoine, the gossip went, was slow to concede the point but gave in to compelling strategy. Van Driesche moved to the carriage house, pending completion of a brick home for him in town.

Medora had the talents required of her high station. She played her square piano by the hour, sending the music of Beethoven and Wagner out over the sage flats. She studied history, wading through Prescott's *Conquest of Mexico* and the works of Flavius Josephus. She made watercolor landscapes and portraits. She was a passionate hunter, traveling to the Big Horns, to Long Lake east of Bismarck, to the elk and bighorn sheep (and mountain lion) country far down the Little Missouri. Antoine built a huge "palace on wheels" for her hunting trips, with bunks, kitchen, parlor and bathroom. She wore trousers like a man on these trips, and a black sombrero with an eagle feather, but she always rode her horse sidesaddle. The marquis boasted that she was a better rifle shot than he was. He told a reporter one day, "She regrets neither the soft skies of Cannes nor the gilded salons of New York."

Most of all, Bad Lands residents enjoyed Medora's delightful extravagances as she went about spending her ninety thousand dollars a year. Every freight train seemed to bring something spectacular and expensive from New York. There were art supplies from Knoedler's

*William Van Driesche, English valet for the marquis (Antoine de Val-
lombrosa), looked more like a cowboy than his master did after a few months
on the Little Missouri, and he began to think of settling down for good
in North Dakota. But the Van Driesche men had dressed the royal Val-
lombrosas for a century. When De Mores returned to France, Van
Driesche went back with him. He even received the marquis's bones when
De Mores was hacked apart in the Sahara by bandits in 1896. (State Historical Society of North Dakota.)*

Galleries, ingenious kitchen aids and curtain rods from Lewis & Conger, coffee urns and silver pitchers from Tiffany, linens and flannels and carpets from Arnold Constable, towels and sheets from B. Altman. The firm of Lord & Taylor shipped a complete set of bedroom furniture and a high chair to be used by the small daughter, Athenais, whom the Baron von Hoffmanns were bringing out in the fall. Crates of exotic foods arrived from Park & Tilford — canned truffles and mushrooms, queen olives, capers, plovers' eggs, woodcock, meringues. Park & Tilford sent Apollinaris water and wine too — sherries and burgundies and champagnes and Fundador, tokays and Moselles, and the marquis's favorite red, Chateau Lagrange, from the St. Julien district of Bordeaux.

But the marquis had less and less time to enjoy Medora and her chateau as the year of '83 wore on into '84. Happiness for him was frenzied creation, then and for months to come. First he had a town to build — a brick business block, boardinghouses for his workers, a hotel, a skating rink, a bowling alley, a Catholic chapel which Medora wanted, a home for his visiting in-laws, warehouses and offices for the Northern Pacific Refrigerator Car Company. He had to provide streets and sell lots. He induced Bob Roberts to close his Little Missouri saloon and move across the trestle to open a hang-out in Medora. Joe Ferris moved his general store there, and the Pyramid Park closed its doors at last, ending the hectic career of the town of Little Missouri. William Van Driesche wasn't doing much valeting now that he had been ousted from the marquis's bedroom. He had himself named postmaster of Medora, trained carrier pigeons, and did a bit of private banking on the side.

While De Mores was in Bismarck buying wheat land, which Hoffmann was forever prescribing as part of the company's investment, he met Arthur Packard, an attractive young reporter for the Mandan paper. Packard had graduated recently from the University of Michigan, where he had specialized in pitching for the baseball team. The marquis liked him and offered him a free office and a full-page ad each week if he would start a paper. Packard thought that the marquis was too impulsive for his own good but admired his drive. He decided to have a go at it, borrowing a press, newsprint, type and so on for his the *Bad Lands Cowboy,* which he began publishing in Medora in February of 1884.

De Mores spent a million dollars of his own and his father-in-law's money on this model meat-packing plant in Medora, which was supposed to revolutionize the industry by eliminating the middleman and reducing meat prices. The plant lasted three years (1883-1886), and a sirloin steak today costs more than ever. (State Historical Society of North Dakota photo.)

Packard's writing had as much flair as the colorful title of his sheet. Editors all over the nation reprinted items like the following:

We neglected in our last issue to mention the Bad Lands minstrel entertainment given by home talent at the rink on the evening of the fourth of July. The variety part of the entertainment would have been a complete success if we had brought our guns along and killed all the performers at the beginning of the first act. The orchestra led by Mose de Spicer was simply indescribable. To escape a popular uprising Mose fled the next morning for the Pacific coast. Two other members of the gang, for this or some other reason, skip tonight for the Big Horn country.

The packing plant absorbed most of De Mores's time and energy from September of '83 on. Its six buildings were costing three hundred thousand dollars and they formed a bewildering conglomerate of engines, boilers, steam pipes, carcass carriers, kill rooms, coolers, a cooper shop and a press to make fertilizer out of the offal. The machine to dry blood cost alone ten thousand dollars. Cattle chutes and corrals surrounded the buildings, and more corrals were prepared at intervals downstream to hold the steers until they could be processed. De Mores put an ice dam above the river ford to produce thousands of tons of ice for the cooling room and refrigerator cars.

The marquis's abattoir was supposed to process two hundred steers a day. But when it began operating in the first week of October, 1883, it managed to take only thirty-five head a day at most. All sorts of problems cropped up that first year — the cattle weren't fat enough or the water wasn't hot enough or the coolers weren't cool enough. If De Mores had plenty of fat cattle and cowboys to drive them through the chutes, then the butchers were in short supply or he didn't have enough buyers, or there might not be enough refrigerator cars to move the meat on its way to the cold-storage plants he was setting up, or proposing to set up, along the route of the Northern Pacific — at St. Paul and Duluth, Fargo and Grand Forks, Bismarck, Miles City, Billings, Bozeman, Helena, The Dalles, Portland. De Mores's idea was to keep the storage plants supplied with fresh meat from the Medora abattoir, for local consumption. In addition, residents could rent space for storing their own vegetables and fruits, as today's housewives rent food lockers.

The marquis instructed the shifty-eyed Paddock to buy some cattle and horses for him, making light of Van Driesche's hints that Paddock looked dishonest enough to work with the region's rustlers. The summer of 1883 had been a splendid time for grass in the Bad Lands, and '84 was a fair hay year too. Paddock bought some fancy horses — Percheron and Clydesdale stallions at two thousand dollars each, for instance. And he bought thousands of cattle to fatten on the De Mores range, though a lot of them turned out to be old cows unfit for slaughter. Having convinced the marquis that there was money in raising sheep, Paddock paid high prices for fifteen thousand Merinos shipped in from South Dakota. Some observers said that many of these sheep "took a turn around the mountain" during the tally, meaning that they were counted twice. In any case, Paddock bought the wrong breed for the climate and half of them died that winter of 1883-1884.

The unusual shining grass encouraged ranchers to overstock the free range, which attracted fresh numbers of cattle thieves. The marquis belonged to the Montana Stockgrowers Association, which met in April of '84 to try to deal with the rustlers. They were said to be led by a man named Axelby. Rumors reached De Mores that Jerry Paddock and others in Medora were informing for Axelby. The marquis denied the rumors but decided in his own mind to do some checking. The association tabled a proposal to fight the rustlers openly, voting to go after them as secret vigilantes. The marquis disapproved, and in doing so showed again, as in the Luffsey affair, how little he understood the Western scene. These cowboy amateurs, he told himself, would bungle the police job. Plainly highly trained professionals were needed — perhaps from one of those big private detective agencies.

In Chicago that summer, the marquis called on W. A. Pinkerton, head of the Western Division of Pinkerton's National ("We Never Sleep") Detective Agency, asking the firm to put all its strength behind an effort to find Axelby and his friends so that they could be brought to justice. Pinkerton declared that he had just the expert to break the case — a man named W. H. Springfield — at a fee of fifty dollars a day and expenses, four hundred dollars payable in advance. The marquis wrote out a check, returned to Medora and got his first written report from Pinkerton on August 27, 1884. It was a stirring document, which showed that things were much worse than anyone in the Bad Lands had believed. The rustling ring, the operative had discovered, was large indeed and included such respected Medora figures as "William Van Driesche, Howard Eaton, Gregor Lang and the saloon-keeper, Bob Roberts." These people were so dangerous that W.H.S. thought "he had better buy riffle and revolvers and has been looking at some but can not get one less than $22 or $23 and will wait untile he gets to Glendive before purchasing." Pinkerton concluded his letter bleakly:

> Your country is full of Indians, theives and murderers, so you can see that the operative W.H.S. has no small task to perform but says he will do his duty and carry it through if possible.

The next Pinkerton report showed how the plot was thickening:

> August 28: The operative arrived at Glendive, Montana, and says he can see from observations that he has before him a hard & dangerous un-

dertaking for the men he will have to deal with are a smart keen and watch-
ful bunch of theives & desperadoes. On the train this day the operative met
two cowboys who used to visit Miles City. They met a prostitute on the
train whom they knew. She got on at Dickerson & rode to Glendive. W.H.S.
told the cowboys that he came from Texas and one of them told the woman,
she then wanted to meet the operative, as she said her father lived at El
Paso Texas and his name was Gregory, he kept a Saloon there. W.H.S.
talked with her and she said if you stop at Glendive long she would like
to see him often & if she heard of a job she would let the operative know.
W.H.S. mentions this woman because she may be of some use to him in
getting acquainted with the men. She said the operative might get a
job with the "Marquis". The operative asked about you and she said
everybody was stealing from the "Marquis" & that you only had a few
good men with you. W.H.S. carries the memorandum you gave him in the
lining in the bottom of his pants where he thinks it will be safe in case he is
ever searched.

It occurred to the marquis that W.H.S. must be getting some information from Jerry Paddock, though Pinkerton's reports made no more
mention of the alleged rustling activities of Van Driesche, Howard
Eaton and others Paddock disliked. The reports pictured vividly all
the entertaining W.H.S. had to do at De Mores's expense:

August 31: Operative has been playing stud poker & he thinks he
has established himself as a tough for since Friday he has been gambling
and drinking all of the time with the toughs of that part of the country.
The Poker game lasted from Friday night until 6:30 A.M. of Sunday. He
pretended he had run horses from Mexico into the States. W.H.S. says there
will be very heavy expenses in this operation as the men he comes in contact with spend their money freely and expect others to do the same.

September 4: Operative pretended to be drunk and layed down on
the floor at Casey's Stable in Glendive to hear the talk. Then he went to
Roberts Saloon in Medoria and met Lloyd Roberts Bob Roberts George
Mathews and several others and back to the Senate Saloon in Glendive.
"Big Fred," the Englishman, was throwing billiard balls and trying to
clean out the place. He landed in the cooler with a bullet in his leg.

September 7: W.H.S. heard Casey tell a man in the stable that he believed the Operative was a horse thief. W.H.S. has telegraphed for $200.00
to continue.

Allan Pinkerton,
PRINCIPAL.
ROBT. A. PINKERTON, GENL. SUPT.
Geo. D. Bangs, Supt., 66 Exchange Pl., N.Y.
R. J. Linden, Supt. 45 South Third St., Philada.
Wm. A. Pinkerton, Supt.,
    101 & 103 Fifth Ave., Chicago.
Clarence A. Seward, N.Y.,   } Attorneys for
Lewis C. Cassidy, Phila.,   }   the Agency.
D. W. Munn, Chicago.   }

Pinkerton's National
WE NEVER SLEEP
Detective Agency.

Chicago Aug 30. 84

Marquis de Morés,
            St Paul Minn.

Dear Sir

            Following you will please find
Continued report of Operative W. H. S.

                                    Monday Aug 25.
Today in St Paul the Operative reports seeing
you & that you mapped out the following plan
for him. that he was to take in the Country
bounded on the East by Bismark, on the north by
Ft Buford, on the West by Glendive, and on the
South by the Black hills. The Operative is to look
this Country & try and find out & bring to justice
the ring leaders in the Cattle & horse stealing business
& the following are the names & residences of those
suspected at Glendive Mike Comfort Country
Commission, Tim O'Brien Butcher, Costello Livery Stable.
On the Yellow Stone & Missouria River, O'Brien Mathew
and Grinnell. Beaver Creek Tom & Mike Rush, on
Little Missouria Rivers Howard Eaton, E. G. Paddock,
Loyd Robberts, Killdear Mountain Tuttle, At Bigfield
Bob Montgomery knows something about it. At
Dickenson Gus Kelly Sheriff. & the following are
despardoes who know more or less about the

The marquis did not trust the Litte Missouri vigilantes to control its
rustlers. He hired Pinkerton's "We Never Sleep" Detective Agency to
send an operative out from Chicago to catch the thieves. The operative,
"W.H.S.," worked hard but caught nothing but a bad case of piles. A
bit of a Pinkerton report is shown here. (Kindness of the State Historical
Society of North Dakota.)

During the rest of September, the marquis observed with growing irritation that W.H.S. was becoming vague as to what he was accomplishing besides playing pool, drinking beer and denying that he was a rustler in the saloons of Miles City, Glendive and Medora. His prostitute informer supplied no more interesting intelligence. W.H.S. stressed in each report that he was in danger of being murdered. He was always on the verge of important discoveries which seemed to lead him further and further away from the terrain under scrutiny. De Mores wearied of mailing large checks to pay Operative's bar bills. Pinkerton's report of September 30 disclosed that W.H.S. was hunting for thieves in the safety of the Army's Fort Buford, some hundred and fifty miles from Medora:

> At Fort Buford today Operative found where Mathew Gummell lives but has not found Mathew Roberts nor McDownell yet, but he has a good excuse to stop here as he has a severe case of piles and can hardly walk and has applied to the doctor at the Fort and he tells him to keep here for a week & in that time he will try to pick up something.

Operative's health problem, the marquis felt, was the last straw. He sent no more checks to the We-Never-Sleep people and Pinkerton recalled his expert to the peaceful precincts of Chicago after his six weeks of peril in the wild and woolly West. In the meantime the cowboy vigilantes of Miles City and Glendive had caught and hung enough thieves to bring the rustling under control in the Bad Lands. With the thieves gone, De Mores had no reason to wonder if Paddock had worked with them. He kept Jerry on as his adviser.

THE MARQUISE DE MORES spent the winter of 1884-1885 at the Hotel Brunswick in New York. Medora was expecting again; her son, Louis de Vallombrosa, was born in March. Her prince was in and out of the city, for he was traveling all over making beef contracts and buying machinery to enlarge the abattoir in Medora. He found time though to go to Newells' on Broadway and buy a dozen piqué-trimmed shirts with monograms and crests, and six pairs of drawers which had to be altered to fit his narrow waist. At Desmond's on Wall Street he paid twenty-eight dollars for a pair of enamel riding boots. A front tooth cost him thirty dollars.

He was twenty-six years old now, and as youthfully enthusiastic as ever, as impatient, as sure that an aristocrat tracing back to the Spain of the King of Aragon could not fail. But he was beginning to understand that brilliant ideas and the money to promote them would not suffice to revolutionize the packing industry. This particular business, he had learned, was as complex as the planet itself, being affected by weather, gravity, eugenics, geology and entomology, to say nothing of the strange ways of middlemen and butchers, the changing tastes of consumers, and phases of the moon.

The abattoir had to be enlarged to earn the wages of its three hundred employees. Medora itself needed a second industry to support the marquis's business properties and to increase the value of his town lots. That was why De Mores bought the rolling stock of a defunct Virginia City stage company and began running stages three days a week to the Black Hills mining camps in South Dakota. The 215-mile stage line was to make all that Black Hills region tributary to Medora and the Northern Pacific. Unfortunately, the Black Hills gold boom expired that winter. De Mores could not get a mail contract out of Washington. The last Concord coach, bearing the Vallombrosa coat of arms, ran in mid-May; the line had been running only seven months.

The marquis was not too disturbed, though by now he and his father-in-law had invested more than a million dollars in the region. De Mores had complete faith in his new abattoir, with its soaring brick chimney and improved coolers. This time he had enough butchers and cowboys, and he had enough buyers. His contract with the Army alone, at Fort Buford, called for delivery of ten thousand pounds of beef. On June 2, 1885, he arrived in Medora with the marquise for the great opening. For the next fortnight the two of them enjoyed the scene spread out along the Little Missouri below their chateau.

De Mores's hotel was full of customers and so were Joe Ferris's store and Bob Roberts's saloon. Arthur Packard had to print extra editions of the *Bad Lands Cowboy*. Everyone was in a gay, good-natured mood. The town laughed when Packard reported:

A visitor to our sanctum this morning under the exhilarating influence of a slight attack of tangle-foot, expressed himself as follows, in regard to the abattoir of Medora. "Zhe odors 'rising from zhe decayed carcasses of defunct animals of zhe slaughterhouse int'posing 'tween zhe pure a'm'sph'r'n my olfact'ry nerves, izh very det'men'al to my plezzure. S'-long, zhenlem'n."

In its third year, 1886, the marquis's town of Medora included the brick house in the foreground which De Mores built for the summer use of his rich father-in-law from Wall Street, Baron von Hoffmann. Near it is Medora de Mores's little Catholic chapel. De Mores's million-dollar packing plant rises in center rear. This is as far as the marquis ever got in his Bad Lands dream to make millions for the restoration of the Bourbons to the throne of France and the greater glory of his own House of Vallombrosa. Young Riley Luffsey was killed near the bend in the Little Missouri, top right of photo. (Harvard College Library photo.)

All of the marquis's creations were working for a change, even the experimental cabbages and alfalfa which were coming up in his big truck garden. Downstream from the chateau he could see corral after corral full of grass-fattened cattle. A string of refrigerator cars stood on the spur track, waiting for their cargoes. Each day two of them, loaded with meat from the new abattoir, were hooked on to a fast freight bound for St. Paul or Chicago or New York. A hundred head were being processed daily, and twice that number would be going through the plant soon.

Would be, *should* be — but weren't. On June 17 there was a sudden, mysterious slowdown. Next day there was a complete stoppage for several hours. The marquis had some trouble finding out why. Nobody wanted to tell him the bad news just when victory seemed to be his. But the truth had to come out. After the first week of operations, it had become clear at the abattoir that the cattle in the marquis's corrals were not fat enough. The butchers had stretched a point, by slaughtering many that were below standard. De Mores's buyers were certain to refuse them.

The butchers explained that the Bad Lands grass in the spring of 1885 was nothing like as plentiful as it had been in the wetter springs of 1883 and 1884. It had failed to put flesh on the stock. Even the color of the meat was wrong. It had a yellow cast that housewives disliked. There was no way out of the impasse. But the loss would be less if De Mores shipped the rest of the cattle East, to be fattened and marketed by the Chicago middlemen in the old inefficient way.

The marquis closed down the abattoir temporarily on June 23. He told his three hundred employees that he would take them back as soon as fat cattle were available.

His heart was broken. The confidence he had brought to the Bad Lands only two years before collapsed. Where were his dreams of a meat packing revolution, of making millions, of returning to France in triumph to help reform the Third Republic? Despair replaced confidence — despair, and a resentment that would grow into something approaching paranoia. He began to feel that all these Bad Lands people who owed so much to him were enemies, particularly after a grand jury indicted him in August for the alleged murder of Riley Luffsey. He was acquitted of course, after a farce of a trial in Bismarck.

Even his father-in-law, though still backing him financially, was doing so without enthusiasm. All that fall of 1885, Hoffmann's book-keepers kept showing up in the Bad Lands to check accounts and inventory of the Northern Pacific Refrigerator Car Company. Only the lovely Medora stood by as staunchly as ever, loving him, comforting him, praising him, encouraging him to fight on. She instituted economies, reducing the chateau's staff from twenty to ten and giving her beloved hunting "palace on wheels" to the town for use as a garbage wagon.

He did fight on, though more from stubbornness than from conviction. The abattoir operated with a small force when cattle were to be had. The rancher Howard Eaton expressed a general Bad Lands feeling when he said, "There was something gorgeous in the marquis's inability to know when he was beaten. His power of self-hypnotism was amazing." He would grasp at any wild scheme for salvation. He tried using his Little Missouri ice to freight refrigerated salmon from Oregon for sale in New York. He planned a huge pottery works based on Bad Lands clay. He planned to fatten his cattle with "brewers' grain" bought from the Milwaukee beer companies.

In January of '86, Medora took her Antoine off to the Riviera for a rest in their honeymoon villa at Juan-les-Pins. While abroad, De Mores agreed to supply beef for a new kind of soup the French Army had invented. The Army did not care about the color of the beef. On their return in March, the marquis opened seven large retail butcher shops in New York City, offering at bargain prices beef shipped directly from Medora. The shops did well at first, and then he was forced to close them one by one. Many housewives refused to patronize them simply because the prices were low. Butchers and ice dealers boycotted them. The railroads raised De Mores's freight rates and gave rebates to his old competitors, the Chicago middlemen. The last New York shop closed in October of '86 while Antoine and Medora were out hunting. The closing was lucky in a way because the abattoir was out of fat cattle again.

The end came on November 16, when Baron von Hoffmann shut down the packing plant for good. The blizzards of the terrible winter of 1886-1887 had already begun. The marquis was still president of the Northern Pacific Refrigerator Car Company but Hoffmann had

When the wealthy Baron von Hoffmann shut off further funds for the wonderful packing plant scheme of his expensive son-in-law, the plant closed down and the Marquis and Marquise de Mores left their chateau as though they were just off for the weekend. They never returned to stay, but the Vallombrosa family hired caretakers for half a century to keep things as they had left them. In the chateau's present museum phase, Medora's bedroom can be seen exactly as it was when she went away in December of 1886. (State Historical Society of North Dakota.)

been paying the bills for months. He felt now that he could do no more for his expensive son-in-law.

Antoine and Medora, still very young and good to look upon, slept in the chateau for the last time on December 1. Next morning they left on the train for New York and Paris — the marquis and marquise, small Athenais, the infant Louis de Vallombrosa, the excellent valet William Van Driesche. They took very little with them. It was as if they had to pretend that in a few days they would be back to this dream home of theirs above their dream town, sheltered by the rainbow ridges and pudding hills of the Bad Lands. If they did not come back, who would watch the garden grow in spring when the Little Missouri bottomland blazed with wildflowers? Who would play Beethoven melodies on the big piano and drink the bottles of Chateau Lagrange on festive evenings? Who would feed Athenais's white rabbits?

As it turned out, they could not bear to come back, and they did not, except briefly and separately. Fifty years later, Athenais's high chair from Lord & Taylor still stood in the ghostly dining room, next to Medora's coffee urn from Tiffany.

WE WILL NOT DWELL LONG on the bitter last years of a young man who failed so often that he was finally driven to destroy himself.

In 1888, the marquis went tiger hunting in India. A year later, he hoped to recoup his Dakota losses by building a railroad in Tongking, China, for France. The plan was frustrated, he thought, by the intrigues of a Jewish engineer and Jean Antoine Constans, French Minister of the Interior. Constans was the arch foe of the popular General Boulanger, who was backed by the marquis and other royalists because he was anti-Republican and demanded revenge for the disaster of 1870.

The Jews! More and more De Mores blamed the Jews for his troubles — packing-house Jews in Chicago, Wall Street Jews in New York, the Jewish engineer in Tongking. He believed that Jewish bankers in Paris caused the Panama scandal, and were ruining France and strengthening England by exploiting the weaknesses of the Third Republic. When Minister Constans managed to drive Boulanger into exile just when he seemed about to overthrow the government, De Mores felt that the time was ripe for a nationalist uprising based on anti-Semitism and opposition to England.

He built up a strange splinter group of royalists, anarchists and national socialists, and dressed them in Bad Lands costumes — white sombreros, purple shirts, silk neckerchiefs. Pathetic nostalgia! In 1890 he drew attention to his cause by inciting workers to riot and going to jail for three months. He made a habit of wild charges, such as his claim that Georges Clemenceau, leader of the Radical Party, was an English spy.

He baited Jews in speeches and in columns of the anarchist paper, *Libre Parole*. He dueled a lot. One duel, on February 2, 1890, was with the Seine deputy Camille Dreyfus, because Dreyfus's paper *La Nation* hinted that the marquise was Jewish and the marquis had married her "in the end of regilding his coat of arms." De Mores shot Dreyfus in the hand. Two years later, on June 23, 1892, the marquis was challenged by Captain Armand Mayer, a Jewish Army officer. Mayer was a huge man and a professional swordsman. But De Mores killed him easily, plunging his blade through Mayer's armpit and lung to the backbone.

By 1894 France was sick of the excesses of De Mores and his Latin cowboys, and they were repudiated by all political parties. The marquis was a powerless, ruined man now, though he refused to admit it. His own father, the Duke de Vallombrosa, deserted him and took steps to prevent him from getting any hold on Medora's fortune. The marquise, of course, remained loyal and so did William Van Driesche. The three of them left Paris to live in Cannes. For many months thereafter, Antoine went often to Algeria and Tunis to campaign against the British, demanding an end of British imperialism in Egypt and the Mediterranean. Nobody took him seriously, though London newspapers reported that "the Marquis de Mores has declared war on the British Empire!"

At last he decided to stop talking and act. In the spring of '96, soon after his fourteenth wedding anniversary, he kissed Medora good-bye. Before leaving Cannes with Van Driesche, he had his palm read. The seeress remarked, "That which I see will not be agreeable to hear. You are going on a trip. You will not return."

In the African ports of Tunis and Gabès, he prepared for the trip. He hired Arab and Negro guides and drivers and interpreters, rented horses and camels and bought tents and food. He was the only white man in the caravan. Van Driesche would wait in Tunis for his return. On May 4, the marquis sent a note to Medora: "I write with your

American portrait before me and with very tender feelings toward you." He wrote his eleven-year-old son, Louis de Vallombrosa, "Life is a Voyage and a Combat. Work and Pray. Seek a productive occupation. Your affectionate Father."

The small De Mores caravan left Gabès and the blue sea on May 14. Its purpose was to explore a military route three thousand miles across the Sahara to the upper waters of the Nile. The marquis believed that once this route was established, France, Spain and Italy would approve his plan to use it to destroy England's hold on Egypt and to drive her from the Mediterranean. All went well for three hundred miles south, to a spot on the Libyan border near Ghadames. There two bands of Touareg and Chambaa tribesmen appeared, demanding tribute which the marquis refused to pay.

On June 9 at 8 A.M. the bands attacked the caravan. A Touareg struck De Mores on the head with his saber, knocking him from his horse. The force of the blow was blunted by a white sombrero which Antoine had bought in Bismarck in 1883. As he crouched on the sand, he blazed away at his attackers with the revolvers he had brought from the Bad Lands. He shot three of them before he died from many knife wounds. He was not quite thirty-eight years old.

An Arab survivor brought word of the tragedy to Van Driesche in Tunis. What was left of the marquis was recovered on June 27 by French soldiers. Van Driesche identified the remains by the thirty-dollar front tooth De Mores had bought in New York. There was a noisy funeral on July 19 at Notre Dame in Paris, with crowds outside chanting *"A bas les Juifs! A bas l'Angleterre!"* The ashes rested briefly at Montmartre before the marquise claimed them for the family plot in Cannes. When officials did nothing to apprehend the murderers, Medora thought of hiring the Little Missouri vigilantes to do the job. Van Driesche dissuaded her and she posted a large reward in Tunis. Three tribesmen were captured later and sentenced to death. The sentence of one of them was commuted to twenty years at Medora's request.

The Marquis and Marquise de Mores, and the excellent valet Van Driesche, are hardly remembered in France today. It is different at Medora on the Little Missouri, where the chateau still stands and people talk still of the long ago when the Bad Lands basked in the brightness of their young dreams.

In Medora's beautiful little De Mores Memorial Park, the marquis's statue in his Dakota garb dominates all. The bas-relief below depicts his wife Medora. And so we have a curious juxtaposition: De Mores, the worshipper of kings, stands in bronze only a few hundred feet from the museum where Theodore Roosevelt, one of the greatest of democrats, is memorialized. (Osborn's Studio photo.)

By the time of his graduation from Harvard, Theodore Roosevelt was sure that he knew the secret of life: Go at it diligently and don't fool around. (Harvard College Library photo.)

8

THE MAKING OF A PRESIDENT

WE HAVE SEEN how Henry Honeychurch Gorringe of the U.S. Navy, having hauled Cleopatra's Needle from Egypt to Central Park, met the Marquis de Morès at the Hotel Brunswick and urged him to buy his property in the Dakota Bad Lands. Some months after, in May of 1883, Gorringe attended a rally at the Free Trade Club in New York to hear a scathing rebuke of sin in politics by Theodore Roosevelt, the very young Republican Assemblyman from the Twenty-first District.

Gorringe had resigned from the Navy by then. He hit it off well with Roosevelt. The two had naval interests in common since Roosevelt had managed to write, partly while a Harvard undergraduate, an exceedingly tedious but favorably reviewed book called *The Naval War of 1812*, which had earned him royalties of $114.75. During their talk, Roosevelt mentioned his desire to shoot a buffalo before the species became extinct. Gorringe said that the last buffalo in the West lived near his Little Missouri ranch. They decided then and there to go hunting together late that summer in the Bad Lands.

But when the time came, Gorringe couldn't, or wouldn't, go. Perhaps he decided to spare himself the pain of looking at his dilapidated Cantonment Comba. So Assemblyman Roosevelt went to Medora and Little Missouri alone, stepping from the Northern Pacific train at three o'clock on the cool Dakota morning of September 7, 1883. He said later that it was "dark as the inside of a cow."

As De Mores and Van Driesche had done six months earlier, he found an empty bed for the rest of the night in the upstairs dormitory of the Pyramid Park Hotel. He slept in his dude clothes, with duffle-bag and big-game rifle close by. The dreams he dreamed were those of a man on his way to becoming one of the greatest of Americans — a man who would be anathema to some, marvelous to others, comic, tragic, ridiculous, noble, but on balance greatly beloved and admired by his countrymen.

TWENTY-FOUR YEARS HAD PASSED since Theodore Roosevelt's birth in New York City on October 27, 1858 (he was four months younger than the Marquis de Mores). His father, also named Theodore, was a well-to-do importer of largely Dutch ancestry, and a member of a first New York family dating all the way back to 1644 and Peter Stuyvesant. His mother, Martha Bullock, had left a Georgia plantation to come North, and she remained a militant Southerner even if she did choose to marry a strong Lincoln Republican. According to Martha, the baby Theodore looked something like a turtle and often seemed about to disintegrate during his first dozen years or so. Roosevelt wrote in his autobiography: "I was a sickly, delicate boy, suffered much from asthma, and frequently had to be taken away on trips to find a place where I could breathe. One of my memories is of my father walking up and down the room with me in his arms at night when I was a very small person, and of sitting up in bed gasping, with my father and mother trying to help me."

The chronic asthma gave him pipestem legs, a half-size body, and made him subject to the whole list of childhood fevers. He was near-sighted and couldn't move without glasses. His muscular reflexes were only so-so. But against his weaknesses he had hidden strengths — vitality, tremendous courage, a quick and retentive mind, a driving will, and a passionate interest in his own life, and his own way of enjoying it. He had a lot of big fine teeth and an eager, flashing smile. He adored his father: "The best man I ever knew." When Theodore, Senior, informed him that he could overcome his weaknesses and build up his weight by clean living, self-control, and exercise, he went at it and stayed at it with awesome diligence.

He became obsessed with exercise and the outdoors. He hiked, ran, rowed, swam, horsebacked, played tennis and hunted in Maine

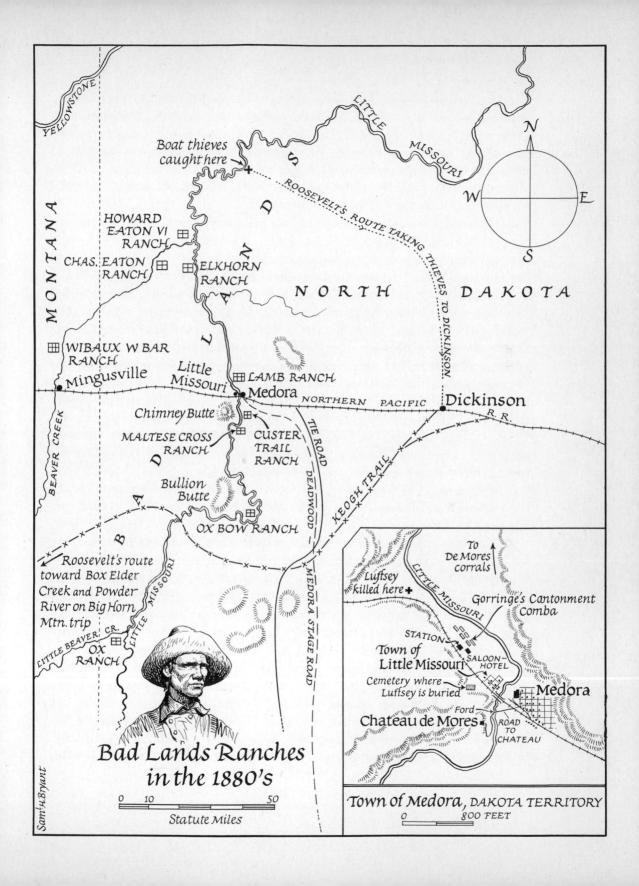

Boat thieves
caught here

YELLOWSTONE

LITTLE MISSOURI

N
W   E
S

ROOSEVELT'S ROUTE TAKING THIEVES TO DICKINSON

MONTANA

B A D   L A N D S

HOWARD
EATON VI
RANCH

CHAS. EATON
RANCH

ELKHORN
RANCH

N O R T H   D A K O T A

WIBAUX W BAR
RANCH

Little
Missouri

LAMB RANCH

Mingusville

Medora

NORTHERN   PACIFIC

Dickinson

R.R.

Chimney Butte

MALTESE CROSS
RANCH

CUSTER
TRAIL
RANCH

TIE ROAD

DEADWOOD

KEOGH TRAIL

BEAVER CREEK

Bullion
Butte

B A D

OX BOW RANCH

MEDORA STAGE ROAD

Roosevelt's route
toward Box Elder
Creek and Powder
River on Big Horn
Mtn. trip

LITTLE BEAVER CR.

OX
RANCH

LITTLE MISSOURI

Sam'l. Bryant

Bad Lands Ranches
in the 1880's

0   10   50
Statute Miles

To
De Mores
corrals

Luffsey
killed here

LITTLE MISSOURI

Gorringe's Cantonment
Comba

STATION

Town of
Little Missouri

SALOON-
HOTEL

Medora

Cemetery where
Luffsey is buried

Chateau de Mores

Ford

ROAD
TO
CHATEAU

Town of Medora, DAKOTA TERRITORY
0   800 FEET

and the Adirondacks. And, sure enough, his self-control conquered the asthma before he entered Harvard College in 1876. That victory convinced him that all one had to do to achieve one's heart's desire was to go at it diligently and not fool around. By going at it and staying at it he got his weight up to 120 pounds as a Harvard freshman, got into Porcellian, the Hasty Pudding, Alpha Delta Phi, and became president of Harvard's Natural History Society.

He used the same formula during his long courtship of seventeen-year-old Alice Hathaway Lee, a small Boston beauty whom he described warily at first as "a very sweet, pretty girl." He was sure that his suit was righteous because, he wrote in his diary, "thank Heaven, I am at least perfectly pure." But the piquant, teasing Alice worried him almost to death before he overcame her resistance by his diligence, just as he had overcome the asthma. He was afraid that he loved her more than was wise or proper, and he suspected that she was a serious threat to his whole credo of self-control. He nicknamed her "Sunshine" and found himself going overboard in his diary, where he called her "my wayward, willful darling" and "a laughing pretty little witch." One diary line read, "By Jove, it sometime seems as if I were having too happy a time to last. I enjoy every moment I live — almost." Alice and Theodore were married in the fall of 1880 after his graduation from Harvard and they settled down in New York City.

Theodore's father had died of cancer in '78, leaving his son $125,000 which allowed him to take his time deciding what to do for a career. He tried law at Columbia, collected spiders and watched birds with the thought of becoming a naturalist. He read books by the dozen and finished writing *The Naval War of 1812*. On a Fourth of July at his mother's home in Oyster Bay he played the bear at a children's party and polished off the day with ninety-one games of tennis. He took Sunshine to Europe and climbed the Matterhorn in three and a half hours because some fool heart doctor advised him to avoid running upstairs. His weight by now was a respectable 140 pounds.

Finally, as Allen Churchill has written, he decided to try politics, joining the Twenty-first District Club of ward heelers, saloon keepers, court clerks, party hacks and loafers. In the fall of '81, the club ran him for State Assemblyman and he was elected, aged twenty-three. During the winters of 1882 and 1883 he served as leader of the Republican reform group, and enjoyed himself immensely. He called spades

At seventeen years of age, the piquant Alice Hathaway Lee (left) caused deep disturbance within the mind of the Harvard undergraduate, Theodore Roosevelt, Jr. (right), who had thought up to then that he could handle anything. He married her in 1880 even though he suspected Alice threatened his whole credo of self-control. The girl in the middle is Rose Saltonstall. (Harvard College Library photo.)

by their right names in frequent shrill speeches addressed to "Mr. Speak-ah." He gave everyone in Albany fits, political sinners and paragons alike.

But the reform business was hard on the nerves. Roosevelt's weight went down into the 120's again. His asthma recurred a little and he had bouts with a fashionable stomach-ache called cholera morbus. Never mind. He would get rid of both out there in Gorringe's Dakota Bad Lands chasing that last buffalo. It was a good time to go. Little Alice was expecting in February, and refused to be seen in public.

AFTER HIS BRIEF SLEEP and breakfast at the Pyramid Park on the morning of September 7, 1883, Roosevelt found an employee of Gorringe's named Joe Ferris who agreed to take him buffalo hunting. For headquarters they would use Gregor Lang's ranch at the mouth of the Little Cannonball, fifty miles up the Little Missouri, where the Bad Lands began merging into the prairie. Ferris was a hard-as-nails lumberjack from eastern Canada who had come out with his brother Sylvane in '81 to cut ties for the railroad. Sylvane was ranching now with another Canadian, William Merrifield, seven miles upstream from Medora at a place which some people called Chimney Butte, for the big rock above it, and some called the Maltese Cross, after the brand.

Joe Ferris took the guide job without joy. This Roosevelt was obviously the worst sort of dude. His Eastern clothes were wrong and so was his rifle. He was skinny and pale and puny-looking and half-grown. His face seemed to be teeth mostly. He wore thick glasses — a sure sign of physical decay. He refused to take a drink or to smoke or to swear. He had a high voice and spoke a weird Eastern dialect. He called Joe "old fellow" and he was always slinging in "jolly wélls" and "bullys" and "by Godfreys." When Joe introduced him to Jerry Paddock and some of the saloon bums he said, "Delighted to meet you!" He expected to be — and was — called *"Mr.* Roosevelt."

That same afternoon of September 7, Joe loaded *Mr.* Roosevelt into a buckboard and trundled him through the maze of mud-pie mesas and hidden pastures to the cabin made of railroad ties at the Maltese Cross. The dude survived the buckboard well enough and surprised Sylvane Ferris and Bill Merrifield in the evening by trouncing them at "old sledge" (high-low-jack and the game). The cramped cabin was short of bunks and he surprised them again by bedding down on the dirt floor wrapped in an old blanket. Next day he scorned Joe's buckboard and bought a buckskin mare named Nell from Sylvane. He rode Nell forty-three miles further — not gracefully but at least he didn't fall off — to the Little Cannonball. The trip had tired Joe Ferris out even though he had ridden in the buckboard, and he went to bed early at Gregor Lang's ranch. But Roosevelt was not tired. He stayed up well past midnight listening to Lang's talk about ranching.

Joe was pleased next morning to find it raining hard and miserably cold — a good day to snooze and get paid for it. But here was his dude again, grinning all over and looking not quite so puny as the day before. He was raring to go after his buffalo. While Roosevelt saddled his mare, Joe complained about the gumbo mud and the poor visibility. The dude just smiled and then he and Nell were fording the river to pick up the eastward trail. Joe trailed along behind, muttering. All that day they sloshed through the drenched coulees and over the ridges in a wild country which looked wilder still in such weather. No buffalo. They slithered back to Lang's after dark and scraped pounds of gumbo from their faces and clothes. After supper Joe went to bed worn out. Roosevelt stayed up for hours again talking about ranches with Lang.

And so it went, bleak day after day for a solid week — rain, rain, rain and still no buffalo to be seen in the murk. As Joe got wearier and more discouraged, the tenderfoot from New York seemed to get stronger and more determined. Ferris could not understand it, though he was certain that he had never misjudged a client so completely. His problem now was to keep up with his dude. At last a day dawned with the sun shining. The land dried out some. In the afternoon, the two hunters were able to get close to three old buffalo bulls. In his excitement, Roosevelt shot too far back and merely injured one bull as all three disappeared over a ridge. They chased them for hours into the open prairie. Then, as twilight fell and a big moon rose from the horizon, they decided to try to run them down on their worn-out horses. Roosevelt wrote later in his *Hunting Trips of a Ranchman:*

> The pony I was on could barely hold its own, after getting up within sixty or seventy yards of the wounded bull; my companion, better mounted, forged ahead, a little to one side. The bull saw him coming and swerved from his course, and by cutting across I was able to get nearly up to him.

Joe Ferris, the Dakota guide, looked without joy at his hunting customer from New York who said his name was Theodore Roosevelt. This dude was small, skinny and puny-looking, and his face seemed to be teeth mostly. He wore thick glasses — a sure sign of physical decay. (Harvard College Library photo.)

But in a matter of months nobody on the Little Missouri called Roosevel[t] a dude any more. He could hold his own with the rest as a hunter and h[e] thought of himself as a genuine frontiersman — as dauntless, tireless an[d] resourceful as any Ned Buntline hero. (Photo courtesy Harvard Colleg[e] Library.)

The ground over which we were running was fearful, being broken into holes and ditches, separated by hillocks; in the dull light, and at the speed we were going, no attempt could be made to guide the horses, and the latter, fagged out by their exertions, floundered and pitched forward at every stride, hardly keeping their legs. When up within twenty feet I fired my rifle, but the darkness, and especially the violent, labored motion of my pony, made me miss; I tried to get in closer, when suddenly up went the bull's tail, and wheeling, he charged me with lowered horns. My pony, frightened into momentary activity, spun around and tossed up his head; I was holding the rifle in both hands, and the pony's head, striking it, knocked it violently against my forehead, cutting quite a gash, from which, heated as I was, the blood poured into my eyes. Meanwhile the buffalo, passing me, charged my companion, and followed him as he made off, and, as the ground was very bad, for some little distance his lowered head was unpleasantly near the tired pony's tail. I tried to run in on him again, but my pony stopped short dead beat; and by no spurring could I force him out of a slow trot. My companion jumped off and took a couple of shots at the buffalo, which missed in the dim moonlight; and to our unutterable chagrin the wounded bull labored off and vanished in the darkness. I made after him on foot, in hopeless and helpless wrath, until he got out of sight.

The tenderfoot and his long-suffering guide stayed out that bitter cold night, trying to rest in clammy blankets and getting up once to chase their horses for half a mile after they had been scared by a wolf. More futile days of hunting eastward from Lang's followed. Then they tried it west, up the Little Cannonball into Montana. Roosevelt described the trip:

A man who is fond of sport, and yet is not naturally a good hunter, soon learns that if he wishes any success at all, he must both keep in memory and put in practice Anthony Trollope's famous precept: "It's dogged as does it." And if he keeps doggedly on in his course the odds are heavy that in the end the longest lane will prove to have a turning. Such was the case on this occasion. Shortly after mid-day we left the creek bottom, and skirted a ridge of broken buttes, cut up by gullies and winding ravines, in whose bottoms grew bunch grass. While passing near the mouth, and to leeward of one of these ravines, both ponies threw up their heads, and snuffed the air, turning their muzzles toward the head of the gully. Feeling sure that they had smelt some wild beast, either a bear or a buffalo, I slipped off my pony, and ran quickly but cautiously up along the valley. . . . The wind was just right, and no ground could have been better for stalking. Hardly needing to bend down, I walked up behind a small sharp-crested hillock, and peeping over, there below me, not fifty yards off, was a great bison bull. He was walking along, grazing as he walked. His glossy fall coat was in fine trim, and shone in the rays of the sun; while his pride of bearing showed him to be in the lusty vigor of his prime. As I rose above the crest of the hill, he held up his head and cocked his tail in the air. The wound was an almost immediately fatal one, yet with surprising agility for so large and heavy an animal, he bounded up the opposite side of the ravine, heedless of two more balls, both of which went into his flank and ranged forward, and disappeared over the ridge at a lumbering gallop, the blood pouring from his mouth and nostrils. We knew he could not go far, and trotted leisurely along his bloody trail; and in the next gully we found him stark dead, lying almost on his back, having pitched over the side when he tried to go down to it.

The dogged hunter jumped on his kill and did an Indian war dance, according to his Bad Lands biographer, Hermann Hagedorn. Then he gave Joe Ferris one hundred dollars in cash. Hagedorn had it from Ferris himself that by now the guide regarded his dude with "a kind of awe, which was not diminished when Roosevelt casually remarked that his doctors back East had told him that he did not have much longer to live, and that violent exercise would be immediately fatal."

That September fortnight of trial and triumph added a new dimension to Roosevelt's view of himself. The pampered New York blue blood, the bookish Harvard grad, the reforming State Assemblyman, seemed to have the stuff of the Western pioneers he had read about — Kit Carson, Buffalo Bill and the rest. He had endured riding hundreds of miles in fair and foul weather over the broken Bad Lands. He had cured his asthma and cholera morbus and put on some weight. He had enjoyed it all — even that wild bitter night in the clammy blankets on the open prairie. The fact was, the pioneer West with its romance and hardship — Robert Service's "the freedom, the freshness, the farness" — was in his blood. Perhaps he ought to invest in a spread on the Little Missouri so that he could go hunting and make money at the same time. Henry Gorringe had had a lot to say about the fortunes still being made out of free-range cattle. This very region was the new El Dorado, Gorringe had said, though the squatters and the Marquis de Mores were claiming the best range on the Little Missouri fast. Gregor Lang, a canny Scot if there ever was one, expressed a similar, if more guarded, optimism during his long talks with Roosevelt. But Lang turned down Roosevelt's request that Lang go into partnership with him in a cattle project. Lang had a partner already, the Englishman Sir John Pender. Lang recommended in his place the Canadians Sylvane Ferris and Bill Merrifield, of the Maltese Cross.

Roosevelt left Medora to return to his pregnant Alice in New York on September 27, 1883. Before leaving, he gave a check for nearly fourteen thousand dollars to Sylvane and to Merrifield so that they could set up the partnership and buy in Iowa some four hundred and fifty head of cattle for the Maltese Cross.

FORTUNE SMILED ON HIM that fall. He spent many hours with his dear Alice planning the new home that they would build near his mother's country place in Oyster Bay on Long Island Sound. It would rise on ninety-five acres of prime land which he had bought, near Cooper's Bluff overlooking the bay and Cold Spring Harbor. It would be called Leeholm, in honor of Alice's family.

In November he was an easy winner for reelection to the New York State Legislature, running on the novel platform of personal integrity. Since the Republicans now held a majority in the Albany Assembly, he could expect to get along with his reforms for the State civil service and the municipal police. He even had hopes of forcing closure of the famous row of bawdy houses on New York's Twenty-seventh Street between Sixth and Seventh Avenues. In his role as the nation's leading Republican progressive he was also absorbed in maneuvers to name the Republican candidate for the fall Presidential campaign. All through January and early February of 1884 he plotted to block the machine incumbent, Chester A. Arthur, and "the political spoilsman," James G. Blaine, in favor of Senator George F. Edmunds of Vermont.

Then the terrible blow came, the inconceivable, the end-of-all. There was no warning. On Wednesday morning, February 13, while he was at work on his bills in Albany, he got a telegram. That afternoon he hurried to his mother's town house in New York, where Alice had just given birth to a daughter. As he entered the house, his younger

This was the log house at the Maltese Cross Ranch a few miles up the Little Missouri from Medora which Sylvane Ferris and Bill Merrifield built for Roosevelt after he went into the cattle business. The second story was removed later when the State of North Dakota bought it and shipped it all over the nation for display. It is in Medora now at the visitor center of Theodore Roosevelt Memorial Park. (Photo from Osborn's Studio, Dickinson, North Dakota.)

brother Elliott met him at the door with, "There is a curse on this house. Mother is dying and Alice is dying too."

At 3 A.M. Thursday, Theodore watched his mother die of typhoid fever on the second floor. She was only forty-eight. He hurried to the floor above. Alice by then could barely recognize him. A poisoning of the blood had developed after the birth of her daughter, and it was killing her. She died in Roosevelt's arms at two o'clock in the afternoon of that same Thursday, February 14, Valentine's Day. The double funeral occurred on Saturday at the Presbyterian Church on Fifth Avenue at Fifty-fifth Street. The baby Alice was taken in for the time being by Roosevelt's older sister Anna.

His world was shattered. And so, it seemed, was his faith in himself — the faith that had kept him at it until he had triumphed over his poor health, the same faith that had kept him at it in the Bad Lands, chasing buffalo until he finally got one. What was the point of faith if the focus of all the effort, his lovely Alice, was gone? He really expected to stop trying, to quit, to live out the rest of his years as a well-heeled vegetable. But he could not. A lot of him was Dutch and, being Dutch, he was not just stubborn; he was impossibly, irrationally, inexorably obstinate. He would keep going, even if he had nowhere to go. A few days after Alice's death he was back in Albany, shrilling "Mr. Speak-ah" and deploring corruption. In June, he went to the Republican National Convention in Chicago as New York's delegate-at-large, furiously backing Senator Edmunds against Blaine, who won the Republican Presidential nomination in a walk.

On June 10, Roosevelt returned to the Maltese Cross. He was still stunned by Alice's death and unable any longer to bear reminders of her in familiar places. He was fleeing from the places, fleeing from New York friends and New York politics, and vowing to make a life far away, as a rancher and hunter. At his ranch, he sought forgetfulness in action, going out of his way to ride bucking horses, though he hated buckers and usually got thrown. He went off alone for a week hunting in remoter Bad Lands, to prove to himself that he could stand the loneliness that had come to him when Alice died.

Some of his grimness abated when he joined a roundup briefly and added a phrase to the lore of the region by pointing to some bolting calves and yelling to a cowboy "Hasten forward quickly there!" as a Harvard substitute for "Head off them cattle!" He even achieved the last word in frontier experience by getting into a brawl at the town of Mingusville (today's Wibaux, Montana), west of Medora. Hermann Hagedorn tells the story. The future President of the United States was looking for strays and approached the small Mingusville hotel to spend the night. He heard shooting in the combined lobby and "rumhole." Inside he found some sheepherders watching a shabby drunk in a sombrero with cocked gun in each hand using the bar clock for a target. Roosevelt moved to a chair behind the stove but the drunk spotted the dude with the spectacles and made cracks about him. Then he came weaving across the room, leaned over Roosevelt and shouted "Four-eyes is going to treat! Set up drinks for the crowd!" Hagedorn continues:

Roosevelt (glamorized considerably, center) made himself a good cowhand, too, even though he was not a graceful rider and could not see well enough to cut out calves for branding. His Dakota experience convinced him that he could make anything of himself — even President of the United States! (Wash drawing by H. Sandham for Roosevelt's book Hunting Trips of a Ranchman, *courtesy Theodore Roosevelt Birthplace National Historic Site.)*

It struck Roosevelt that the man was foolish to stand so near, with his heels together. "Well, if I've got to, I've got to," he said, and rose to his feet, looking past his tormentor. As he rose he struck quick and hard with his right just to one side of the point of the jaw, hitting with his left as he straightened out, and then again with his right. The bully fired both guns, but the bullets went wide as he fell like a tree, striking the corner of the bar with his head. It occurred to Roosevelt that it was not a case in which one could afford to take chances, and he watched, ready to drop with his knees on the man's ribs at the first indication of activity. But the bully was senseless. The sheepherders hustled the would-be desperado into a shed.

At the Maltese Cross that June of '84, Roosevelt found that Sylvane Ferris and Bill Merrifield had replaced the dirt-floor shack made of railroad ties with a comfortable log ranch house. The wet spring had brought the cattle through in good shape, which encouraged him to go on with a plan he had been considering for months. Roosevelt was a discovering sort of man, and when he "discovered" something — ranching, for instance — he had to share it with others, even if he had to shove it down their throats. In his Harvard days he had gone on hunting trips three times in the birch-and-balsam wilds of Maine north of Bangor, along the Mattawamkeag River. His guides had been the expert canoe- and lumbermen Bill Sewall and his nephew, Wilmot Dow, who had spent all their lives at Island Falls. They were prototypes of a Maine breed which can become legendary even on brief acquaintance — legendary for succinct and colorful language, for dry humor, for a kind of rustic nobility, for quiet mastery of a beautiful land.

Roosevelt decided that Bill Sewall and Wilmot Dow ought to know the joys of ranching in the Bad Lands. Perhaps Alice was at the root of it somehow. Unconsciously he may have liked to have part of her New England background with him. He proposed to set them up on the Little Missouri with cattle and buildings. If they made a go of it on shares, all well and good. If they didn't, Roosevelt would foot the bill. Sewall hinted by letter that he and Wilmot were not enthusiastic about leaving Island Falls to go away and hell and gone out West to learn the cattle business. But Roosevelt didn't take hints when he was bent on pushing a discovery on people. In the end, Sewall agreed for himself and Wilmot to give the Bad Lands a whirl.

In mid-June, Roosevelt gave Sylvane Ferris and Bill Merrifield a check for twenty-six thousand dollars to buy a thousand more Iowa cattle for the Maltese Cross and for his Maine novices. That raised his total Bad Lands investment to more than forty thousand dollars — a very large amount of money in 1884. Then he rode north in search of unoccupied free range for his second ranch — north down the Little Missouri, where the Bad Lands were several hundred feet deeper below the prairie and more strangely beautiful than they were south of Medora. His Maltese Cross neighbor, Howard Eaton, had suggested a tract some thirty-five miles from town on the west bank of the river short of the mouth of Beaver Creek. The trail crossed and recrossed the thin muddy stream, passing corrals where the Marquis de Mores was holding cattle for his abattoir-to-be. The stream wound by and struggled over the coulees and ridges of the Bad Lands which French-Canadian *voyageurs* of the eighteenth century had called *"mauvaises terres pour traverser."* Roosevelt came to Blacktail Creek on the river's east bank, rounded a hill and found a river ford. On the west bank he saw a pair of interlocked elk antlers. Beyond was a row of big cottonwoods with quivering, gray-green leaves, and a stretch of rich pasture. Magpies were gossiping and doves were cooing and the air had a fragrance of juniper. It was exactly what he wanted for himself and for Sewall and Dow. He even had a name for it — Elkhorn Ranch.

He described the setting later in his *Ranch Life and the Hunting Trail:*

> The general course of the stream here is northerly, but, while flowing through my ranch, it takes a great westerly reach of some three miles, walled in, as always, between chains of steep, high bluffs half a mile or more apart. The stream twists down through the valley in long sweeps, leaving oval wooded bottoms, first on one side and then on the other. . . . The bluffs that wall in the river-valley curve back in semi-circles, rising from its alluvial bottom generally as abrupt cliffs, but often as steep, grassy slopes that lead up to great level plateaus; and the line is broken every mile or two by the entrance of a coulee, or dry creek, whose head branches may be twenty miles back. Above us, where the river comes round the bend, the valley is very narrow, and the high buttes bounding it rise, sheer and barren, into scalped hill-peaks and naked knife-blade ridges.

During July, after staking out his squatter's claim to Elkhorn, Roosevelt made a visit to Oyster Bay and Boston, returning at the end of the month with Bill Sewall and Wilmot Dow in tow. He wrote his sister Anna on August 12 of their reactions, or what he thought were their reactions, to the Bad Lands:

I had great fun in bringing my two backwoods babies out here. Their absolute astonishment and delight at everything they saw, and their really very shrewd, and yet wonderfully simple remarks were a perpetual delight to me. . . . I started them at once off down the river with a hundred head of cattle, under the lead of one of my friends out here. . . . Sewall tried to spur his horse which began kicking and rolled over with him into a washout.

Meanwhile, Sewall expressed "absolute astonishment and delight" in somewhat different terms in a letter to his brother in Island Falls:

It is a dirty country and very dirty people on an average, but I think it is healthy. The soil is sand or clay, all dust or all mud. The river is the meanest apology for a frog-pond that I ever saw. It is a queer country, you would like to see it, but you would not like to live here long . . . think the country ought to have been left to the animals that have laid their bones here.

Sewall and Dow were fine axe men and carpenters, for all their limitations as cowboys. While they were building the log ranch house and stable at Elkhorn in late August and September, the proprietor went off to the Big Horns hunting with Bill Merrifield and a small, garrulous French-Canadian cook named Norman Lebo who, Roosevelt wrote, "possessed a most extraordinary stock of miscellaneous misinformation upon every conceivable subject." From near the Maltese Cross, the little caravan of horses and chuck wagon followed the Fort Keogh Trail into Montana toward Miles City as far as Box Elder Creek. Then the hunters angled southwest over the rolling prairie to Powder River. They moved up that willowed waterway and into the cool lodgepole forests of the Big Horns — the mountain stretch by way of Crazy Woman Creek, on the ancient Sioux Indian trail which led eventually to South Pass and Green River. Each day brought new adventures. They survived a storm and whirlwind — "sheets of hailstones as large as pigeons' eggs striking the earth with the velocity of bullets" — and won a friendly shooting match with some Cheyenne Indians. The September weather was crisp and tonic. From their mountain camp on Crazy Woman Creek they could see the snows of Cloud Peak glittering some ten miles to the northwest. The elk and deer and grouse and cutthroat trout were plentiful but Roosevelt

Roosevelt's Elkhorn Ranch house, which those two lumbermen from Maine, Bill Sewall and Wilmot Dow, built for him, was some thirty-five miles down the Little Missouri from Medora. That was far enough away so that the young author could get some writing done without the interruptions which had bothered him at the Maltese Cross. (Wash drawing by R. Swain Gifford for Hunting Trips of a Ranchman, *courtesy Theodore Roosevelt Birthplace National Historic Site.)*

wanted a grizzly bear above all. At last they cornered in a thicket a twelve-hundred pound male, which they had lured near the camp with an elk carcass. Roosevelt described the event in *Hunting Trips of a Ranchman:*

> When in the middle of the thicket we crossed what was almost a breast-work of fallen logs, and Merrifield, who was leading, passed by the upright stem of a great pine. As soon as he was by it he sank suddenly on one knee, turning half round, his face fairly aflame with excitement; and as I strode past him, with my rifle at the ready, there, not ten steps off, was the great bear, slowly rising from his bed among the young spruces. He had heard us, but apparently hardly knew exactly where or what we were, for he reared up on his haunches sidewise to us. Then he saw us and dropped down again on all fours, the shaggy hair on his neck and shoulders seeming to bristle as he turned toward us. As he sank down on his forefeet I had raised the rifle; his head was bent slightly down, and when I saw the top of the white bead fairly between his small, glittering, evil eyes, I pulled trigger. Half-rising up the huge beast fell over on his side in the death throes, the ball having gone into his brain, striking as fairly between the eyes as if the distance had been measured by a carpenter's rule. The whole thing was over in twenty seconds from the time I caught sight of the game. . . . It was the first I had ever seen, and I felt not a little proud, as I stood over the great brindled hulk.

THE PURPOSE OF IT ALL — the Elkhorn Ranch, the strenuous, month-long Big Horns trip, the whole plan of a pioneering career in the West — was therapy. Roosevelt, the stubborn Dutchman, would get over the tragedy of Alice's death or kill himself trying. During that summer of 1884 he had written a family memorial to her which closed with the lines, "Fair, pure and joyous as a maiden; loving, tender, and happy as a young wife; when she had just become a mother, when her life seemed to be but just begun, and when the years seemed so bright before her — then, by a strange and terrible fate, death came to her. And when my heart's dearest died, the light went from my life for ever."

That would be his last word. Having written it, he went to work to try to recapture the light. No more on Alice. He would discipline himself not to think of her. He would not speak of her, not even to her daughter. He would take the view that Sunshine had never existed, and perhaps the time would come when he would believe it. But it was hard going. It depressed him that October when he went back to New York to have to push along with building the Oyster Bay home, its name changed now from Leeholm to Sagamore Hill. He was depressed still more when he decided to be a loyal Republican, which meant making campaign speeches in favor of James G. Blaine for President — the man whose nomination he had opposed with all his strength. And still he cheered up during the winter. He did some politicking in Albany but spent most of the time in New York. Writing, he found, was salvation — the hard work of writing day and night on his book *Hunting Trips of a Ranchman*. He finished it late in March, for July publication by G. P. Putnam. But the work routine set him back physically. When he arrived at Medora to resume ranching on April 5, 1885, he looked as thin and as frail as he had looked that first time in '83 when he had come to shoot a buffalo.

But there was a world of difference in how he felt. He was not a dude now. He knew one end of a cow pony from the other. He could ride off alone for a week in the labyrinthine Bad Lands, living off the country and without getting lost. He had cowboy friends who accepted him almost as one of them even if he did brush his teeth and shave every morning. As one of them said, "He was not a purty rider, but he was a hell of a good rider." And he was going to complete his Dakota education by attending the big spring roundup this time — all five weeks of it — in his role as boss of the Maltese Cross and the Elkhorn.

Of course he was soft and would have to build himself up. That was easy during the wet April, with all the streams in flood. His muscles hardened during days of toil hauling his cattle out of bogs. The fords of the river could be crossed only by swimming the horse over. Roosevelt liked the drama of swimming. One day in Medora he refused to take the easy way across by riding his horse Manitou over the narrow plank between the tracks of the railroad trestle. Instead he put Manitou to crossing on the submerged ice dam which the Marquis de Mores had built. In midstream, Manitou slipped off the dam — or maybe the dam had washed away. Horse and rider plunged into the yellow torrent. Roosevelt threw himself free and swam to shore, guiding Manitou and protecting the horse's head from floating blocks of ice.

The big roundup began on May 25 at the mouth of the Little Missouri tributary Box Elder Creek, a hundred miles south of Medora. The Maltese Cross men joined the other Little Missouri outfits there

— Gregor Lang's and Howard Eaton's and the Three Sevens, Hash-knife, Dantz Ranch and so on. Roosevelt had picked his cowboys on the basis of friendship — Sylvane Ferris, Bill Merrifield, Bill Sewall, Wilmot Dow, the fine trail cook Walter Watterson, the good-natured "Dutch" Wannigan who had tangled accidentally with the Marquis de Mores in the Luffsey killing, and several more. Each Maltese Cross cowboy, the boss included, drew eight or ten ponies by lot from Roosevelt's horse herd. The hard work began at once, sixteen hours of it a day as the men worked down the drainage of the river, combing the coulees and the prairies back from them for cattle. Roosevelt took his turn riding the long circle (the gathering process), herding the captured cattle by day and by night, wrestling calves to brand them. He did plenty of roping, though he was not good at it. But he did not try to cut out calves and their mothers from the herd because he was too nearsighted to be able to read the brands properly. A man had to be able to read brands from a fair distance.

Roosevelt had not been lucky in drawing his string of ponies. He recalled in his autobiography:

Three or four of the animals I got were not easy to ride. The effort both to ride them and to look as if I enjoyed doing so, on some cool morning when my grinning cowboy friends had gathered round "to see whether the high-headed bay could buck the boss off," doubtless was of benefit to me, but lacked much of being enjoyable. The time I smashed my rib I was bucked off on a stone. The time I hurt the point of my shoulder I was riding a big sulky horse named Ben Butler, which went over backwards with me. When we got up it still refused to go anywhere; so, while I sat it, Sylvane Ferris and George Meyer got their ropes on its neck and dragged it a few hundred yards, choking but stubborn, all four feet firmly planted and plowing the ground. When they released the ropes it lay down and wouldn't get up. The round-up had started; so Sylvane gave me his horse, Baldy, which sometimes bucked but never went over backwards, and he got on the now re-arisen Ben Butler. To my discomfiture Ben started quietly beside us, while Sylvane remarked, "Why, there's nothing the matter with this horse; he's a plumb gentle horse." Then Ben fell slightly behind and I heard Sylvane again, "That's all right! Come along! Here, you! Go on, you! Hi, hi, fellows, help me out! he's lying on me!" Sure enough he was; and when we dragged Sylvane from under him the first thing the rescued Sylvane did was to execute a war-dance, spurs and all, on the iniquitous Ben. We could do nothing with him that day; subsequently we got him so that we could ride him; but he never became a nice saddle-horse.

The roundup had a satisfactory climax near the Maltese Cross, where two thousand cattle went crazy in a midnight storm and stampeded across the Little Missouri. The scene was Wagnerian. The thunder crashed and the cattle bawled and the rain clattered in the cottonwoods. Roosevelt and the rest galloped after the herd, with only great jagged flashes of lightning to see by. It was a matter of trying to stay with the cattle without taking a fall and getting trampled to death. One cowboy's horse killed itself by running into a tree, though the rider survived. Other horses sank in the river's quicksand and had to be rescued with ropes. The herd stopped stampeding at daylight many miles from camp. The job then was to drive the animals back to camp. When that was over, Roosevelt had been riding for forty-eight hours. He was worn out, but a night's sleep restored him. Thereafter he held his own until the roundup was disbanded in late June near his Elkhorn Ranch.

And when he left Medora to do some business in New York he seemed quite another person. He had gained thirty pounds since March. His chest had barreled out. His face had taken on a weathered, brown cast. He looked rugged, and in fact he was. It seems likely that the roundup of '85 did mark his emergence from childhood frailties. At last he had achieved the strength his father had talked about — physical strength and endurance to match his vitality. And yet the tragedy of Alice stayed with him, causing moods when everything seemed futile. The antidote was thinking about his ranches. In the spring he had sent Sewall and Dow to Minnesota to bring back fifteen hundred more cattle for the Elkhorn and the Maltese Cross, raising his investment to well over eighty thousand dollars. The total was huge, but ranching, Roosevelt still thought, was his life's work. He was certain of that when he returned to the Elkhorn in late August. He recalled in his autobiography how he felt about it:

I do not believe there ever was any life more attractive to a vigorous young fellow than life on a cattle ranch in those days. It was a fine, healthy life, too; it taught a man self-reliance, hardihood, and the value of instant decision — in short, the virtues that ought to come from life in the open country. I enjoyed the life to the full. After the first year I built on the

Elkhorn ranch a long, low ranch house of hewn logs, with a veranda, and with, in addition to the other rooms, a bedroom for myself, and a sitting-room with a big fire-place. I got out a rock-chair — I am very fond of rock-chairs — and enough books to fill two or three shelves, and a rubber bath-tub so that I could get a bath. And then I do not see how any one could have lived more comfortably.

The one slight flaw in Roosevelt's ranching was the Marquis de Mores. The two young men were of the same age and had met each other in Medora because of their acquaintance with ex-Commander Gor-ringe. De Mores had supported Roosevelt in December of '84 when the latter had organized the Little Missouri Stockmen's Association as a step toward ending anarchy in Medora and Billings County. The Mar-quis had vouched for Roosevelt when he had applied for membership in the Montana Stockgrowers' Association. On the other hand, they had squabbled over the extent of Roosevelt's squatter's rights both at the Maltese Cross and at the Elkhorn. And De Mores's adviser, Jerry Paddock, had tried to make a sucker out of Roosevelt by demanding five hundred dollars for an abandoned shack on the Elkhorn which he claimed was his.

But something more basic kept the New York aristocrat on the de-fensive where De Mores was concerned. The marquis was a Latin. The Puritan Roosevelt supposed that all Latins were untrustworthy and traditionally immoral. De Mores believed in the divine right of kings and spoke hopefully of putting an Orleanist on the throne of France. His attitude toward Roosevelt was courteously patronizing, as though he were aware that his nobility dated back to the King of Ara-gon in the fourteenth century, whereas Roosevelt's humble Dutch an-cestor did not reach Manhattan Island until the seventeenth. And whereas Roosevelt was just a well-educated American, the marquis was a cultured European. He spoke several languages fluently, knew French wine, read Dostoievski and had a wife who played Mozart by the hour and painted watercolors. In some infuriating way, the marquis made Roosevelt feel like a country bumpkin whenever he had him to lunch at the De Mores chateau above Medora.

This was their relationship in late August of 1885 when the marquis was indicted at last for the murder of Riley Luffsey and jailed in Bis-marck pending trial. Some of Roosevelt's cowboys, including "Dutch" Wannigan, were expected to testify for the prosecution. Then one day

Roosevelt's mail contained a letter, quoted here from Carleton Putnam's *Theodore Roosevelt*. The original letter is on file in the Theodore Roosevelt Collection at the Harvard College Library.

Northern Pacific Refrigerator Car Company
Bismarck, Dak.
Sept. 3, 1885

My dear Roosevelt:

My principle is to take the bull by the horns. Joe Ferris is very active against me and has been instrumental in getting me indicted by furnishing money to witnesses and hunting them up. The papers also publish very stupid accounts of our quarrelling — I sent you the paper to New York. Is this done by your orders? I thought you my friend. If you are my enemy I want to know it. I am always on hand as you know, and between gentlemen it is easy to settle matters of that sort directly.

Yours very truly,
MORES

I hear the people want to organize the county. I am opposed to it for one year more at least.

After reading this plaintive missive several times, Roosevelt concluded that it just might be the subtle way in which a European gentleman challenged another gentleman to a duel. He knew that he stood no chance with pistols against an expert like the marquis. Still, if his honor was at stake he would have to go through with it. He wrote his reply with great care, to fit the bill whatever De Mores meant.

Medora, Dakota
September 6, 1885

Dear De Mores:

Most emphatically I am not your enemy; if I were you would know it, for I would be an open one, and would not have asked you to my house nor gone to yours. As your final words, however, seem to imply a threat it is due to myself to say that the statement is not made through any fear of possible consequences to me; I too, as you know, am always on hand, and ever ready to hold myself accountable in any way for anything I have said or done.

Yours very truly,
THEODORE ROOSEVELT

There is no record of the marquis's reply but its tone must have been friendly and conciliatory. As Bill Sewall recalled, he apologized for the last line in his first letter which sounded like a challenge where none was intended. Instead of the word "directly" he should have written "without trouble."

Pleasant days for the young master of Elkhorn. Roosevelt hunted when the spirit moved him, watched the golden fall come along, made notes for an ambitious history, *The Winning of the West.*

And still he had not erased the memory of Alice.

He had nearly courted another girl of the same age once. He had grown up in New York with Edith Kermit Carow. She had been fond enough of him when he married Sunshine in 1880 to find nothing to admire about her. Edith was as beautiful as Alice in her quiet way. She was wise and dependable and predictable. She had all the virtues Alice had lacked. She had too much respect for a man's ego to assault his personality, to demand equal time, to threaten his self-control.

Alice's death may have filled Edith with Victorian feelings of guilt. Roosevelt the widower had bad reactions too. As a result, they avoided each other, which took some doing since Edith was a friend of his sister Anna and came to see Anna often in her Madison Avenue house. Late in October of 1885, Roosevelt returned from Medora to ride with the Meadowbrook Hunt. He broke his arm riding. Then he stopped unexpectedly at Anna's, and there was Edith standing in the hall. She looked at the arm in its sling and they smiled at each other.

They fell in love then and there and became secretly engaged on November 17, though they did not marry for another year.

EVERY PRESIDENT OF THE United States has had his prophets. The first in Roosevelt's case was his buffalo guide, Joe Ferris, who had barely survived the effects of the tenderfoot's persistence. As early as 1884, Joe told friends in his Medora store that he wouldn't be surprised if Roosevelt was President some day.

Life in the Bad Lands did contribute to the qualities that made Joe so sure of his man. It solved Roosevelt's physical problem certainly, the indifferent health, the mediocre reflexes. During those many months of hardship in the saddle, he became permanently rugged and proved to himself that the steadfast spirit triumphs over physical handicaps. In the meantime he observed how freedom flowered in a classless society and, flowering, produced self-reliant men. By coming to understand his Bad Lands cowboys he was able to emerge from his narrow Eastern world so that he could understand the aspirations of Americans everywhere. And on the Maltese Cross and the Elkhorn he began to develop ideas of conservation which he would use to bring about some of the great achievements of modern America.

The boat-stealing incident near the end of his Bad Lands days foreshadowed the great Teddy Roosevelt to come — the swashbuckling Teddy who would risk his life to oppose wrongdoing in high and low places, and risk it again charging up San Juan Hill just for the fun of it, the color of it, the crazy juvenile drama of it.

The Bad Lands had their dregs of society. One of them was a red-headed, noisy drifter of middle years named Mike Finnegan who lived in a shack twenty miles up the Little Missouri from the Elkhorn. Mike made whiskey money by hunting and petty theft. His shackmates were a muscular half-breed, Edward Burnsted, and a half-witted old German whose last name was something like Pfaffenbach, or maybe Wharfenberg. It was easier to call him Chris.

On March 19, 1886, Roosevelt returned from New York to find winter still hanging thick around the Elkhorn. The Little Missouri was full of ice which jammed at the turns and made the water high. He was rather pleased about the high water since he had bought a fine rowboat in St. Paul and he could cross the river if he wanted to. On March 24 he wanted to very much. A mountain lion was killing game in the area and he hoped to track it down.

But he discovered that somebody had stolen his boat the night before.

The thief was Mike Finnegan, of course. Probably he and his pals were skipping the Bad Lands bound for the Missouri, St. Louis and more congenial climes. They must have floated down in their leaky old scow as far as the Elkhorn and had traded the scow for the new boat.

It was blizzard weather but Roosevelt decided to go after them. Sewall and Dow, the Maine woodsmen, built a large flatboat. By March 30 the storm had abated enough so that the three of them could cast off from Elkhorn, carrying a fortnight's provisions. Roosevelt, always improving himself, took along a book of Matthew Arnold's poems and Tolstoy's *Anna Karenina,* which the Marquise de Mores had urged

Nobody was going to steal Roosevelt's new boat and get away with it, for he regarded stealing, big or little, as a threat to the Constitution of the United States. Here is the fearless posse which set out from Elkhorn Ranch after the thieves — Wilmot Dow (left), Roosevelt and Bill Sewall. It was in March of 1886 and cold enough to bundle up in fur. (Theodore Roosevelt Birthplace National Historic Site photo.)

him to read. After three days of acute misery winding fifty miles or so down through those deeper Bad Lands, they spotted the stolen boat. Old Chris was on shore near it by a campfire. He did not resist and Sewall sat down to guard him. Roosevelt and Dow hid below the

And they got their men! Roosevelt is shown holding his "big stick" over the boat stealers, Mike Finnegan (center), Edward Burnsted, the half-breed, and the old German, Chris (standing). (Theodore Roosevelt Birthplace National Historic Site photo.)

stream bank and waited for Finnegan and Burnsted, who were off hunting. Just before dark, the hunters walked right into the short range of their rifles. Roosevelt ordered them to hold their hands high and stripped them of guns, knives, boots and coats. Then he made all three of them lie down under a single buffalo robe, since it was much too cold to tie them up. They had to stay with the robe to keep from freezing.

That was on a gloomy April 1. Next day was gloomier still. The policemen put the thieves in the flatboat to float them down to the Missouri and so on to Mandan. But the scheme seemed more and more ridiculous as the bad weather continued. Because of the ice jams ahead, they hardly moved at all for six days. Roosevelt had time to read Arnold's poetry but found no comfort in it. Tolstoy's lax attitude toward morality irritated him. The Bad Lands never looked so tortured and depressing. Why should sane men endure all this discomfort and sleeplessness and tension to punish the likes of Mike Finnegan?

On top of everything else, they began to run short of food. Roosevelt went to get help eastward, away from the river, in the foothills of the Killdeer Mountains. He found a ranch and returned to the boats with a rented wagon and a cowboy to drive it. The thieves were transferred to the wagon. Sewall and Dow said good-bye to Roosevelt and floated off downstream in the two boats, bound for Bismarck. The cowboy driver headed the wagon southeast to strike the road to Dickinson, which was some sixty miles away. Roosevelt, the implacable guard, did not ride in the wagon. He trudged along close behind it, his rifle loaded and aimed at the prisoners. When they put up in a cabin that night he did not sleep. Late next day, April 12, he turned Finnegan and the others over to Dickinson's justice of the peace, who locked them up on theft charges.

Then Roosevelt called on Dr. Stickney to have his blistered feet treated. He was half frozen and caked with gumbo, but there was a quality about him which later would astound and amuse the whole nation. He should have been worn out after two hundred miles of tramping and guarding in bitter weather — the last forty-eight hours without sleep. He *looked* worn out — "all teeth and eyes," Stickney said. But he was wide awake and brimming over with joy and boyish bravado. The reason was simple. He had seen to it that right triumphed over wrong against terrible odds.

For him, the principle was and would always be the thing, whether bringing Mike Finnegan to book, or United States Steel.

HE MAY HAVE REALIZED, that summer of 1886, that his Bad Lands career was just about over. He enjoyed himself hunting and writing but his center of gravity had shifted. His thoughts now were of Edith Carow back East and of the life they would have, with lots of children in the big place at Oyster Bay. The Bad Lands ranching outlook was very poor. It had not rained since April. The Little Missouri free range was burned up. Prices in Chicago were lower than the cost of raising the cattle. The Marquis de Mores's packing house was failing. Arthur Packard's newspaper the *Bad Lands Cowboy* was on its last legs. Because of the dark future, Roosevelt was almost relieved when one day in September Bill Sewall and Wilmot Dow got his permission to leave the Elkhorn and return to the sylvan charms of the Mattawamkeag River in Maine. He made a four-year contract the same day with Sylvane Ferris and Bill Merrifield to manage the Elkhorn as well as the Maltese Cross.

On October 3 he left Medora for New York to run for Mayor on the Republican ticket. He knew he could not win. It was just a gesture for the good of the party. He had "a bully time" and he was especially pleased about comments on his campaign in the Sioux Falls (Iowa) *Press:* "Theodore is a Dakota cowboy and has spent a large share of his time in the Territory for a couple of years. . . . When he first went on the range, the cowboys took him for a dude, but soon they realized the stuff of which the youngster was built."

He married Edith Carow in London on December 2. The fatal winter of 1886-1887 had begun its work of nearly destroying the free-range cattle industry, weakened already by drouth and overstocking. While he and Edith honeymooned in Europe the Bad Lands filled with snow and hundreds of thousands of cattle died there, unable to get to the grass. In March of '87, Bill Merrifield rode out from the Maltese Cross after a Chinook thaw; he could not find a single live cow or steer.

Roosevelt lost sixty thousand dollars' worth of cattle in the disaster of '86. But he held on to the Maltese Cross and the Elkhorn for years and returned to hunt again and again. Meanwhile back East, as Civil Service commissioner, as head of police in New York, as Rough Rider, as Governor, as President, he handled problems in ways he had learned while bagging buffalo or stopping a cattle stampede or putting down a drunk in Mingusville. The world plied him with honors but nothing delighted him more than the spurs he had won as a cowhand whom nobody cared to call "dude" or "Four-Eyes" after the roundup of 1885.

He loved the Bad Lands all his life and poured out affection on his human and animal friends back there. One day in 1906 Joe Ferris got this letter from the White House about an animal friend:

> Dear Joe:
> Can't Muley be kept up during the winter? I feel that he is entitled to a pension. I will of course pay all expenses connected with it.
> Give my regards to Mrs. Ferris and all the family.
> Sincerely yours,
> THEODORE ROOSEVELT

And he never tired of talking about his debt to the Bad Lands. "The romance of my life," he said in Medora, while campaigning for Vice President, "began here."

9

THE MILKMAN OF BROADMOOR

OUT IN THE SPACIOUS residential area of Broadmoor, near Colorado Springs, Colorado, there is a street called Pourtales Road. It runs from near the Broadmoor Hotel for half a mile, past a number of large homes which lie in a cover of old trees along Spring Creek. The name Pourtales is pronounced in three syllables with the accent on the second, and it is not some sort of bad Spanish as you might suppose. Instead it honors a German nobleman, Count James Pourtales, because he created Broadmoor.

That occurred in the 1880's but we start his story long before. Pourtales's forebears were Huguenots who left France at the time of the revocation of the Edict of Nantes and settled in the Swiss principality of Neuchâtel, under the rule of the King of Prussia. Jacques Louis de Pourtales made a stack of money during the eighteenth century and spent some of it to strengthen the hold on Neuchâtel of the next Prussian king, who made him and his progeny counts and countesses.

In 1814, Neuchâtel joined the democratic Swiss Confederation, which meant that Prussia would lose its principality in time. The several Pourtales counts in Neuchâtel had been opposing Swiss Republicanism but they knew that the jig was up, and they began moving themselves and their assets to more congenial environments — to France and Alsace and Bohemia and Prussian Silesia (now in Poland).

One of these emigrants, James Pourtales's grandfather, bought in Silesia a former monastery, Glumbowitz, which had nine villages dangling from it. Our Count James, born in 1853, was a current count briefly, having nothing to be count of after 1857 when Frederick William IV of Prussia renounced sovereignty over Neuchâtel. Still, James was called count by courtesy, and so were his cousins in France — the French branch having the prefix *de* in front of Pourtales.

Count Pourtales lost his father at an early age and became owner in 1881 of the moldy monastery, a lot of needy peasants, big mortgages and other problems such as sick cows, bad harvests and drought. He was not alarmed. He was a big, cheery, positive, stubborn man who ate and drank and played and worked with gusto. He had a knack for business and a creative feeling about it. He loved to think up bold schemes and to gamble his shirt on them. As he studied Glumbowitz, he concluded that his father had been a poor businessman because of his classical education — too much Goethe and Schiller and Kant and not enough study of interest rates. It was the reason why, in his view, Germany as a whole lagged behind England and America in economic growth. So young Pourtales discarded the cultural traditions of his father and patterned himself on his shrewd French ancestor, Jacques Louis de Pourtales — the one who had made all the money. Count James would pick up a fortune in the United States and return to the Fatherland as a shining example of what all German youngsters should do to regenerate the nation.

He crossed the Atlantic first in April of 1884 on a North German Lloyd steamer, amusing himself during the six-day trip by calculating the boat's coal consumption, how much it cost to feed the crew and how much money the company lost because German bartenders could not make a decent American cocktail. He found New York City to be thrilling, writing of it later:

> The impression which I received as I entered New York harbor was overwhelming. It occurred at evening. The first lights had flashed on in the houses and on the piers; our steamer swept with slow majesty through the wide harbor against the current of the Hudson River. The hustle and bustle in the harbor is absolutely indescribable. Hundreds of small steamers, sailing vessels, transatlantic steamers, inbound and outbound, cross paths. The ferry boats from New York to New Jersey and Hoboken churn the waters at a mad speed. Giant passenger steamers glide under

Everybody liked Count James Pourtales when he came to Pikes Peak from Silesia in 1885 to make a fortune. They liked his pipe and his accent and funny clothes and, of course, they revered his title. (H. S. Poley photo, Denver Public Library Western Collection.)

the well known, hanging Brooklyn Bridge continuing their journey to Boston and New York on the East River. I have seen other big harbors; those in England, some on the French coast, the harbors of Toulon, Marseille, Genoa, Naples, Brindisi, Alexandria, and, of first importance, the harbors of Bremen and Hamburg; but none of these can be compared with the harbor of New York.

He searched the whole country for business opportunities, journeying to Washington and Philadelphia and Chicago, where he looked in at the Republican National Convention — the one Theodore Roosevelt was attending on his way to Medora. From Chicago, the Count went to St. Louis, to Denver and to Colorado Springs. The latter — population, two thousand — did not impress him then. He stopped merely to call on a French cousin of his, Count Louis de Pourtales, who, to correct a tendency toward intemperance, was ranching some miles up Ute Pass. Louis had grown up in Washington, and then in Boston, where his father was an associate at Harvard with the Swiss-born scientist A. E. Agassiz.

From the Springs, Count James went on to San Francisco, to Portland, to Yellowstone Park, and on back East through St. Paul, Detroit and Niagara Falls. He wound up in Boston in August of '84 to call on Louis de Pourtales's sister, Countess Berthe de Pourtales, whose marriage to a Boston financier, Sebastian Schlesinger, had gone on the rocks. Berthe was going to Colorado Springs with her two small daughters to be near her brother and to forget her marital troubles. She was a tall, slender, stunningly beautiful creature rather on the order of the Venus de Milo. She seems to have been the one thing in the United States that Count James studied without reference to his interest tables.

On his homeward voyage, Pourtales dreamed often of Berthe. Back in Silesia he continued to dream of her while raising capital through more mortgages on Glumbowitz. In January of '85 he returned to the States for further study of business opportunities. He discarded Florida as a field of operations and made his way to Pikes Peak to begin a campaign to win a fortune and Countess Berthe's heart.

THE GERMAN DUDE was intrigued by a number of things about the town which General William Jackson Palmer of Philadelphia had created in 1871, five miles out on the plain from the mountain. Saloons were

Count James had a beautiful French cousin, Berthe de Pourtales, who was visiting in Colorado Springs. He married her in 1889 after she shed her rich Boston husband. Then the count named a Broadmoor street after her, Berthe Circle. (Colorado Springs Pioneer Museum photo.)

banned. Liquor had to be bought in drugstores, specified "medicinal." The top of Colorado Springs society was composed of pioneer English families who had their tea at five each afternoon, put on Gilbert and Sullivan operettas and maintained the high moral tone of the community. Everyone called it "Little London." Residing among the English were numbers of well-heeled Americans from New York and Philadelphia, from Newport and Boston and Baltimore. They had come West to recover from tuberculosis or some such convenient disease which did not prevent them from playing polo or tennis or from hiking up Pikes Peak by moonlight or dancing all night long. Then there were odd characters around, such as Berthe's brother Louis, who had distinguished himself by serenading General Palmer's wife Queen at her bedroom window with what a contemporary called "songs of unrequited passion as persistently melancholy as the call of a mourning dove."

From the start, Pourtales was popular with the Pikes Peak Americans. They revered his title and liked the jokes he told in his comical English, and his quaint getup and his stubby pipe. One American, Anne Parish, a quite good artist from Philadelphia, painted his portrait. Her husband, Tom Parrish, got him in to the exclusive El Paso Club where he soon learned everybody's business.

Colorado Springs, Count James observed, would be booming soon because residents were making fortunes from the silver mines of Leadville and Aspen to the west. He had meant to invest a maximum of twenty-five thousand dollars in sound mortgages at twelve per cent interest. But, one fateful day in December of '85, he met William J. Willcox, Anne Parrish's brother. Willcox piled him in a buggy and took him on a tour of his dairy farm. The name of the farm was Broadmoor. It began on a treeless mesa a couple of miles or so south of town and extended west along a little stream, Spring Creek, to the foot of a singularly lovely spur of Pikes Peak called Cheyenne Mountain.

Willcox confided to the count that he had been losing money on the Broadmoor Dairy Farm for four years. His cows wouldn't settle half the time and gave much less milk than they should to pay for the huge amount of hay they ate. The butter made from their milk tasted funny and brought low prices. Pourtales took notes as they rode about in the buggy — notes about the farm's water rights, about the wages paid to milkers, and about the blood lines of the cows and bulls. He translated

William Willcox of Philadelphia started the Broadmoor Dairy Farm but Pourtales said Willcox was doing everything wrong. When the count got through expanding, the place stretched all up and down Spring Creek. Cheyenne Mountain shows at right center. (Picture from the Pourtales autobiography Lessons Learned from Experience, *kindness of Colorado College.)*

the farm's acres into hektar and morgen, tons of alfalfa into centner of alfalfa, and dollars and cents into marks and pfennigs, so that he could tell where Willcox stood in German. In this way he was able to inform the worried Philadelphian that same afternoon that everything was being done wrong at the Broadmoor Dairy Farm. But he added that it had a bright future because of the coming boom if someone with horse sense was in charge. Willcox, an amiable soul, thanked the count for his excellent advice. In the next breath, he offered him a half interest in the business and a free hand to run it — for twenty-five thousand dollars.

Pourtales's gambling instinct flamed. He took the offer. Here was a challenge which he felt a young German of the new progressive type must accept. And he did not see how he could fail to make big money. There was no first-class dairy in the Rockies. His friends at the El Paso Club would pay through the nose to buy milk and butter sold by a nobleman. He could experiment with the cows at Broadmoor and apply the resultant knowledge at Glumbowitz. All the while he could woo Berthe, who was involved in divorce proceedings.

He did not hurry. Sound husbandry took time. Early in 1886, he bought two cows in Denver, set them up comfortably in a barn in Colorado Springs and recorded their reactions hour by hour — their consumption of carbohydrates and water, their state of mind under varying barometric pressures, the frequency and ardor of their sex urges. He worked out measures for efficient churning and ordered a modern centrifugal churn. He timed with a stopwatch how long it took his Negro research assistant to milk a pail full. In the spring he got rid of the worst of Willcox's cows, bought eighty new cows, bought two tracts of land with water rights on Cheyenne Creek below Broadmoor, and planted alfalfa. His researches indicated that twenty centner (one ton) of hay costing three dollars and a half produced fourteen dollars worth of lamb if put into a sheep and only ten dollars worth of beef if put into a steer. He bought a flock of sheep.

By the fall of '86, things at Broadmoor were doing so well that he wrote out instructions for Willcox to follow and returned to Silesia. Though the count enjoyed the creative phase of enterprise, humdrum management bored him. He planned to work for a year on Glumbowitz while his new house was going up in the Springs and Berthe was shedding Sebastian Schlesinger. But a frantic cable from his partner reached him in Germany before the spring of '87 had barely begun. Willcox reported that every one of the eighty new cows had come down with contagious abortion. Many of the sheep were lame from trampling on Spanish bayonet. The town was booming all right, but dairy competition was fierce and the price of milk had fallen from eight to seven

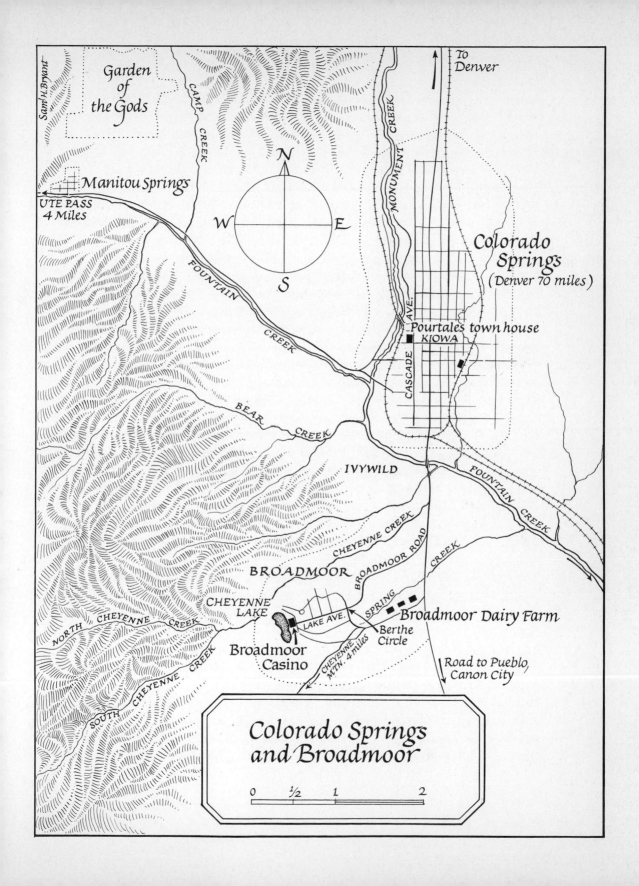

Colorado Springs
and Broadmoor

cents a quart. The centrifugal churn had cracked. The count's friends were turning up their noses at his Broadmoor Gilt Edge Crown Butter. Even the steward of the El Paso Club was buying his milk from the Garden Ranch, north of town.

The news put Pourtales in a rage and he caught the next North German Lloyd steamer for New York. Back at Broadmoor he went furiously to work to meet competition. He increased the farm's size to two thousand four hundred acres and imported a cheese genius from the famous Darlington Dairy in Philadelphia to improve that part of the business. He sold the sick cows and bought two hundred healthy ones, building new barns to house them and getting formulas for their diet devised by the German scientist Professor Emil Wolff. He conducted a barn-by-barn canvass of the Pikes Peak region to find high-altitude milkers. If he found a cow giving more than twenty quarts a day, he would pay as much as a hundred dollars for her.

Such fine cows deserved to get the very best service. He had five imported Brown Swiss bulls shipped from the East, all bearing the name of the legendary Swiss Republican, William Tell. The bulls brought much publicity to Broadmoor when people learned that Pourtales had paid the fantastic price of a thousand dollars for Wilhelm Tell, Jr. Jokes flew around town about the prowess of Thaddeus Tell and Prince Tell, and how Duke Tell and Melchior Tell were feuding over one of Broadmoor's flirtatious heifers. Sales of Broadmoor milk, butter and cheese picked up. Pourtales decided to live at the farm to sustain the improvement. He moved Willcox and his family to his new house downtown and moved himself into Willcox's house at Broadmoor.

All the while, Colorado Springs was growing very fast, especially after the local tycoon, James J. Hagerman, finished his Colorado Midland Railroad up Ute Pass and beyond to Leadville and Aspen. The residential area was pushing north, and it occurred to the count that he ought to urge residents to come south to live in Broadmoor instead. He felt that the beauty of Cheyenne Mountain was a big attraction. And he knew that his El Paso Club friends were complaining of General Palmer's Little London, where whiskey was sold only as medicine in drugstores and rules of decorum were laid down by the English pioneers who were getting stuffier with age. An uninhibited community at Broadmoor, Pourtales concluded, just might appeal to

The count felt that good cows deserved good service. He paid a thousand dollars for the Brown Swiss champion William Tell, Jr., imported from the East. The man with the beard standing on the fence is Duncan Chisholm, manager of the dairy farm. (Photo from Pourtales's book Lessons Learned from Experience, *kindness of Colorado College.)*

people, platted on French lines with radiating streets and all, and no Union Jacks fluttering around on Boxing Day.

Count James married Countess Berthe in the spring of '89 and took her to Glumbowitz for a honeymoon. Before leaving Pikes Peak he set up a real estate firm called the Cheyenne Lake, Land and Improvement Company. The property of this modest "Broadmoor" consisted of two hundred and forty acres around the source of Spring Creek, at the west end of the Broadmoor Dairy Farm. The count marked out his radiating streets with a plow. Since there wasn't a tree in miles, he gave some of the streets tree names — Maple, Elm, Beech, Walnut, Hazel, Holly, Lime — as a promise that there would be trees some day. He implemented the promise by planting two thousand saplings. He named one of the streets Lake Avenue, which suggested that he had a lake somewhere. So he spent ten thousand dollars building Cheyenne Lake and filling it with water drawn by pipeline from Cheyenne Creek. The radiating streets were tied together by Lake Circle on the west and Berthe Circle on the east. They were bound by Broadmoor Avenue on the south and Mesa Avenue on the north.

Pourtales was happy to hire as his new farm manager one of the leading lights of the El Paso Club, a big, hearty Scot named Duncan Chisholm. This left William Willcox with nothing to do, which Pourtales seemed to feel was the safest job for him during his own absence. While honeymooning in Silesia, the count was shocked to discover one day that he had spent $180,000 in Broadmoor so far, instead of the maximum $25,000 which he had expected to invest four years earlier. And still the great fortune eluded him. And Duncan Chisholm's reports brought no joy. The city of Colorado Springs was stealing Pourtales's share of the water in Cheyenne Creek. The theft had caused Cheyenne Lake to run dry and all the saplings had died. And whenever a prospect was about to buy a Broadmoor lot, somebody got killed at the unguarded Nevada Avenue railroad crossing and the prospect lost interest through fear of driving his buggy over the crossing.

There was nothing for the count to do but curtail his honeymoon and rush into the breach once more. Returning with Berthe to Pikes Peak, he found that the Springs population was nearing eight thousand. A four-fold increase in five years! The north end of town was getting the benefit, with lots bringing a hundred and fifty dollars a front foot. Heroic measures were needed to turn the tide from the

For his bride, Pourtales built a fine home at Cascade Avenue and Kiowa Street in Colorado Springs, with gables and cupolas typical of the '80's. He had to sell it in a few years to try to keep afloat financially. (From the Pourtales autobiography Lessons Learned from Experience, *kindness of Colorado College.)*

north to Broadmoor in the south. The count decided to shoot the works, pledging the dairy farm and all else as security for a loan of two hundred and fifty thousand dollars which he obtained in New York from the London and New York Investment Company.

Then he began expanding Broadmoor into "Broadmoor City"— six hundred acres all told, with its own power plant and water system. Each acre lot was priced at fifteen hundred dollars or better. During that fall and winter of 1889-1890 he forced Colorado Springs to stop stealing his water, replaced the two thousand saplings with ten thousand, and refilled Cheyenne Lake. He promised twenty thousand dollars to the new electric streetcar company to extend its line from the Springs to Cheyenne Mountain and to build an underpass at the Nevada Avenue railroad crossing. Word reached him that a new men's club might be formed at Austin's Bluff north of town to enhance

To lure people to Broadmoor, Pourtales gave land on Lake Avenue to be used for the new Cheyenne Mountain Country Club. It opened in 1891, and still flourishes there, though it was remodeled in 1964. (Colorado Springs Pioneer Museum photo.)

real estate values out that way. He nipped it in the bud by giving the organizers a larger acreage at Broadmoor. And so the Cheyenne Mountain Country Club began, the lively indoor and outdoor games of which continue to this day.

To cap the climax, Count James announced plans to build a spectacular palace of pleasure called the Broadmoor Casino. Its design would recall the great casinos of Aix-les-Bains and Monte Carlo and it would have a fine French restaurant, a ballroom and, for certain sure, an excellent bar where a man could buy a drink without mumbling that it was for medicinal purposes. The whole Broadmoor City layout had as its focal point the ten-acre Cheyenne Lake, held in place by an earth dam twenty feet high and one hundred and ten feet thick. On a warm and sunny morning in April of 1890 Pourtales rode from the dairy farm to enjoy the lake's beauty against the red and green contour of

Cheyenne Mountain. To his horror, the water was missing. He found that it had leaked away through hundreds of prairie-dog holes.

He gathered all his milkmen and cheese makers and plugged the holes with clay. The lake was empty again within a week. More holes were plugged and the Broadmoor herd of sheep were pastured on the lake bed so that leaks would be closed by their tramping. Still the water drained off. At last Portales paid a contractor nearly twenty thousand dollars to coat the lake bed with special clay. The coating worked. But as the lake filled to the top, some of the rival North End realtors spread word that Pourtales was preparing Broadmoor for another Johnstown Flood. Everybody remembered that Pennsylvania disaster of May, 1889, when three thousand people drowned because a dam — just like this one, the rumor went — had collapsed. Pourtales worried for months before he found an answer to the slander. When he began building the Casino in February of 1891, he put it right on top of the dam. The flood talk died with this proof of his faith in the dam's stability.

But the fates remained unkind. Pourtales came down with tuberculosis and for eight weeks had to supervise the Casino's construction from a bed in a nearby shack. The weather was mild. The fifty-thousand-dollar birthday cake of a building went up rapidly. An eight-acre elliptical park was laid out along the front of the dam. The furniture came and Pourtales hired Rosner's famed Hungarian Band for the proposed June 1 opening. Willcox went to New York and had the good luck to engage maître d'hôtel W. A. Kelly, late of the Lotus Club, and the superb French chef Emile Hertzog, formerly of Delmonico's. Colorado newspapers were full of glowing Casino stories. A reporter's chance phrase for Broadmoor, "a sunny place for shady people," caught on and gave it a jaunty air.

Encouraged by these events, Count James got out of bed, feeling optimistic again. Perhaps he should have known better. M. Hertzog turned up and wouldn't so much as boil an egg except on his own *fourneau de cuisine,* which was lost in transit. Maître d'hôtel Kelly was in a vile humor because the Casino was not like the Lotus Club. When M. Hertzog's special stove arrived, the Casino chimney to which it was attached refused to draw. While Pourtales redesigned the Casino to fit the chimney, he had to postpone the grand opening until July 1, his thirty-eighth birthday.

The musicians in Rosner's band arrived from San Francisco punctually on June 1, to start drawing their salary of three hundred and seventy-five dollars a week. There were ten of them — Hungarians, Austrians, Germans. Five had American wives along, and the count soon found that each of the players and each of the wives had to have his or her special food. He took on an extra chef to keep them happy at mealtime.

Trouble, trouble, trouble. Still, the July 1 grand opening was a brilliant success. And the people of Colorado Springs showed real pride in the Casino and gave it support all through that month. They praised the decor, Rosner's music, the fine food and wines, the flashing fountain, the variety and excellence of the American cocktails. Pourtales began to hope that he was going to win his rash million-dollar Broadmoor gamble. His joy reached a peak on July 11, 1891, when the town's civic leaders, assembled by Tom Parrish, gave a banquet honoring Willcox and himself.

But the month's-end accounting revealed unhappy truths. Three thousand dollars' worth of Casino liquor was missing. The employees had put away the liquor during gay parties in the kitchen after the midnight closing. Careless waiters had tossed quantities of silverware out with the garbage, though Duncan Chisholm recovered some of it in the Broadmoor Dairy Farm pigpen, where the garbage was dumped. Maître d'hôtel Kelly had won the hearts of pretty women customers by giving them spoons engraved with the Pourtales coat of arms as tokens of his esteem. The count dismissed Kelly and his aides, and hired more honest if less expert help from Denver. Things did not improve during the remaining eight weeks of the summer. Nobody appeared to buy residential lots. The Broadmoor Casino was twenty-five thousand dollars in the hole when Pourtales closed down on October 1 and went off hunting with Berthe in the White River country of western Colorado.

The season of '92 brought no improvement. The count was saddened when William Willcox was killed in a riding accident. Duncan Chisholm told the count that he was resigning soon as manager of the Broadmoor Dairy Farm. Temperance people in Colorado Springs rebuked Pourtales in the *Gazette* letter column for calling Rosner's Sunday concerts at the Casino "sacred concerts," and then serving wine at them. Pourtales arranged an answering letter signed "Justice" which argued that the Casino's customers were mainly lungers who

In 1891, Count James built the spectacular Broadmoor Casino at Cheyenne Mountain (center building with carriages), along the lines of this artist's sketch. It stood on the dam of his lake exactly where the Broadmoor Hotel stands now. A photograph of the building, which burned down in July, 1897, is below. The count went broke before he could add the resplendent hotel shown on the other side of the lake, and the covered walks around the lake leading to it. (Photo above from the Pourtales book Lessons Learned from Experience, kindness of Colorado College. Hook photo below kindness of Robert E. McIntyre and the Broadmoor Hotel.)

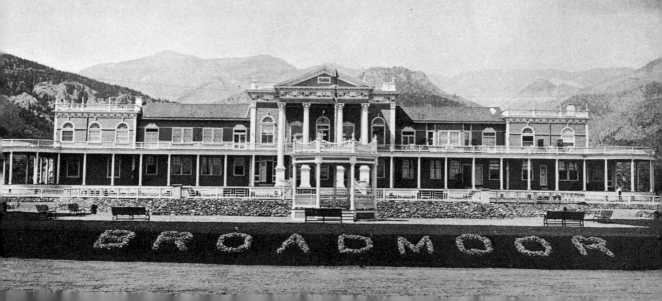

needed a drink even on Sunday to make their lives more bearable. To meet his payroll and mortgage interest, the count sold his downtown house to an old prospector named Sam Altman who had struck pay dirt at the alleged new gold camp of Cripple Creek on the other side of Pikes Peak. Then Pourtales raised thirty-five thousand dollars more with which to build a hotel facing Cheyenne Lake, directly across from the Casino.

This fresh money came from five young playboy friends of his who bought Willcox's share of Broadmoor and agreed to run the Casino while the count was busy elsewhere. They were full of ideas, and the results of their eager enterprise were spectacular. A lady balloonist gave a parachute demonstration and almost drowned when she fell in Cheyenne Lake. A tightrope artist with firecrackers in his act performed near the Casino and set the porch on fire. The partners held rowboat races and children's parties and musical soirees. They couldn't seem to find time to build the proposed Broadmoor Hotel, which was what they were supposed to be doing. And when, late in the season, Pourtales checked the unpaid Casino bar chits of his partners, they almost equaled their total investment.

Somehow Broadmoor City and the stately Casino bumbled along for another year. Then the mints of India stopped coining silver and the Panic of '93 began. As Colorado's main industry, silver mining, ceased, Pourtales opened the Casino for the summer but he could not stand the pressure of his creditors. On August 17, he had to give up. He turned over those two thousand four hundred Broadmoor acres, and everything he had created on them in seven years of nerve-wracking toil — dairy farm, Casino, Broadmoor City, Cheyenne Lake, saplings, the Tell bulls, the streetcar right-of-way — to the London and New York Investment company to satisfy its $250,000 mortgage. When he and Berthe moved back to town he left pieces of his heart along the full course of Spring Creek.

THOSE LAST TWO YEARS at the Casino would alone have been enough to send the count to his grave. But all the while he was leading two lives, both of them unendurable. His second life found him embroiled on the other side of Pikes Peak at the aforementioned gold camp of Cripple Creek. Gold camps were an old story in Colorado. All the high country was speckled with the ghosts of them. Hundreds of thousands of argonauts had been picking up the stuff in stream beds or blasting it out of rock since 1858 — at Central City and Idaho Springs, in South Park and Breckenridge, and south along the soaring Continental Divide all the way to the Silverton region of the San Juan Range. During thirty years, prospectors had poked over every inch of Pikes Peak on their way to real diggings elsewhere.

Wild rumors about Cripple Creek — its obscure promoters called it "the greatest gold camp on earth" — began in the spring of '91. As the summer wore on, the count's mining friends in the El Paso Club denounced the place as a hoax. There just could be no gold on Pikes Peak at this late date. Pourtales, of course, was the rankest of tyros. He had never even seen a gold mine. But he was desperate, and unable to resist a gamble, as we know. The bills he ran up to keep the Broadmoor Casino afloat piled higher. Pure gold lying on the ground! It wouldn't cost him anything to have a look, and it would be good to get away from Cheyenne Lake for a day or two.

On a bright golden September morning he donned his Bavarian hunting costume and rode the Colorado Midland train up Ute Pass around the great brown north face of the peak. He left the train after thirty-five miles, at the little cow town of Florissant. He rented a buckboard there and rode it twenty miles up the steep old cattle trail, south and east to the beautiful high pasture of gulches and round hills under Pikes Peak where Levi Welty had summered cattle for two decades. One of Welty's calves had lamed itself crossing the tiny stream and he had named the stream Cripple Creek.

Around a source spring of the stream Pourtales found "the greatest gold camp on earth." It consisted of Welty's log ranch house, a log store and a log "hotel" twenty feet square. A couple dozen mine owners lounged around whittling and spitting. Most of them seemed to be cowboys from Florissant and they did not seem to know how to develop their bonanzas. With their help the count examined placer diggings on Mineral Hill to the north and bought shares in two of them for a few dollars. He spent two sleepless nights in the "hotel" with fourteen overpoweringly odorous prospectors and then returned to Broadmoor, convinced that Cripple Creek was a sure-enough fraud.

And still he wondered. In November, after his White River hunting trip with Berthe, he went back to Cripple Creek, taking along his old friend Tom Parrish, who was something of a mining man. They found quarters in the Welty ranch house, owned now by George and Emma Carr of Florissant. Cheerful Emma, the only woman in the camp, rather liked the big master of Glumbowitz who informed her that she reminded him of those female sirens, the Lorelei. Emma returned the compliment by letting him sleep on her kitchen table. If he slept late she made her biscuits anyhow, propping apart the count's large feet so that she could get her dough board between them while Pourtales snored away. The count could sing with gusto, if not with accuracy. One night, he astounded the miners by presenting the score of *Fidelio,* singing all the parts himself.

For a week or so, Pourtales and Parrish climbed around Cripple's ten thousand acres. They avoided the surface gold placers this time, looking instead for veins in solid rock, especially a mile or two east and southeast on Bull Hill and Battle Mountain. They spent some hours with a carpenter who had built many houses in Colorado Springs. His name was Winfield Scott Stratton and he claimed to have something good in a Battle Mountain hole which he called the Independence. However Pourtales had hired an Aspen expert, Wolcott Newberry, for advice, and Newberry told him to forget about the Independence and every other hole in Cripple Creek with the dubious exception of a Bull Hill mine called the Buena Vista. Its owners were asking the absurd price of a hundred thousand dollars for it. The count dickered with them and bought the Buena Vista at last for two thousand dollars down, which was that much more than he and Parrish had on hand. The owners were to get seventy-eight thousand dollars more at the end of a year, plus twenty per cent royalty on the mine's production.

News of this Buena Vista sale came out in the Colorado papers on November 10, 1891. That date coincided with the low point in the camp's history. Even the Florissant cowboys were giving up "the greatest gold camp on earth" as a lost cause. The newspaper stories said nothing about the small down payment of two thousand dollars, reporting merely that Pourtales had paid eighty thousand dollars cash — an unimaginable sum for an unproven mine. The count was quoted as saying that the Buena Vista contained a million dollars' worth of gold in sight, and that the district had at least a hundred other claims of equal richness.

Because of the count's social prestige and the glamour of his name, the Buena Vista news changed everybody's attitude toward Cripple

Desperate for cash, Pourtales took a fling at the gold camp of Cripple Creek on the other side of Pikes Peak in its earliest days. He bet what little money he had left on the Buena Vista Mine, Bull Hill. That gamble did not pay off either. (Photo from the Pourtales book Lessons Learned from Experience, *kindness of Colorado College.)*

Creek overnight. Bankers and rich playboys from Colorado Springs and Denver sent engineers by the dozens up Levi Welty's steep trail from Florissant to the cow pasture. Nothing succeeds like success. The same cowboys who had almost abandoned their claims in October of '91 raised their asking prices for them in November ten and twenty times. The carpenter Winfield Scott Stratton, who had tried hard in the spring to exchange his Washington mine for five hundred dollars, unloaded it for eighty thousand dollars. Bob Womack, the actual discoverer of gold at Cripple Creek, had sold his half-interest in the El Paso Discovery Lodge for three hundred dollars. Now he watched its price rise to fifty thousand dollars and more.

The snowballing of confidence helped everyone up there except the two gamblers, Pourtales and Parrish, who had created the confidence with their Buena Vista purchase. All history shows that there is nothing quite like a gold rush for excitement, for joy, for heartbreak, for the spectacle of what happens when human beings ignore common sense, caution and moral scruples, and go flying along an unmarked course guided by hope alone. Count Pourtales, who was virtually bankrupt on two continents, saw the rainbow and saw his pot of gold at the foot of it. He set out in the usual frantic race of mining finance, raising his two-thousand-dollar down payment by selling pieces of the Buena Vista to Charlie MacNeill and other El Paso Club friends of his.

In January of 1892, he organized a stock company and peddled shares in the mine, as money was needed to dig out his alleged "million dollars worth of gold ore in sight" and get it shipped to Denver and refined in the mill there. Tom Parrish was out of his depth financially. Winfield Scott Stratton was absorbed in his Independence. Pourtales sought partners among members of the Cheyenne Mountain Country Club, including the handsome Philadelphian Spencer Penrose, who had arrived in Cripple Creek to run a branch of Charles L. Tutt's real estate company. Penrose and Tutt were tied up in a mine on Cripple Creek's Poverty Gulch. But the count did bring in Duncan Chisholm and Horace Devereux, the Colorado polo pioneer and former Princeton football star.

Through that spring and summer of '92, the money Pourtales raised never seemed to be quite enough. Today's great expectations became tomorrow's bad luck. High assays of Buena Vista ore did not prove out at the Denver smelter, indicating that the assays were wrong or that highgraders along the way were stealing the rich stuff and substituting dump rock. The vein in the mine kept pinching out or getting lost. Surrounding claims had to be bought to avoid lawsuits. The Buena Vista's miners got hurt or were hired away or asked more wages. Though the price of the stock rose a bit, Pourtales's percentage of ownership fell and fell. The question was, could he get the Buena Vista to start paying dividends while he still held control?

It turned out that he could not. In December of '92, he was forced to ask the Aspen silver millionaire, James J. Hagerman, to bail him out. When Hagerman bailed out a mine, he always wound up controlling it. He put in $225,000 and consolidated all Pourtales's Bull Hill properties as the Isabella Gold Mining Company. Hagerman picked the name Isabella because the year 1892 was the four hundredth anniversary of America's discovery by Columbus, grubstaked by Queen Isabella of Spain.

After the consolidation, the Buena Vista began to pay dividends and Pourtales's minority interest gave him a modest income. He and Berthe went off to Glumbowitz for the winter. As we have seen, they returned in June of '93 to their "sunny place for shady people" only to endure the agony of final defeat. For two years more, the count was in and out of town promoting a milling process and trying to set up a mill so that Cripple Creek ore could be treated near Colorado Springs instead of being sent to Denver. In January of 1896, he reached the end of that road. He sold his 125,000 Isabella shares for $62,500, took a last look at his Casino in stagnating Broadmoor City, and went on his way with the beautiful Berthe at his side. Instead of making a fortune for the greater glory of Glumbowitz and the Fatherland, he had lost something like two hundred thousand dollars.

So ENDED A FORGOTTEN DECADE in Pikes Peak history. Spencer Penrose's statue stands at the Broadmoor Hotel. Winfield Scott Stratton's statue is in the grounds of the Myron Stratton Home at the foot of Broadmoor. There is no statue of Count James Pourtales. Not one Broadmoor resident in fifty knows for whom Pourtales Road was named.

And yet it was Pourtales who showed the way, both at Broadmoor and at Cripple Creek. His purchase of the Buena Vista saved Cripple Creek from collapse by attracting new capital for development. Within two years, "the world's greatest gold camp" was proving itself to be just that. The boom continued at white heat for a quarter century. To date, the camp has produced nearly a billion dollars worth of gold at current prices. Its survival in '91 gave Winfield Scott Stratton the time he needed to trace the vein in his Independence. He sold it for eleven million dollars, the highest price ever paid to one person for a single mine of any kind.

In 1896, the count's friends Spencer Penrose, C. L. Tutt and Char-

Count James Pourtales drew up a very thorough plan for Broadmoor in 1890-1891 but he was a quarter-century ahead of time and he went broke. Spencer Penrose picked up that plan around 1915-1916, built the Broadmoor Hotel (central building in photo) in 1918, and pushed Broadmoor successfully as a residential area. After Penrose's death in 1939, the hotel was expanded in all directions to its present dimensions. But the lake just behind the hotel is the Cheyenne Lake which Pourtales built and the hotel sits on the dam of the lake exactly where Pourtales placed his casino. Cheyenne Mountain is mostly out of view at left. The central mountain is Mount Rosa (named for Isabella Bird's friend Rose Kingsley). (Robert E. McIntyre and Broadmoor Hotel photo.)

lie MacNeill followed his lead and managed to set up a profitable gold mill near Colorado Springs. When Stratton died in 1902, his estate bought Broadmoor City as an investment. Later Penrose made a vast copper fortune in Utah and bought Broadmoor City from the Stratton Estate. He moved the Casino off the count's dam in 1918, converted the Casino into a golf house, and built the Broadmoor Hotel on the dam. Residential lots sold rapidly thereafter, along Lake Avenue and Berthe Circle and the count's tree streets. Today few lots remain for sale on the rolling mesa of the Broadmoor Dairy Farm where the Tell boys had flirted with the heifers. The Broadmoor Hotel has burst like a skyrocket all over the banks of Cheyenne Lake to become one of the world's great palaces of hedonism.

The count failed at Pikes Peak. But be of good cheer. Soon after he left in '96, Spencer Penrose's geologist brother Dick sold him a tenth interest in a mine at Pearce, Arizona, the Commonwealth. Praises be! It produced thirty million dollars' worth of gold and silver before it was exhausted in 1905. Pourtales's share of the profits made up for his Pikes Peak loss and gave him a million dollars besides.

And so he returned with Berthe to Silesia in the role of conquering hero and proceeded to restore Glumbowitz along guidelines learned at Spring Creek. He died in 1908, aged fifty-five, cheery and stubborn to the last — and certain that a study of interest rates benefited a man more than any amount of Goethe, Schiller and Kant.

NOTES AND SOURCES

Scotsman on the Green

Mrs. Clyde (Mae Reed) Porter, of Kansas City, Missouri, spent twenty years delving into the life of Sir William Drummond Stewart. Much of my material has been gleaned gratefully and admiringly from *Scotsman in Buckskin* (Hastings House, New York, 1963), which she wrote with Odessa Davenport. Accounts of Mrs. Porter's discovery in 1935 of one hundred Alfred Jacob Miller sketches at the Peale Museum in Baltimore, of her detective work at Murthly, of her search for information about Sir William's adopted son Franc Nichols, are as exciting as her Stewart discoveries. Her enthusiasm for Miller's painting and her knowledge of Stewart led Bernard De Voto to make Sir William the central figure of his fur trade classic *Across the Wide Missouri* (Houghton Mifflin Co., Boston, 1947). Mrs. Porter found and encouraged the publication of Field's New Orleans *Picayune* articles of Stewart's 1843 trip, which became *Prairie and Mountain Sketches* (University of Oklahoma Press, Norman, 1957).

In 1964, my good Colorado Springs friend Maxwell McRoberts went to Murthly on my behalf and relayed to me much information about Sir William from Murthly's present owner, Steurt Fothringham.

I found more Stewart material in *Persimmon Hill,* by William Clark Kennerly (University of Oklahoma Press, Norman, 1948); *The Life and Adventures of James P. Beckwourth,* by T. D. Bonner (Harper and Brothers, New York, 1856); and *Narrative of a Journey Across the Rocky Mountains,* by John K. Townsend, as reprinted from the 1839 original in *Early Western Travels,* edited by R. G. Thwaites, Vol. XXI (Arthur H. Clark Co., Cleveland, 1904-1907). I read Stewart's *Altowan* in the Harper & Brothers 1846 edition. The second novel, *Edward Warren,* was published in London in 1854 by G. Walker.

As Shakespeare students know, Macbeth spoke of Birnam Wood removing to Dunsinane in *Macbeth,* Act V, scene 3.

The Travels of Prince Max

Prince Maximilian's study of the Upper Missouri, first published by subscription in German at Koblenz (1839-1840), was issued in a three-volume French edition at Paris (1840-1843), and then in a one-volume English edition translated from the German by H. Evans Lloyd and printed by Ackerman & Co. in London (1843-1844). The English title is *Travels in the Interior of North America.* The original Lloyd translation was bought in 1858 by the State Historical Society of Missouri at Columbia. This Lloyd translation of Max's text comprises Volumes XXII and XXIII of *Early Western Travels* (Arthur H. Clark Co., Cleveland, 1904-1907). Volume XXIV contains eighty-one reproductions of Bodmer's watercolors as they appeared originally. Some years ago, M. Knoedler & Co. of New York sent William Davidson to Neuwied where he discovered and purchased from Prince Max's descendants practically the entire results of Max's Upper Missouri tour. In 1962 the collection was acquired for the Northern Natural Gas Company of Omaha, Nebraska, by its chairman, John Merriam, as a public service to

Omaha and all the Missouri Valley. It was placed in the care of Omaha's Joslyn Art Museum, Eugene Kingman, director, where it is now on permanent exhibition as the Maximilian-Bodmer Collection, with Miss Mildred Goosman as curator. It is magnificent — certainly one of the greatest of treasures dealing with the American West. It includes 427 original watercolors by Bodmer, first editions of Maximilian's work in German, French and English, sixteen drawings and watercolors by the prince himself, and all his diaries, contracts, maps and handwritten texts.

Major Alexander Culbertson's impression of Prince Max is found in *Affairs at Fort Benton from 1831 to 1869* (from Lieutenant Bradley's journal), Volume III, Contributions to the Historical Society of Montana (State Publishing Co., Helena, 1900). There is a good description of Fort McKenzie in *Audubon and His Journals* (two vols.) by Maria R. Audubon and Elliott Coues (John C. Nimmo, London, 1898). You may recall that John James Audubon declined to accompany Sir William Drummond Stewart to Yellowstone in 1843, visiting the Upper Missouri instead.

Some data about Kenneth McKenzie, the so-called King of the Missouri, has been borrowed from *Forty Years a Fur Trader on the Upper Missouri* (two vols.) by Charles Larpenteur (Francis P. Harper, New York, 1898). Larpenteur asserts that in 1836 at Fort Union McKenzie discovered his pretty Cree wife in his own bed with a yellow-haired, twenty-year-old French-Canadian named Augustin Bourdonnais. McKenzie grabbed his "sprig of a shillelah" and went at the man with a cuckold's fury. Bourdonnais retreated from the house so fast that "the tail of his surtout (frock coat) stretched horizontally to its full extent." Later, Bourdonnais staged a one-man attack on the fort and McKenzie had him shot.

An interesting appraisal of the paintings of Alfred Jacob Miller, Karl Bodmer and George Catlin appears in James Thomas Flexner's *That Wilder Image* (Little, Brown and Co., Boston, 1962).

ORDEAL OVER YELLOWHEAD

The quotations in this chapter are taken from *Cheadle's Journal of a Trip Across Canada, 1862-1863*, with introduction and notes by A. G. Doughty and Gustave Lanctot (Graphic Publishers, Ltd., Ottawa, Canada, 1931); and from *The North West Passage by Land*, by Viscount Milton and Dr. Cheadle, *Being the Narrative of an Expedition from the Atlantic to the Pacific Undertaken with the view of Exploring a route across the Continent to British Columbia through British Territory by one of the Northern Passes in the Rocky Mountains* (Cassell, Petter and Galpin, London, published June 1, 1865, with at least five editions thereafter). The latter book seems to have been printed privately at first, under the title *An Expedition across the Rocky Mountains into British Columbia by the Yellow Head or Leather Pass*. Though Lord Milton is listed as joint author, he had nothing to do with the writing. Dr. Cheadle dedicated the book to the mothers involved, "The Countess Fitzwilliam and Mrs. Cheadle, who took so great an interest in the success of the Travellers." This second book has a strong political slant, castigating Hudson's Bay Company for holding back the development of Rupert's Land (Hudson Bay drainage) and urging the unification of all of Canada as "a means of more rapid and direct communication with China & Japan."

The brief data about Lord Southesk is from *Saskatchewan and the Rocky Mountains, A Diary and Narrative of Travel, Sport and Adventure during a Journey through the Hudson's Bay Company's territories in 1859 and 1860* by the Earl of Southesk (Edmonston and Douglas, Edinburgh, 1875). Southesk revealed himself to be a delightful observer and an incredibly avid reader. During his rugged circuit he managed to plow through at least five plays of Shakespeare and Bulwer-Lytton's *My Novel*. The Rocky River–Brazeau River area of eastern Jasper Park abounds with landmarks which he named, such as Southesk Pass, Mount Southesk and Southesk River. Mount Lindsay and Mount Balcarres honor his friend Lord Lindsay, Earl of Balcarres. Mount Toma, Mount La Grace and Mount McBeath were named for his pack-train employees. Mount Dalhousie memorializes the eleventh Earl of Dalhousie. There is even a Thistle Mountain near Jasper Park's east border, since Southesk was a Knight of the Thistle.

It may be stressed that Mount Robson is the highest mountain only in the Canadian Rockies, not the highest in Canada. Mount Logan in the Yukon is Canada's highest, at 19,850 feet above sea level. When Milton's party reached the North Thompson, they were barely a hundred miles as the crow flies southeast of Barkerville and the Cariboo, but the icefields of the soaring Premier group of mountains (Mount Stanley Baldwin, etc.) intervened and the travelers would have perished if they had tried to cross them. Today a motor road of sorts and the tracks of the Canadian National Railway follow the three-hundred-mile route which they took from Jasper, Yellowhead Pass and Tete Jaune Cache to Kamloops, including the awful forest passage of sixty miles or so between present Thunder River Station and Vavenby Station. In 1962 Mount Robson Motor Village at Mount Robson, British Columbia, issued a bulletin on this road, reading in part: "Much of the road is on the old tote road used by horse and mule drawn freight wagons to haul supplies for the construction of the Canadian Northern and Grand Trunk Pacific railroads (now the Canadian National), in the early 1900's. These dirt portions have been little changed since that time, and in places are narrow and winding." The Porte d'Enfer Canyon section of the present road, near where Bucephalus fell off the cliff, is described this way: "First 18 miles very narrow and winding, side hill road. Have to back up to pass other cars in places. Slow going to Avola. You may find some water on the road on the lower end of this section during high water, or when the beaver have dammed the culverts."

The "Overlanders" party of Cariboo argonauts was the first amateur group of record to reach Kamloops from Yellowhead Pass, arriving on October 13, 1862. They rafted down the North Thompson, the flowing condition of which must have been much less dangerous than it was a year later. Among them was the highly pregnant Mrs. August Schubert, who called for a tent as they floated into Kamloops and produced a daughter then and there on the shore — the first white child born in interior British Columbia.

Back in England, Milton and Cheadle heard that the Assiniboine and his wife and son returned to Fort Pitt and were there accused of having eaten their employers. The residents assumed that that was how they got Bucephalus and other things which the dudes had given to them.

A GRAND DUKE FOR DENVER

The American tour of Grand Duke Alexis Alexandrovitch, to give him his full name, is a researcher's delight. I found newspaper accounts in January, 1872, copies of the *New York Times*, of *The London Times*, the *Rocky Mountain News*, the *Denver Tribune*, and the *Colorado Transcript* (Golden). The Kansas State Historical Society's *Comprehensive Index to Publications 1875-1930* led me to J. A. Hadley's *His Buffalo Hunt*, and Chalkley McCarty Beeson's *A Royal Buffalo Hunt*. At the Western Collection of the Denver Public Library I picked up data in Bayard Henry Paine's *Pioneers, Indians and Buffaloes;* in M. A. Otero's *My Life on the Frontier*, and in DeWitt Harris Winget's

Anecdotes of Buffalo Bill — all privately printed. Winget wrote that he posed as a bootblack at Camp Alexis and walked off with the grand duke's boots, which he returned polished but with the spurs missing. Winget snitched them for souvenirs. I looked at Buffalo Bill's biographies and was helped especially by Don Russell's *The Lives and Legends of Buffalo Bill* (University of Oklahoma Press, Norman, 1960). The description of Alexis which appeared in Frank Leslie's *Illustrated Newspaper* on February 10, 1872, was a clumsy parody. For the grand duke's later years I dipped into *The Court of Russia in the 19th Century* (Methuen & Co., London, 1908), and *Behind the Veil at the Russian Court* by Count Paul Vassili (John Lane, New York, 1914). There may be some fact in these gossipy books.

The site of Camp Alexis, on Red Willow Creek, is reached today by driving ten miles northeast from the little county seat of Hayes Center, Nebraska, to the Clifford Ranch and getting permission from the ranch's amiable co-owner, Walter Bower, to walk a mile or so in to the spot. The campsite is quite near the Hayes Center Recreation Area. In 1931, the Nebraska Historical Society put up a red sandstone marker near the great cottonwoods where Alexis had smoked the peace pipe with Spotted Tail, Sheridan and Custer. It is a heavenly spot still, with bobwhites whistling in the thick grass and the frost daisies blooming amid the soapweed and red-fruited cactus. The little sandstone marker — rarely visited any more — shows a buffalo at the top. Below it are these words:

> COMMEMORATING
> CAMP   GROUND
> FAMOUS BUFFALO HUNT
> GRAND DUKE ALEXIS
> OF RUSSIA 1872
> SPONSORED BY
> BUFFALO BILL CODY
> GEN. SHERIDAN
> GEN. CUSTER   CAP. HAYS
> CAP. EGAN   WITH SPOT-
> TED TAIL AND TRIBE
> AND OTHER NOTED
> BUFFALO HUNTERS AS GUESTS

The back of the monument contains the legend: *Buffalo Bill died Jan. 10, 1917. Last of the Old West.*

The American House at Sixteenth and Blake Street, Denver, which John W. Smith built in 1868, was torn down in 1933. Alexis's visit was the great event of its sixty-five-year career. The wallpaper of Room 25 sold at a very high price during demolition. Two of the Denver Republicans who handled details of the grand duke's stay had troubles thereafter. President Grant removed Governor McCook in 1873 for alleged fraud in Indian affairs, reappointed him in 1874 and let him go for good some months later when Colorado went Democratic to protest his regime. U.S. Marshal Shaffenburg was caught collecting money on false subsistence vouchers for prisoners and went to the penitentiary. The sister of Mrs. McCook, Mrs. Charles Adams, whose low-necked dress put a gleam in Alexis's eyes at the ball, was the wife of General Adams. He became a national hero in 1879 by rescuing Arvilla and Josie Meeker from Ute Indians who held them hostage after the Meeker massacre.

LOVE IN THE PARK

Altogether, Isabella Bird wrote seventeen letters about her Colorado adventure to Henrietta between September 9 and December 11, 1873, and toned them down for publication during 1878 in the magazine, *Leisure Hour.* She edited them still more to make her book, *A Lady's Life in the Rocky Mountains,* which John Murray of London published in 1879. Putnam published the first American edition that year and there have been many American editions since, including that of the University of Oklahoma Press, with printings in 1960, 1962 and 1965. Miss Bird told a lot about Mountain Jim in the book but did not disclose the extent of her romance with him. In 1952, the John Murray magazine the *Cornhill* published an Isabella Bird article by Dorothy Middleton, of the Royal Geographic Society, a well-known English writer on exploration. Harold M. Dunning of Longmont, Colorado, read the article, which mentioned the existence of unpublished Bird letters. He spoke of the letters to Mrs. Louisa Ward Arps, and to Miss Ina Aulls of the Denver Public Library's Western Collection. Miss Aulls wrote to the present John Murray in London and was overjoyed to receive from him for the Western Collection photostatic copies of most of Isabella's original letters to Henrietta. They covered the period October 19 to December 4, 1873, and contained passages about her love affair with Jim which she deleted in her book. Mrs. Arps typed up the handwritten letters and published "Letters from Isabella Bird" in the 1955-1956 *Colorado Quarterly* (University of Colorado). The quotations used in this chapter are taken from Mrs. Arps's transcript of the letters. Mrs. Arps's "Tracking Isabella Bird," published in the December, 1956, *Roundup* of the Denver Westerners, gave me more data. In 1965, Dorothy Middleton sent me new Bird material and put me on to her delightful book, *Victoria Lady Travellers* (E. P. Dutton & Co., New York, 1965), which has a section on Miss Bird.

I had no trouble getting accurate data on Isabella and Jim's route to the top of Longs Peak. My Colorado Springs neighbor, Paul Nesbit, has climbed the mountain at least *a hundred and fifty* times. His excellent *Longs Peak: Its Story and Climbing Guide* is the standard work. He told me about Jim's Grove, the Dog's Lift and all the other things Isabella encountered.

Much of Griff Evans's ranch is now under the water forming the south side of Estes Lake. The beauty of Estes Park has been disgracefully marred by the hundred-foot towers of a power line down the middle of it. But Isabella's trail in, State Route 66 from Lyons, is as lovely as ever. Jim's cabin stood near the buildings of today's Meadowdale Ranch, some four miles from Estes. Isabella left the park for good by the trail which became the Pole Hill stage road to Loveland. The shorter Estes Park–Loveland road through Big Thompson Canyon, today's U.S. 34, was not built until 1903. I am indebted to B. R. Newkirk of Roosevelt National Forest for sending me a sketch of this Pole Hill Road past Panorama Peak, Rattlesnake Park and Pinewood School. A few miles of it just east of Estes is open to the public but the long middle part is closed, being on private land.

Isabella's South Park trip from Colorado Springs is easily followed. Take U.S. 24 west up Ute Pass a mile and a half beyond Divide, and fork left on the gravel Twin Rocks Road, which rejoins U.S. 24 at Florissant. The Twin Rocks Road still supplies the fine views Isabella mentioned — the Sangre de Cristo Range to the south, and the Continental Divide westward. Just beyond the Platte River bridge at Lake George, leave U.S. 24 and drive north on the charming Tarryall River Road to U.S. 285 and to Como, where in summer the Boreas (Breckenridge) Pass road approximates Isabella's rugged route to the Tarryall's source and the top of the Continental Divide. Returning to Como, you will move east over Kenosha Pass on U.S. 285 to Webster (near Hall's Gulch) and to Denver pretty much along the route Isabella took in '73.

THE DUDE FROM LIMERICK

My view of the fourth Earl of Dunraven is based on his own writings, beginning with his remarkable book, *The Great Divide, Travels in the Upper Yellowstone in the Summer of 1874*. I used the second edition (Chatto & Windus, London, 1876). The earl went to the English artist Valentine W. Bromley for illustrations, giving him photos of Rockies scenes, and his own rough sketches of particular incidents to give Bromley the idea. *The Great Divide* came out when books on hunting in the West were in huge demand, much as science fiction is today. Of its reception, Dunraven wrote later, "Some clergy bought *The Great Divide* supposing it to be a theological work expounding the separation of the sheep and the goats; but, if I remember right, the book did not rely much on that, and had a pretty good sale."

Some Dunraven data came from his "A Colorado Sketch" (*Appleton's Journal*, New York, November, 1880). There was more in his *Canadian Nights, Being Sketches and Reminiscences of Life and Sport in the Rockies, the Prairies and the Canadian Woods* (Charles Scribner's Sons, New York, 1914). The earl's adventures were summarized in his autobiography, *Past Times and Pastimes*, in two volumes (Hodder and Stoughton, London, 1922) — a mellow work of great charm, written four years before he died.

I used also *Notes on Sport and Travel* by the earl's hunting companion, Dr. George Henry Kingsley (Macmillan and Co., London, 1900). As we noted in Chapter 5, Kingsley advised Isabella Bird to visit Estes, but neither Kingsley nor Dunraven mentioned Miss Bird in their writings. They may have come to dislike her because in her book, *A Lady's Life*, she berated them for revealing the whereabouts of Estes in a magazine article which they wrote for the *Field*. Then, too, the two sportsmen had little sympathy for her hero, Mountain Jim Nugent.

I followed the Dunraven party through Yellowstone Park with the help of *Report of a Reconnaissance from Carroll, Montana Territory, on the Upper Missouri to the Yellowstone Park and Return in the Summer of 1875*, by William Ludlow (Washington, Government Printing Office, 1876). I found Dunraven data in *Over Hill and Dale*, in two volumes, by Harold Marion Dunning (Johnson Publishing Co., Boulder, Colorado, 1956 and 1962); in *The Earl, the Artist and Estes Park* by Dorothy Dengler (1956 Brand Book, Denver Westerners, 1957); in *Denver in Slices* by Louisa Ward Arps (Sage Books, Denver, 1959); and in articles by Hazel E. Johnson, published in *Greeley* (Colorado) *Sunday Journal*, June 19 and June 26, 1960.

Since Lord Dunraven died without male issue, his title and estates in Ireland and Wales passed to a cousin. Our fourth earl's daughter, Aileen May, married the thirteenth Earl of Meath in 1908, and their son and daughter-in-law, the present Earl and Countess of Meath, have been most helpful in supplying Dunraven pictures. Their twenty-year-old daughter, the Lady Lavinia Brabazon, came to Colorado on a Greyhound bus from New York in 1965 just to see Estes Park. I am indebted to Irene M. Spry of London, author of *The Palliser Expedition*, for putting me in touch with the Meaths and for telling me of John Palliser's visits to Adare when the fourth earl was a child.

Mrs. Alys Freeze, head of the Western History Department, Denver Public Library, conducted a search of her own for Dunraven material, and had word from Sir Desmond Fitzgerald (the Knight of Glin), a grandnephew of the earl's. Sir Desmond reported from Ireland that "letters and effects of Lord Dunraven were sunk when his yacht Valkyrie III was run down in the Clyde." Mrs. Freeze had a second letter from Sir Roy Harrod, nephew of Valentine Bromley (Dunraven's illustrator), stating that the Bromley family has no Dunraven letters or journals in its possession.

Theodore Whyte built the English Hotel with the aid of a carpenter imported from England, John T. Cleave. Cleave took land near the hotel but could not stand the guests' racket so Dunraven gave him a tract further away. That Cleave tract is where the town of Estes Park stands now. In 1886, Theodore Whyte, a widower, married Lady Maude Ogilvy, daughter of the Earl of Airlie. They set up housekeeping in Dunraven's Fish Creek cottage. Lady Maude's brother, Lyulph Gilchrist Stanley Ogilvy, was a famous Colorado character for half a century. During most of that time he wrote a farm column for the *Denver Post* under the by-line Lord Ogilvy.

The English Hotel was renamed the Estes Park Hotel in 1893. It burned down on August 4, 1911. A disgruntled bellhop was said to have set fire to it. Dunraven's hunting lodge in Dunraven Glade is long gone, and so is the whiskey, probably. Griff Evans's ranch house was removed in 1948 when the space it occupied was flooded in the creation of Lake Estes, a storage reservoir in the Bureau of Reclamation's Colorado–Big Thompson irrigation and power project. Only the Fish Creek cottage still stands. It is called Camp Dunraven and is owned by the Camp Fire Girls.

O TEMPORA! O MORES!

The author of this book and his wife spent a very happy week in the library of the North Dakota Historical Society at Bismarck wading through the Society's wealth of De Mores materials, including letters, clippings, bills, and family scrapbooks, which the couple pasted up in the early 1880's. They read also the marquis's complete file of A. T. Packard's the *Bad Lands Cowboy*, from its first issue early in '83 to its last on December 23, 1886. The researchers were helped in every way by Miss Margaret Rose and her staff, including Miss Mary Halloran especially. More help came from the superintendent of the Historical Society, Ray H. Mattison, a former National Park Service historian who is the authority on the Little Missouri Bad Lands.

Basic data was found in Arnold O. Goplen's "The Career of Marquis de Mores," which appeared originally in *North Dakota History*, Vol. 13, Nos. 1 and 2, January-April, 1946. More data came from Charles Droulers's sympathetic biography, *Le Marquis de Mores* (published in French by Librairie Plon, Paris, 1932) and Usher L. Burdick's *Marquis de Mores at War in the Bad Lands* (Fargo, North Dakota, 1930). A fine study of De Mores's political career was found in Robert F. Byrnes's "The First National Socialist," in *Review of Politics*, Vol. 12, No. 3, July, 1950.

It is not known precisely how the marquis and his father-in-law, Baron von Hoffmann, set up the Northern Pacific Refrigerator Car Company or what their exact losses were. The assumption has always been that they lost something over a million dollars, with the marquis contributing $400,000 out of Medora's half-million-dollar dowry. It is possible that Hoffmann lost very little. When he closed the plant in '86, he seems to have retained for himself twenty thousand acres of wheat land around Bismarck which the marquis had bought for less than fifty thousand dollars. Its value would have increased hugely in a decade or so. Though the marquis failed, his packing-plant scheme was sound. In this day of heavy irrigation, many Great Plains areas can provide enough feed to fatten cattle near their birthplace — on wheat and sugar beet tops, for instance. Such cattle are slaughtered in the same area.

After the marquis's death, his widow paid the bills to keep the chateau on the hill above Little Missouri exactly as it had been when they left it in 1886. Some business buildings, the little Catholic chapel in Medora, and the empty packing plant were maintained too. The plant burned down on March 17, 1907, leaving only the great brick chimney. When the marquise died in Cannes in 1921, her son Louis, who had become the Duke de Vallombrosa, continued maintenance until 1936, when he gave the chateau, the packing-plant site, and one hundred and thirty acres of land around them to the North Dakota Historical Society. In the next few years, the properties were restored into public memorials by the Historical Society, the National Park Service, the State Parks Committee, and the Civilian Conservation Corps. Today the chateau with its original furnishings is open to the public daily under the management of Mr. and Mrs. Harry Roberts. The packing-plant site is marked on an excellent diagram at the entrance showing where everything was in the early 1880's.

A charming feature of Medora is De Mores Memorial Park, a landscaped area some one hundred and fifty feet square, bounded by a natural stone wall and iron pickets and shaded by Russian olive and cottonwood trees. Its paths lead to P. M. Poisson's bronze statue of the marquis in his cowboy clothes, somewhat larger than life size. The statue was cast in Paris by F. Barbedienne and given to the town by the Duke de Vallombrosa. Below the statue is a bas-relief head representing the marquise. The inscription on the base reads:

IN MEMORY OF
ANTOINE MANCA DE VALLOMBROSA
MARQUIS DE MORES
LIEUTENANT FRENCH CAVALRY
BORN IN PARIS 1858
KILLED IN NORTH AFRICA 1896
AND HIS WIFE
MEDORA
WHO FOUNDED THIS TOWN IN 1883

After De Mores's death, his political friends had a statue made of him which they hoped to erect at the gates of La Villette, in the slaughterhouse quarter of Paris, but the Paris Municipal Council refused them permission. Family records do not reveal whether this statue is the same as that in Medora. The town lies a hundred and thirty miles west of Bismarck on Interstate 10, beyond the Heart River valley. As the next chapter shows, it has added historical interest because Theodore Roosevelt ranched in the region at the same time De Mores was there.

One last note. Nobody in Medora today believes that the marquis killed Riley Luffsey, though he took the responsibility for it. According to local hearsay, Jerry Paddock confessed on his deathbed that he fired a shot at Luffsey from across the river and that shot could have killed him.

THE MAKING OF A PRESIDENT

Tons of books have been written about Theodore Roosevelt, in addition to the million words he wrote about himself. Every day of his life seems to have been accounted for, though debates arise as to whether something happened at two or three o'clock of an afternoon. For this chapter, I have relied on Hermann Hagedorn's classic *Roosevelt in the Bad Lands* (Houghton Mifflin Co., Boston and New York, 1921) and *Theodore Roosevelt, the Formative Years* by Carleton Putnam (Charles Scribner's Sons New York.

1958). I found much data also in Ray H. Mattison's studies for the State Historical Society of North Dakota, including *Roosevelt's Dakota Ranches* and *Ranching in the Dakota Bad Lands.* For bits of color I am indebted to *Bill Sewall's Story of T.R.* by William Wingate Sewall (Harper and Brothers, New York and London, 1919) and *Ranching with Roosevelt* by Lincoln Lang (J. B. Lippincott Co., Philadelphia and London, 1926). Roosevelt himself wrote marvelously well in his mid-twenties. I was particularly inspired and instructed by his *Hunting Trips of a Ranchman* (G. P. Putnam's Sons, New York, 1885) and his *Ranch Life and the Hunting Trail,* with fine illustrations by Frederic Remington (Century Co., New York, 1888). I found flavorsome correspondence and anecdotes in the Roosevelt file at the State Historical Society Library in Bismarck.

I have discussed in my De Mores notes the marquis's chateau and other De Mores landmarks in Medora. It is astonishing that such an out-of-the-way spot can boast *two* great tourist attractions, plus much restoration of Medora itself by Harold Schafer of Bismarck. Much of the Little Missouri Bad Lands which Roosevelt knew can be seen by car in the north and south units of Theodore Roosevelt National Memorial Park. Roosevelt's two ranches did not touch either of these units, but he had to ride through the south unit to get to the Elkhorn and he got very close to the north unit during his adventure with the boat thieves.

Park headquarters and the Roosevelt museum are at Medora, and so is the cabin which Sylvane Ferris and Bill Merrifield built at the Maltese Cross. Joe Hild owns the Maltese Cross Ranch and he doesn't mind if visitors hunt up his place, a few miles south of Medora down a back road. There is nothing left at the site of the Elkhorn Ranch, some thirty-three miles north down the Little Missouri from Medora Park headquarters. The road is paved for several miles beyond headquarters within the south unit, but after that it is rough and dusty and lonely. The Elkhorn site is a small island of Park property, and to reach it by car you have to drive across a ford of the Little Missouri, and that isn't possible at times of high water. My wife and I got to the Elkhorn because we had the luck to stop at the One Equals One Ranch of Mr. and Mrs. Leslie Connell, across the river from it. They put us in their pickup and hauled us to the river's edge and it was easy to wade across to the big cottonwoods where the ranch house had stood.

Now and then someone suggests that Roosevelt didn't spend enough time in the Bad Lands to become much of a cowboy. Well, a rough tabulation shows that he made twelve visits to the region between September, 1883, and the fall of 1887, spending a total of something close to six hundred and seventy days there, most of that time in the saddle.

Perhaps you wonder, as Roosevelt wondered, how the Bad Lands got the way they are. Wilson M. Laird, North Dakota State geologist, has explained it. As the Rocky Mountains lifted through the dried-up ocean eons ago, the rivers of present Montana and Wyoming washed seabed sediments eastward to form the northern plains. Heavy sediments settled near the mountains. The lighter flour-stuff — clay, lignite and such — floated hundreds of miles east to make the prairies of eastern Montana and the Dakotas. The Missouri, the Yellowstone and their branches, including the Little Missouri, drained north to Hudson Bay in those days. But the Ice Age came and went, shunting the Missouri so that it flowed south into the Mississippi.

The Little Missouri, rising on the prairie of northeastern Wyoming near present Devil's Tower National Monument, had been a branch of the Yellowstone. After the glaciers of the Ice Age had scrambled the topography, it ran four hundred miles into the Missouri instead of into the Yellowstone. The altitude of its Missouri mouth was hundreds of feet lower than its Yellowstone mouth. But it was easy for the Little Missouri to compensate for the difference in altitudes by cutting a gash for itself through the soft flour-stuff of the prairie. The Little Missouri Bad Lands resulted — one hundred and fifty miles of them, winding along with the river in a south-to-north gash averaging twenty miles wide. The erosion still goes on, but the rain does most of it now as it flows from the clay sides of the gash into the river.

THE COUNT OF BROADMOOR

During the past decade I have touched on Count James Pourtales's career many times in books and articles, basing some of my impressions on items of the period in the *Colorado Springs Gazette*. The standard source is the charming book which the Count wrote in German about his Pikes Peak adventure for his relatives at the turn of the century with the title *Durchlebte Erfahrungen*. The book was published in 1955 by the Colorado College in a fine English translation prepared by Margaret Woodbridge Jackson and entitled *Lessons Learned from Experience*. Spencer Penrose's estate, El Pomar Foundation, paid for that publication. The count's foreword concluded: "Work is a blessing and will harm no one. We all came to this earth equally naked. First consider, then dare. Do not be a monkey, be an eagle. Always remember that you are a German and will remain such; that even if you live in foreign lands for years, your roots will remain at home."

Nothing remains of the old Broadmoor Dairy Farm buildings — there were a dozen of them — except bits of metal and building material among the Spanish bayonet. Visitors to Colorado Springs can reach the headquarters site by driving out South Nevada Avenue and through the braided intersection on State Route 115 to the intersection at the top of the hill, half a mile from the braided intersection. A *left-hand* turn here leads to the Myron Stratton Home and Winfield Scott Stratton's statue. A *right* turn puts you on Cheyenne Mountain Road. The dairy farm buildings began about a quarter of a mile west along this road, on the right, between the road and the present dam end of Stratton Reservoir (a later damming of Spring Creek). Cheyenne Mountain Road runs into Pourtales Road half a mile further west, and Pourtales Road leads to the Broadmoor Golf Club, Broadmoor Hotel and Spencer Penrose's statue. Cheyenne *Mountain* Road should not be confused with plain Cheyenne Road, which borders Broadmoor along Cheyenne Creek on the north.

The big Casino which Pourtales built burned down in July, 1897. The London and New York Investment Company replaced it a year later by a smaller Casino. It is this second Casino which Penrose moved in 1918 from the dam of Cheyenne Lake to use as a golf club. It serves as the Broadmoor Golf Club still.

The portrait which Anne Parrish made of Count Pourtales hangs over the main fireplace of the Cheyenne Mountain Country Club on Lake Avenue today. Anne and Tom Parrish produced a remarkable child, also named Anne Parrish, who would grow up to write *The Perennial Bachelor* and other distinguished novels.

The name of Sebastian Schlesinger, Berthe de Pourtales's first husband, interested me since this Schlesinger was a Bostonian and Berthe's father had taught at Harvard. So I wrote the historian Arthur M. Schlesinger, Jr., President Kennedy's aide, who is of Harvard and Boston. Mr. Schlesinger replied: "Sebastian Schlesinger was no known relative. My father's father came from Germany in 1860 and settled in Ohio. When we came to Massachusetts in 1924, the Sebastian Schlesinger family was well established in Brookline with the result that Boston is the only place where the name is properly pronounced, but no family ties appeared to exist."

INDEX

Page numbers in italic refer to illustrations.

ADAMS, MRS. CHARLES, 109, 278

Agassiz, Alexander E., 250

Alexis Alexandrovitch, Grand Duke of Russia, *96, 103, 105, 108, 113, 114, 116,* 277-278; background as Romanoff, 95-97; visits New York City 1871, 97; Washington visit and Western trip arranged, 98-100; to Camp Alexis (Neb.), 101; Nebraska buffalo hunt with Cody and Custer, 101-104; Denver visit, 106-110; Colorado hunt, 111-115; return to Russia, later career, 115-117

Altowan (Stewart's first novel), 11, 12, *14,* 22, 25

American Fur Company (AFC), 6, 35, 38-64

America's Cup race, 176

Ames, Mary Clemmer, 98

Arthur, President Chester A., 226

Ashley, General William H., 7, 23, 37

Assiniboine (AFC steamer), 40, 62, 64; Prince Max's trip on, 47-50

Assiniboine, the. *See* Battenotte, Louis

Astor, John Jacob, 6

Audubon, John James, 26, 276

Bad Lands Cowboy (Medora newspaper) 198, 205, 245, 281

Bates, Mayor (of Denver), 108, 112

Battenotte, Louis (the Assiniboine), *77, 85, 89,* 277; guides Milton to Kamloops, 78-90; in Victoria, 92

Beeson, Chalkley McCarty, 112, 115, 275; suggests Alexis's Colorado hunt, hired as guide, 111

Bell, Dr. William A., 137

Bennett, James Gordon, 99

Bierstadt, Albert, 171, *172,* 175; story of Longs Peak painting, *173;* to Estes Park with Dunraven 1876, 174

Bird, Isabella Lucy, *120,* 150, 156, 279-280; visits New Zealand, Hawaii 1872-1873, 119-121; to Colorado and Estes Park 1873, 121-126; Evans Ranch and Mountain Jim, 127-129; climbs Longs Peak, 130-133; to Denver and Colorado Springs, 135-136; rides around Pikes Peak, 137-140; last weeks at Estes Park, 141-144; later life, 145

Bishop, Dr. John, marries Isabella Bird, 145

Blaine, James G., 226, 228, 235

Bodmer, Karl (Charles), *45,* 275, 276; to St. Louis with Prince Max 1832-1833, 35-37; to Fort Pierre (Dakota), 38-47; at Fort Clark (Dakota), 48; arrives Fort Union (present Mont.), 50; on the *Flora,* 52; at Fort McKenzie (Mont.), 53-56; down Missouri 1834, 58; later career, member Barbizon school, 64-65

Bogstick, Mahogany, 159, 162

Bonneville, Captain Louis Eulalie de, 12, 17

Boteler, Fred, 160, 162, 163, *164,* 165, 170

Bourdonnais, Augustin, 276

Brady, Mathew, 98

Braunsberg, Baron (Prince Max's alias), 37, 62

Brazeau, J. E., 58

Brevoort House (New York City dude rendezvous), 148, 170

Bridger, Jim, 6, 22, 23, 28, 159; at 1833 rendezvous, 12; with Stewart to Taos 1833-1834, 15; Dr. Whitman removes arrowhead, 18

Bridger Wilderness Area (near Pinedale, Wyo.), 11, 23

Broadmoor Casino (Colorado Springs), 260, 261-264, *263,* 269, 271, 283

Broadmoor City, 259-264, 269, 271; laid out by Pourtales 1889, 258

Broadmoor Dairy Farm, 252-256, *253*, 262, 271, 284

Broadmoor Hotel, 176, 247, 264, *270*, 271

Bromley, Valentine W., 145, 281

Bruneau, Athanese, 75, 77

Brunswick Hotel (New York City dude rendezvous), 186, 204, 215

Bucephalus (Cheadle's horse), 74, *82*, 85-92, *85*, *86*, 277; naming of, 73; mountain named for, 83

Burnsted, Edward, steals Roosevelt boat, 241-244, *243*

Butler, General Benjamin Franklin, 69

Byers, William N. (editor, *Rocky Mountain News*), 106, 107, 110, 129, 136

CAMBRIDGE UNIVERSITY (England), 67, 68, 69, 72, 78, 92, 162

Campbell, Robert, 6, 12, 21, 40; heads RMF train to 1833 rendezvous, 7; at 1834 rendezvous, 16

Cariboo Gold Fields (British Columbia), 67, 68, 80, 92, 277

Carow, Edith Kermit. *See* Roosevelt, Edith

Carr, Emma and George, 266

Catacazy, Count (Russian ambassador with Alexis), 98

Catlin, George, 38, 40, 64, 65, 276

Chalmers, Thomas, 122, 124

Charbonneau, Baptiste (Sacajawea's son), 28

Charbonneau, Toussaint (Sacajawea's husband), *45*, 48, 60

Charpiot's Restaurant and Hotel (Denver), 107, 136, 153

Cheadle, Dr. Walter Butler, *77*, *82*, *86*, *89*, 165, 276-277; ancestry, early career, 67-68; meets Milton, 68; Liverpool to Minnesota 1862, 67-72; to Fort Garry (Winnipeg), 72; to Fort Carlton, 73-75; winters at Jolie Prairie, 76; over Yellowhead Pass to Fraser River, 80-85; accident at Canoe River, 86-88; hunger on North Thompson, 88-90; arrives Kamloops, B.C., 90; returns to England 1864, later career, 90-92

Cheyenne Mountain Country Club (Colorado Springs), *260*, 268, 284

Chisholm, Duncan, *257*, 258, 262, 268

Chouteau, Pierre, Jr. (head of AFC), 6, 38, 40

Clark, George, 108

Clark, Jefferson, 28

Clark, General William, 6, 33, 34, 37, 38

Cleave, John T., 280

Clemenceau, Georges, 211

Clement, Antoine, *19*; meets Stewart at 1833 rendezvous, 12; at 1835 rendezvous, 18; to New Orleans with Stewart winter 1836-1837, 21; to Murthly, Scotland, with Stewart 1838, 22-26

Cody, William F. (Buffalo Bill), *103*, 278; hired by General Sheridan 1871, 99-100; with Alexis on Nebraska hunt, 101-104, 115; carriage runaway, 106; guides Dunraven 1871-1872, 150-153, 160, 179

Colorado Springs (Colo.), 136-137; 247-271

Comba (U.S. Army cantonment at Little Missouri, Dakota), 186, 187, 215

Commonwealth Mine (Pearce, Ariz.), 271

Constans, Jean Antoine, 210

Corbie (Stewart's valet), 28

Corkscrew Club (Denver), 153-154

Cripple Creek (Colo.), Pourtales there 1891-1893, 264-271

Culbertson, Major Alexander, 35, 52, 54, 276

Custer, General George Armstrong, 15, *113*, *114*, 188, 278; joins Alexis 1871, 100-101; leads Nebraska hunt, 102-104; at Denver, 108; leads Colorado hunt, 111-115

DALHOUSIE, ELEVENTH EARL OF, 277

Delmonico's Restaurant (New York City), 148

Denver (Colo.), 106-111, 136, 153

Devereux, Horace, 268

De Voto, Bernard, 22, 275

Dickinson, Anna E. (first woman up Longs Peak, 1873), 129, 132, 157

Dow, Wilmot, *242*; at Elkhorn Ranch, 230-236, 237, 245; chases boat thieves with T.R., 242-244

Downer, S. S., 128; guides Isabella Bird to Estes Park, 124; climbs Longs Peak with Isabella, 129-133

Dreidoppel, (King) David, *55*, 64; to St.

Louis with Prince Max 1833, 34-37; on the *Yellowstone*, 40; at Fort Pierce, 47; arrives Fort Union, 50; to Fort McKenzie, 52-54; return journey 1834, 58

Dreyfus, Camille, wounded by De Mores, 211

Duden, Gottfried, 34

Dunmore, Lord (brother-in-law of Lord Southesk), 73

Dunraven, Lady Florence (Dunraven's wife), 148

Dunraven, Windham Thomas Wyndham-Quin, fourth Earl of, 121, 144, *146, 154, 161, 164, 169, 177, 178*, 280-281; early life, 147-148; hunting at North Platte 1871, 150-153; to Estes Park 1872, 154-155; buys land at Estes, 156-158; Yellowstone Park expedition 1843, 159-170; brings Bierstadt to Estes, 171-174; last years, 175-179

EATON, HOWARD (pioneer dude rancher), 188, 201, 202, 208, 231, 236

Edmunds, George F., 226, 228

Edward Warren (Stewart's second novel), 12, 25

Elkhorn Ranch (Roosevelt's place on the Little Missouri), 231-235, *233*, 237-238, 240-241, 245, 283

El Paso Club (Colorado Springs), 252, 253, 256, 265, 268

English Hotel (Estes Park), 174, *175*, 176, 281

Estes, Joel, 121, 126

Estes Park (Colo.), 121-145, 153-179, 279, 280-281

Evans, Griffith, 121, 122, 136-138, 140-144, 158, 176, 279, 281; hosts Isabella Bird 1873, 127-128; guide to Anna Dickinson, 129; host to Dunraven, 153-155; sells ranch to Dunraven, 156; shoots Mountain Jim, 157

Evans, Jinny, 128, 144

Evans, ex-Governor John, 106, 107

FERRIS, JOE, 198, 205, 239, 246; guides Roosevelt, 220-225; predicts Roosevelt presidency, 240

Ferris, Sylvane, 188, 220-221, 230, 236, 245,

283; hired by Roosevelt, 226

Field, Matt, 28, 29, 153

Finnegan, Mike, *243;* steals Roosevelt boat, 241-244

Fitzgerald, Sir Desmond, 280-281

Fitzpatrick, Thomas, 6; at 1833 rendezvous, 12; with Stewart to Big Horns 1833, 15; leads train to 1836 rendezvous, 18-21; leads 1837 caravan to Green River, 22

Fitzwilliam, Countess (Lord Milton's mother, the former Lady Frances Harriet Douglas), 68, 73, 276

Fitzwilliam, William Thomas Spencer Wentworth, sixth Earl (Lord Milton's father), 68

Flora (keelboat), Prince Max's trip on, 50-54

Fodder. *See* Haig

Forsythe, General George A., arranges Nebraska hunt for Alexis, 100-101

Forts: Buford, 204, 205; Carlton, 73-77; Clark, 48, 58, 62, 64; Edmonton, 68, 77, 78-80, *79*, 90; Ellice, 73, 158-160, 170; Garry, 68, 69, 72, 79; Hall, 159; Hayes, 100, 101; Keogh, 232; Laramie, 21-25; Leavenworth, 44, 62; McKenzie, 48-57, *56*, 62, 274; McPherson, 99-101, 150-153; "Milton," *66*, 76, 77; Piegan, 48, 53; Pierre, 40, *41*, 47, 62; Pitt, 77, 78, 85, 92, 277; Tecumseh, 40; Union (Mont.), 38, 40, 44, 47, 48, 50, *51*, 276; Vancouver, 17; Wallace, 100, 112

Fothringham, Steurt, 275

Frémont, Lieutenant John Charles, 23

Friedrich Karl, Prince of Wied-Neuwied (Prince Max's father), 33

GARDEN OF THE GODS (Colorado Springs), 136

Geyserland. *See* Yellowstone Park

Glass, Hugh, 44

Glenlyon, Lord George, 4, 6

Glyn, Elinor (novelist), 179

Gore, Sir St. George, 68, 101, 148

Gorringe, Commander Henry Honeychurch, 186-189, 215, 220, 225, 226, 238

Grant, President Ulysses S., 95-99, 106, 278

Grymes, John R., 184

HADLEY, JAMES A., 102, 104

Hagedorn, Herman (T.R.'s biographer), 225, 228

Hagerman, James J., 256, 269

Haig (alias Mr. Fodder, Dunraven's dude agent), 144, 156, 174

Hamilton, James Archdale. See Palmer, Lord Archibald

Harmony Society: visited by Prince Max at Economy (Pa.), 37; at New Harmony (Ind.), 62

Harrison, Dr. Benjamin, 7

Harrison, General William Henry, 7

Harvard College, 218, 230, 239

Hayden, Dr. F. V., 129, 155

Heath, Colonel, woos Isabella, 135-139

Hertzog, Emile, 261

Hoffman, Athenais Grymes von (Medora's mother), 184

Hoffmann, Baron Louis von (Medora's father), 184, 186, 198, 281; backs De Mores, 190; shuts down packing plant 1886, 208

Holmes, George, 12, 76

Holmes, Oliver Wendell, 98

Home, Daniel Dunglas, 148

Hudson's Bay Company (HBC), 7, 17, 54, 68, 69, 73, 84, 90, 128, 153, 276

Hunt, A. H., 121, 122, 136, 137

Hutchings, Ella, 30

INDEPENDENCE ROCK, 21

Indians: Arikaras, 44, 48, 62, 64; Assiniboines, 50-64; Blackfeet, 11, 18, 44, 48, 50, 54, 64; Bloods, 53, 54, 56, 57, 60; Botocudos, 60; Cheyennes, 232; Crees, 40, 50, 56, 73; Crows, 11, 14, 15, 48, 160, 161, 162; Flatheads, 11; Gros Ventres, 53, 54, 64; Iowas, 44; Kootenais, 54; Mandans, 48, 49, 60, 64; Minnetarees, 48, 60, 64; Nez Percé, 11; Omahas, 44; Pawnees, 44; Piegans, 50-60; Ponchas, 44; Sarsis, 54; Sauk and Fox, 37; Shushwaps, 85, 90; Sioux, 23, 47, 48, 99, 104, 159, 232; Snakes, 11, 21, 23, 25, 28; Tapuyans, 44; Utes, 11, 107; Wood Crees, 76

Isabella Gold Mining Company, 269

JACKSON HOLE (Wyo.), 11, 28

James, Dr. Edwin, 34

Jones, Colonel D. Floyd, 111

KELLY, W. A., 261, 262

Kennerly, William Clark, 28-30, 275

Kingsley, Canon Charles, 121

Kingsley, Dr. George Henry, 121, 146, 159, 161, 164, 169, 170, 280; to North Platte with Dunraven 1871, 150-153; at Estes Park 1873, 156-158; to Yellowstone Park with Dunraven, 162-163

Kingsley, Rose, 121, 135, 136, 137

Knickerbocker Club (New York City), 184

LAKES: Bear, 155; Cheyenne, 258-261, 264, 270, 271; Erie, 62; Estes, 279; Fremont (Stewart), 23, 28, 29; Grand, 128, 129; Island, 23; Jackson, 17; Jasper, 84; Lily, 129, 130; Long, 196; Mary, 168; Moose, 83; New Fork (Loch Drummond), 16, 23, 28, 29; Stonehammer, 23; Yellowhead (Buffalo Dung), 83; Yellowstone, 29

Lander, Frederick W., 174

Lang, Gregor, 201, 220-226, 236

Langford, N. P., 158

La Ronde (Cheadle's guide), 73-77

Lebo, Norman, 232

Lee, Daniel and Jason, 16

Lewis, Captain Meriwether, 6, 33, 38, 47, 48

Liller, J. E., 137, 143

Lindsay, Lord, Earl of Belcarres, 277

Little London. See Colorado Springs

Little Missouri Stockmen's Association, 238

London and New York Investment Company, 264, 284

Long, Major Stephen, 34

Loveland, W. A. H., 111

Lowell, James Russell, 98, 115

Luffsey, Riley, 201, 207, 236, 238, 282; shooting of, 193-194

McCOOK, GOVERNOR AND MRS. EDWARD, 106, 108, 109, 278

Mackenzie, Alexander, 40

McKenzie, Kenneth, 58, 276; with Prince Max on Yellowstone, 40-50

McLoughlin, Dr. John, 17

MacNeill, Charles, 268, 271

Maltese Cross (Roosevelt's ranch on the Little Missouri), 180, 220, 226-232, *227*, 235-238, 241, 245, 283

Mansel, Emily (second Mrs. Cheadle), 92

Maria (keelboat of *Assiniboine*), 47

Martineau, Harriet, 3

Maximilian, Alexander Philip, Prince of Wied-Neuwied, *59*, *63*, 275-276; early life, 33-34; takes Dreidoppel and Bodmer to St. Louis 1832-1833, 34-37; to Fort Pierre 1833, 38-47; meets Mandans, 48; arrives Fort Union, 50; to Fort McKenzie on the *Flora*, 52-54; battle at Fort McKenzie, 56; winters at Fort Clark 1833-1834, 58-62; later years, 64

Maxwell (Dunraven's valet), 159, *164*, *169*

Mayer, Captain Armand, killed in duel with De Mores, 211

Medora (N.D.), 190-208, *206*, 226-245, 281

Merrifield, William, 188, 220, 230, 236 245, 283; engaged by T.R. to run Maltese Cross, 226; grizzly hunt, 234

Messiter ("of Oxford," Cheadle and Milton's traveling companion), 69-75

Meyer, George, 236

Miller, Alfred Jacob, *5*, 35, 65, 275; meets Stewart, 22; trip to Green River, 23-25; to Murthly, 26

Milton, Lord William, Viscount, *77*, *82*, *89*, *91*, 276-277; ancestry, early life, 67-68; meets Cheadle, 68; Liverpool to Minnesota 1862, 67-72; to Fort Garry (Winnipeg), 72; to Fort Carlton, 73-75; winters at "Jolie Prairie," 76; to Fort Edmonton, 77-79; over Yellowhead Pass to Fraser River, 80-85; accident at Canoe River, 86-88; hunger on the North Thompson, 88-90; arrives Kamloops, 90; to England 1864, later life, 90-93

Mitchell, David, 50, 52-54

Montana Stockgrowers Association, 201, 238

Moran, Thomas, 158

Mores, Marquis Antoine-Amédée-Marie-Vincent Manca de, *182*, *195*, 215, 216, 226, 231, 235, 236, 245, 281-282; early life and marriage, 181-184; arrives U.S., 186; begins Bad Lands adventure 1883, 187-189; founding of town Medora, 190; killing of Luffsey, 192-194; the chateau, 194-198; the packing plant, 199-207; end of Bad Lands operation 1886, 208; last years and death, 210-212; letter to Roosevelt, 238-239

Mores, Athenais de (daughter of Antoine and Medora, born 1883), 190, 198, 210

Mores, Marquise Medora de, 179, *185*, 281-282; marries the marquis 1882, 184; daughter born 1883, 190; occupies chateau, 194-196; son born 1885, 204; end of Bad Lands enterprise, later years, 208-212

Mountain passes: Bozman, 159, 160; Breckenridge (Boreas), 138, *139*; Bridger's, 15; Dunraven, 165, 170; Fall River, 128, 129; Green River, 23; Hayden's Divide, 138; Kenosha, 138, 280; Monida, 159; Pryor's Gap, 15; Sangre de Cristo, 15; South, 7, 17, 23, 25, 28, 174, 232; Southesk, 277; Teton, 17; Two Ocean, 28; Union, 23, 28; Ute, 137, 265, 279; Yellowhead, 67-69, 80, 83, 90, 276, 277

Mountain peaks: Battle, 266; Balcarres, 277; Bingley, 83; Bucephalus, 83; Bull Hill, 266; Cheyenne, 252, *253*, *263*, *270*; Cloud Peak, 232; Dalhousie, 277; Dunraven, 155-156; Emigrant, 160; Fitzwilliam, 83; Fremont, 11; Gannett, 11, 23; High Tor, 62; Hood, 174; La Grace, 277; Laramie, 174; Lindsay, 277; Logan, 277; Longs, *127*, 128-133, *131*, *134*, 141, 143, 145, 153, 155-157, *172*, *173*, 174, 176, 279; Mauna Loa, 120, 129; McBeath, 277; O'Beirne, 83; Olympus, 155; Pikes Peak, 15, 121, 136, 137, 140, 259, 264, 265; Pyramid, 83; Robson, 83, 84, 277; Rosa, *270*; Sacajawea, 11; Silverheels, 138; Sir Donald, 174; Southesk, 277; Spanish Peaks, 15; Squaretop, 23; Stanley Baldwin, 277; Thistle, 277; Toma, 277; Twin Sisters, 155, *173*; Washakie, 11; Washburn, 165, 170; Whitney, 174

Mountain ranges: Absaroka, 15, 28, 163; Atlas, 145; Bearpaw, 52, 56; Big Horn, 15, 159, 196, 232; Bitterroot, 111; Blue, 17; Catskills, 62; Centennial, 28; Gallatin, 159, 163; Gros Ventre, 11; Highwood, 53; Judith, 52; Larb Hills, 52; Little Rockies, 52; Madison, 159; Mummy, 130, 155; Never Summer, 130; Premier, 88, 277; Rockies, 22, 38, 45, 52, 53, 58, 80, 99, 121, 122, 130, 144; San Juan 265; Sangre de Cristo, 138, 278; Selkirk, 68, 174; Snowy, 126, 141; Tarryall, 138; Teton, 11, 17, 28; Tobacco Root, 159; Touchwood Hills, 73; Wind River, 7, 11, 15, 174; Wyoming, 11

Muggins Gulch (Estes Park), 121-142, 153, 155

Murgatroyd, Anne (first Mrs. Cheadle), 92

NAPIER, SIR ROBERT, 148

Newberry, Wolcott, 266

Nichols, E. B., 18, 21, 30

Nichols, Franc (Stewart's adopted son), 30, 275

Nilsson, Christine, 98

Ninoch-Kiaui (Piegan chief), 54, 56

North West (Fur) Company, 84

Northern Pacific Refrigerator Car Company, 198, 208

Nugent, James (Mountain Jim), 121, 122, 124, 135-138, 145, 153, 155, 279, 280; meets Isabella Bird 1873, 125; early life, 128-129; guides Isabella up Longs Peak, 129-133; last courtship of Isabella, 140-144; refuses to sell to Dunraven, 156; death, 157

Nuttall, Thomas, 17

O'BYRNE (companion of Cheadle and Milton), *81*, 83-85, *86*, 93; joins Cheadle party, 78-80; accident at Canoe River, 86-88; loses Bucephalus, 89-90

O'Donald, Frank, 192, 194

O'Fallon, Major Benjamin, 38

Ogilvy, "Lord" Lyulph Gilchrist Stanley (*Denver Post* writer), 281

Ogilvy, Lady Maude, 281

Old Boy (Wood Cree chief), 76

Omohundro, Texas Jack, *151, 164, 169,* 179; guides Dunraven 1871-1872, 150-153, 159-170

Otero, Miguel, 112, 115

Oxford University (England), 69, 72, 147, 148, 160

PACKARD, ARTHUR (editor, *Bad Lands Cowboy*), 198, 199, 205, 245, 281

Paddock, Elbridge G. (Jerry), 190, 200-202, 204, 220, 238, 282; hired by De Mores 1883, 188; shooting of Luffsey, 193-194

Palliser, Captain John, 148, 158

Palmer, Lord Archibald, 50, 58

Palmer, Queen, 252

Palmer, General William Jackson, 121, 136, 250, 252, 256

Parker, Samuel, 18

Parrish, Anne (Mrs. Thomas), 252, 284

Parrish, Thomas, 252, 262, 268, 284; at Cripple Creek with Pourtales, 265

Pender, Sir John, 226

Penrose, Richard A. F., Jr., 271

Penrose, Spencer, 176, 268-271, 284

Pfaffenbach, Chris, steals Roosevelt boat, 241-244

Phelps, Alfred C., 109

Pierre's Hole (Idaho), 53

Pinkerton's National Detective Agency, 201, 204

Porter, Mae Reed (Mrs. Clyde), 4, 30, 275

Pourtales, Countess Berthe de (Count James's cousin and wife), 250, *251,* 253, 262, 264, 265, 269, 271, 284; married to Count James 1889, 258

Pourtales, Count Jacques Louis de, 247, 248

Pourtales, Count James, *249,* 284; early life, 247-250; dairy farm at Colorado Springs 1885, 250-256; marriage, 258; "Broadmoor City" and Casino 1889, 259-264; at Cripple Creek 1881-1883, 265-269; acquires Commonwealth Mine 1896, 271

Pourtales, Count Louis de, 250, 252

Powell, Major John Wesley, 129

Putnam, Carleton, 239

RAILROADS: Canadian National, 86, 90, 277;

Canadian Northern, 277; Chicago and Northwestern, 72; Colorado Central, 111; Colorado Midland, 256, 265; Denver Pacific, 106, 121; Denver and Rio Grande, 121; Grand Trunk Pacific, 277; Kansas and Northwestern, 100; Kansas Pacific, 111; Northern Pacific, 186-190, 200, 205; Pennsylvania, 99, 115; Union Pacific, 100, 153, 159

Randolph, George E., 109

Reed, Bill, 104

Rendezvous: explained, 7; 1833 at Green River and Horse Creek, 7-15; 1834 on Green River at Ham's Fork, 15-17; 1835 at New Fork on Green River, 17-18; 1836 at Green River and Horse Creek, 21; 1837 between New Fork and Horse Creek on Green River, 23; 1838 on the Popo Agie, 25

Rivers: Arkansas, 100, 136; Assiniboine, 73; Athabasca, 80, 83, *84*; Bear, 17; Big Thompson, 121, 122, 126, 128, 141-143, 155, 158; Bighorn, 11, 15, 123; Canoe, 86, *86*, *87*; Clearwater, 90; Columbia, 17; Fall, 155; Firehole, 168; Fish Creek, 155; Fraser, 67-69, 80-86; Frenchman, 100; Grand (Colorado), 129; Green, 7-38, 232; Hudson, 62, 98; Judith, 53; Kamloops, 86; Kansas, 7; Little Bighorn, 15, 101; Little Blue, 7; Little Cannonball, 220-224; Little Missouri, 186-210, 220-241, 283; Little Nemehaw, 46; Little Thompson, 125, 143; Marias, 48, 53, 56; Mattawamkeag, 230, 245; Medicine Creek, 100-102, 153; Middle Thompson, 155; Miette, 81, 83; Milk, 52; Mississippi, 6, 40, 72; Missouri, 7, 38, 40, 46, 50, 52, 53, 64, 187; New Fork 17, 23; Niobrara, 47; North Platte, 7, 101, 152; North St. Vrain, 125; North Thompson, 80-90, 277; Ohio, 37; Platte, 7, 18, 22, 25, 38; Popo Agie, 25; Portneuf, 17; Powder, 232; Qu'Appelle, 73; Raft, 90; Red, 72; Red Willow Creek, 100, 101, 278; Republican, 99, 100; Rocky, 83; Rosebud Creek, 15; St. Lawrence, 69; Salmon, 11; Saskatchewan, 73, 77, 78; Snake, 17; South Platte, 101, 136, 138; Southesk, 277; Sweetwater, 7, 23; Tarryall, 138, 279, 280; Tongue, 11, 15; Washita, 100; White, 34; Wind, 23, 25; Yellowstone, 11, 23, 28, 48, 50, 153, 159, 163, 168, 170

Roberts, Bob, 190, 193, 198, 201, 202, 205

Robertson, Colin, 84

Rocky Mountain Fur Company (RMF), 7, 12, 15, 32

Rogers, Platte, 128; guides Isabella to Estes, 124; Longs Peak climb with Isabella, 129-133

Roosevelt, Alice (daughter of T.R.), 227

Roosevelt, Alice Hathaway Lee (T.R.'s first wife), *219*, 230, 234, 237, 240; courtship, marriage to T.R., 218-220; death in childbirth, 226-228

Roosevelt, Anna (sister of T.R), 227, 240

Roosevelt, Edith Kermit Carow (T.R.'s second wife), 240, 244, 245

Roosevelt, Elliott (brother of T.R.), 227

Roosevelt, Martha Bullock (T.R.'s mother), 216, 227

Roosevelt, Theodore, *214*, *219*, *222*, *223*, *229*, 235-237, *242*, *243*, 250, 282-283; early life, marriage, 215-220; first visit to Bad Lands, 220-225; sets up Maltese Cross 1883, 226; death of Alice, 226-228; back at Medora, 228-230; sets up Elkhorn, 230-234; engaged to Edith Carow, 240; pursuit and capture of boat thieves, 241-244; remarriage, end of Bad Lands 1886-1887, 245-246

Roosevelt, Theodore, Senior (T.R.'s father), 216

Russell, Don, 104, 106

SACAJAWEA (Snake Indian heroine), 28, 48

Saxe-Weimar, Duke Bernhard of, 34

Say, Thomas, 34, 37

Schlesinger, Sebastian, 250, 253, 284

Selkirk, Thomas Douglas, fifth Earl of, 68

Sewall, William, *242*, 245, 283; from Maine to Elkhorn Ranch, 230-236; chases boat thieves with T.R., 242-244

Shaffenburg, Mr. and Mrs. Mark A., 106, 109, 278

Sheridan, General Philip Henry, 98, *114*, 150, 278; arranges Alexis's Nebraska hunt 1871, 99-101; at Camp Alexis, 101-104; at Denver with Alexis, 106-110; arranges Colorado hunt, 111-115

South Park (Colo.), 137, 138, 153, 279

Southesk, James Carnegie, ninth Earl of, 68, 73, 83, 276

Spalding, Reverend and Mrs. Henry, 21

Spotted Tail (Sioux chief), with Alexis on Nebraska hunt, 99-104, 278

Springfield, W. H. (W.H.S.), sleuths for De Mores, 201-204

Stanley, Freelan O., 176

Steck, Judge Amos, 109

Stewart, Sir Archibald, inherited title, 30

Stewart, Lady Catherine (Sir William's mother), 4

Stewart, Lady Christina (Sir William's wife), 10, 11, 32; meets Stewart, 4; birth of George, marriage, 6; dies, 30

Stewart, Sir George (Sir William's father), 4

Stewart, George (son of Sir William), 6, 30

Stewart, Sir John (Sir William's brother), 4, 18, 21; dies, 35

Stewart, Sir William Drummond (Captain), *2*, *13*, *19*, *20*, *24*, *27*, 33, 37-38, 48, 52, 65, 67, 68, 101, 153, 158, 275, 276; early life, 3-6; to Western U.S., 6-7; to 1833 Green River rendezvous, 10-15; 1834 Ham's Fork rendezvous, 15-17; 1835 New Fork rendezvous, 18; 1836 Horse Creek rendezvous, 20-21; hires Albert Jacob Miller, 22; to 1837 Green River rendezvous with Miller, 23; 1838 Popo Agie rendezvous, 25; returns to Murthly, 25-26; Yellowstone expedition 1843, 26-30; later career, 30-32

Stone Walls (on Upper Missouri, Mont.), 53, *61*

Stratton, Winfield Scott, 176, 266-271, 284

Sublette, William, 6, 7, 18, 21, 25, 40; at 1834 Ham's Fork rendezvous, 16; sends buffalo to Murthly, 26; leads Stewart's Yellowstone trek, 26-28

Supernat, Baptiste, 77, 80

Sutter, John A., 25

Thing, Captain Joseph, 17

Tocqueville, Count Alexis de, 3

Townsend, John Kirk, 17

Trollope, Frances, 3

Tutt, Charles L., 268, 271

Two Lance (Sioux chief), 104

Vallombrosa, Duke and Duchess of (De Mores's parents), 183, 211

Vallombrosa, Louis de (De Mores's son), 205, 210, 211, 282

Van Driesche, William, 188, 190, 196, *197*, 201, 202, 216; early years with De Mores, 183-186; to Dakota 1883, 187; postmaster at Medora, 198; later years, 210-212

Victoria, Queen, of England, 26, 68, 124, 176

Wannigan, "Dutch," 193, 194, 236, 238

Ward, Medora Grymes (Mrs. Sam), 179

Ward, Sam, 179, 184

Washburn, Henry D., 158

Watterson, Walter, 236

Webb, J. Watson, 25-26

Welty, Levi, 265, 267

Whistler, James McNeill, 179

White Castles (on Upper Missouri, Mont.), 52

Whitman, Dr. Marcus and Narcissa, 18-23

W.H.S. *See* Springfield, W. H.

Whyte, Theodore, 155, 170, 280; tells Dunraven about Estes 1872, 153; manages Estes property for Dunraven, 156-158; leases Estes from Dunraven, 175-176

Wilde, Oscar, 179

Willcox, William J., partnership with Pourtales, 252-256; killed 1892, 262

Womack, Bob, 267

Württemberg, Duke Paul Wilhelm of, 34, 37

Wyeth, Nathaniel, 15, 16

Wynne, Captain C., 165, *169*, 170

Yellowstone (AFC steamer), 38, *39*, 40, 44-47

Yellowstone Park (Wyo.), 28, 67, *166*, *167*; Stewart visit 1843, 29; Dunraven visit 1874, 158-160, 163, 165-170; Pourtales visit 1884, 250

Zear (Milton's guide), 74, 75